The Media and Public Life

The Media and Public Life

A History

John Nerone

polity

First published in 2015 by Polity Press

Polity Press
65 Bridge Street
Cambridge CB2 1UR, UK

Polity Press
350 Main Street
Malden, MA 02148, USA

ISBN-13: 978-0-7456-6020-2
ISBN-13: 978-0-7456-6021-9(pb)

A catalogue record for this book is available from the British Library.

Library of Congress Cataloging-in-Publication Data
Nerone, John C.
The media and public life : a history / John Nerone.
pages cm
Includes bibliographical references and index.
ISBN 978-0-7456-6020-2 (hardcover : alk. paper) – ISBN 0-7456-6020-7 (hardcover : alk. paper) – ISBN 978-0-7456-6021-9 (pbk. : alk. paper) – ISBN 0-7456-6021-5 (pbk. : alk. paper) 1. Mass media–Social aspects. 2. Journalism–Social aspects. I. Title.
HM1206.N47 2015
302.23–dc23

2014043775

Typeset in 10.5 on 12 pt Sabon
by Toppan Best-set Premedia Limited
Printed and bound in the UK by Clays Ltd, St Ives plc

For further information on Polity, visit our website: politybooks.com

Contents

Figures

Acknowledgments

I wrote this book over many years in various places, and owe thanks to many people who directly or indirectly contributed. Among the institutions who hosted me while doing research for this book are the American Antiquarian Society, which awarded me an NEH fellowship, and where John B. Hench and Caroline Sloat were especially generous; the University of Texas at Austin, where Ellen Wartella and Chuck Whitney were my hosts; and the University of Bergen in Norway, where Martin Eide was my host. Several colleagues were especially important as interlocutors: Kevin Barnhurst, Sandra Braman, Richard Campbell, James Carey, Clifford Christians, Norman Denzin, Fernando Elichirigoity, Kathy Forde, Barbara Friedman, James Hay, Robert McChesney, David Nord, Kent Ono, Dan Schiller, Mira Sotirovic, Bill Solomon, Inger Stole, Angharad Valdivia, and Barbie Zelizer deserve special mention.

The Institute of Communications Research at the University of Illinois at Urbana-Champaign has been my intellectual home since 1983. The most important part of my involvement there has been working with several generations of extraordinary graduate students, many now well advanced in distinguished academic careers. Among those who contributed significantly to this book are John Anderson, Jon Bekken, Tabe Bergman, Scott Berman, Jack Bratich, Wenrui Chen, Richard Craig, Matt Crain, Letrell Crittenden, Ian Davis, Kevin Dolan, Brian Dolber, Kelly Gates, Dong Han, Andrew Kennis, Holly Kruse, Nina Li, Chunfeng Lin, Sascha Meinrath, Molly Niesen, Mark Nimkoff, Andrew O'Baoill, Jeremy Packer, Victor Pickard, Carrie Rentschler, Paul Riismandel, Craig Robertson, Gretchen

Soderlund, Jonathan Sterne, Mandy Troger, and Fred Wasser. Many others helped shape my thinking.

Polity Press has been supportive and efficient; Andrea Drugan and Helen Gray have edited with great discretion. They have earned my gratitude. I also thank the anonymous readers, whose comments were substantial, useful, and often wise.

Finally, family members have materially contributed to the book. Ivy Glennon edited passages for style, encouraging me to be more direct and assertive on the page. Miranda Glennon-Nerone, who was born a few months after this project was conceived, graduated from high school shortly after its last revision. As an infant and toddler, she burst into tears every time I turned to a keyboard; as a new adult, she drew up roughs of three of the diagrams included in the book. It would have been a very different book without their support.

Introduction

This book sits at the intersection of the history of the public sphere, journalism history, and normative media theory. Partly a social history, partly a history of institutions, and partly a history of ideas, it addresses the particular task that a media system is supposed to perform in governance, and especially in democracies. It understands that task as public intelligence.

Both "public" and "intelligence" have a range of meanings. Public can mean *of and for The People*, and it is a common though sloppy habit to refer to the people as the public. Public can also mean *open*, as in, there to be seen by everyone. Intelligence can refer to a particular kind of information, the kind that allows a special insight into affairs – this is the Intelligence in the Central Intelligence Agency. More commonly in our time, it refers to the capacity to make sense of things. What I mean by public intelligence is a combination of all these meanings. In any political order, there has to be a mechanism that makes sense out of things by sifting through information in a way that can be presented publicly as both worthy of guiding policy and as the sort of thinking that really represents the way the public thinks and the way people would think if they had enough time and knowledge.

The part of "public intelligence" that's easiest to study and the readiest subject for a historical narrative is the media system, and especially the news media. As a result, much of this book looks like what is called "journalism history." But it's weird journalism history, because its purpose is to deconstruct journalism as it is commonly known and rethink it as a particular formation of practices involving public intelligence. So one of the arguments of the book is that journalism as we know it is a very recent phenomenon – not much older than me – and that it has deformed governance in part because its practitioners consistently misrecognize it.

Instead of treating journalism as a profession, and looking for its origins, this book treats journalism as a set of practices involved in what I call the representation of public opinion. This approach is meant to turn the common sense of journalists on its head. Journalists believe that they should and do make democratic government possible by making information available to people, who then discuss it and think about it and make up their minds and vote. It would be nice if that were the way things work, but we know people don't pay much attention to news, and forget what little they learn within a very short time. In other words, journalism doesn't make governance work by making people smarter. Rather, journalism works by representing the public. It represents the public in two ways. First, journalists stand in for the public in the halls of power. They speak and are spoken to on behalf of the public. Second, journalists depict the public, both explicitly when they describe the public mood or predict public reactions to events, and implicitly when they assume an agenda on behalf of the public, treating some things as relevant and others as trivial.

So public opinion really does matter in governance. But it matters not because that's what people think. It matters because the people who run things accept the fact that they have to answer to a universal supervising intelligence that is represented by journalism, among other things. This notion of a supervising public works as a "regulative fiction," to borrow a term from Nietzsche. Journalism has worked well in supporting this regulative fiction when it has been able to point to an overwhelming consensus, and when there has been a powerful movement that journalists see as righteous. Thus, by the mid-1960s, US journalists had come to portray the Civil Rights movement as a manifestation of a right-thinking public (Alexander, 2007). But professional journalists do a very poor job of representing an intelligent public in cases of partisan division or when the glamor of expertise misleads them. Foreign-policy elites continually misled journalists during the Cold War, leaving them baffled and stunned by the collapse of the Soviet empire. Journalists do an execrable job of holding candidates accountable during election campaigns, retailing talking points while showing off their chops by gaming the strategy behind them. A commitment to neutrality or objectivity makes journalists vulnerable in such cases. By default, they end up representing the public as indifferent or, worse yet, an idiot.

Journalism has been the most compelling mechanism for representing public opinion in my lifetime, but it has never held a monopoly, and its authority is weakening. There are older mechanisms, of course. Voting is one of them. Other forms of news practices have also represented public opinion, like partisan newspapers. Before the age of the public-opinion poll, if a politician wanted to assess the likely outcome of approaching elections, he (usually) would read a bunch of newspapers to find out what their editors were arguing. Beginning in the 1930s, public-opinion polling and other forms of social science began replacing these more vernacular ways of representing public opinion. By now such techniques have reached a level of precision that politicians no longer have to extrapolate from a sample to an abstract demography; instead, they can build databases of every voter, with enough individual data points to accurately predict behavior (Issenberg, 2012).

This means that journalism's representation of public opinion can be immediately refuted and discarded when it suits the purposes of the people who run things. The supervising public is no longer a regulative fiction, at least in the advanced western countries. In its place, ever more naked calculations of advancing interests have come to replace pretensions toward rational debate; the people who run things no longer need to clothe their maneuvers with appeals to the common good. It is this fact, rather than a lack of information or the weakness of the legacy news-media business model, that troubles public intelligence today.

Don't take the grumpiness of this position as indicating nostalgia for the old press establishment. For a US American of my generation, which came of age in the years when journalists routinely and cynically passed on disinformation about race relations and the war in Vietnam, today's disarray should be refreshing, even hopeful. The more powerful press of the second half of the twentieth century did an inadequate job of keeping the powerful in check, arguably because it tried too hard to be professional. The press made it easy for the Nixons and Thatchers of the world to slap it around.

The book explains this by tracing a long history. The history is too big, however, to be told without violent simplification, and my treatment makes no pretense to being encyclopedic. Instead, I've chosen to construct a narrative around a series of moments, using the term "moment" in the way that a physicist would, as a particular line of force. After explaining how and why news systems tend to function in governance generally, I turn to the rise of European printing and the invention of the newspaper form. The book then looks at transformations of news or publicity coming out of larger political and social changes.

The first transformative moment was the rise of liberal political regimes in the Age of Revolution. This moment appears in the narrative as a North Atlantic story, concentrated in the UK, the US, and France. It produced a fantasy about public politics in which the media system was supposed to function as a frictionless space for public information and deliberation. This fantasy animated policy in the US and elsewhere, and continues to be productive, but has always been at odds with unruly realities. Today we notice its naivety about social inequality. In earlier centuries, many pointed out its conflict with the partisan uses of the press, first, and then the commercial uses of the press.

Politicization and commercialization are the second and third moments I discuss. Politicization means the integration of the press into emerging systems of mass politics; commercialization means integration into emerging market systems. Both are large and complex moments, taking different forms in different places. I have simplified these by concentrating on the US and the UK experiences. More on this choice in a minute.

The fourth moment is industrialization, which transformed the infrastructure and mode of production of news media even as it worked to transform social relations more broadly. The rise of industrial media organizations in industrial societies caused a general reorganization of public life. For news media, this prompted the moment of institutionalization, in which the press became a supposedly expert, professional element of the governing process (Cook, 1998). This fifth moment produced what Dan Hallin (1992) has called journalism's "high modern" moment.

The decline of high modernism is sort of the sixth moment the book discusses. It's hard to call this a "moment," because the broad social process remains unclear at the time of writing. I've variously called it "corporatization," "digitization," and "globalization." But these are lines of force that operate in different ways, and it's not clear to me which one drives the changes under way now.

I've chosen to talk about "moments" rather than periods or stages. As lines of force, moments don't stop operating when another one emerges. This conceptual framework makes it easier to understand the first half of the nineteenth century, then, when politicization and commercialization operated simultaneously, driving change in sometimes harmonious and sometimes dissonant ways. Periodization has long been a problem in journalism histories that want to see a "partisan" period ending at a precise point when a "commercial" period begins.

Another way of understanding how moments transform the media system is to think of media as networks of relationships (Barnhurst and Nerone, 2001). Kevin Barnhurst and I have applied this term in our analysis of the development of newspaper forms, which we see as constituted out of a collection of tubes, as it were – some carry content, some revenue – that converges in the newspaper office but embeds the medium itself in the larger society. We identify particular formations of media-as-networks-of-relationships, each explained by a master metaphor. The printer's newspaper (master metaphor = the town meeting) became the editor's paper (the courtroom), the publisher's paper and the industrial paper (the department store), the professional paper (the social map), and now the corporate (or digital) paper (the index). The printer's paper had a relatively simple set of relationships. Printers took content from letters, official documents, and other newspapers, assembled them into digests, produced printed newspapers in craft shops, sold them to gentlemen readers, and exchanged them with other printers. The rise of partisan editors added a set of relationships with parties and voters to this network. Commercialization added intensified relationships with advertisers, who related to readerships as consumers rather than voters. Industrialization transformed the relations of production in the pressroom and the newsroom, and situated news organizations within a growing infrastructure of content providers – wire services and features syndicates, obviously, but also industrialized financial entities like stock exchanges and cultural complexes like the entertainment industry. Industrialization introduced new economies of scale that produced bottlenecks that in turn required and supported professionalization among newsworkers. The framework of this book differs slightly in that it focuses on one dimension of these formations, the mode of production, and relates them to networks of relationships that include but can go beyond newspapers.

This narrative usefully makes the point that news practices don't disappear. Rather, new moments and new relationships augment the overall formation. There is an editor's paper buried within the layers of content that go into the making of a corporate paper. The conceptual framework also makes it easier to talk about news media other than newspapers, which tend to respond to the same lines of force and to be constituted out of similar relationships. I also hope that the conceptual framework can be applied outside the specific historical episodes that this book dwells on.

This is a parochial book with a guilty conscience. Although it begins and ends with discussions of global developments, the concrete stories that the book tells are mostly confined to the English-speaking part of the world, and especially the US. The practical reason for this is that it's the history I know best. The justification for it is that the English-speaking world and, since the second half of the nineteenth century, the US have exercised hegemony in the development of news systems and political life. These are sound reasons, but different sound reasons would also support other decisions. Hence the guilt.

I've tried to shape the narrative so that it doesn't present Anglo-American history as normative. I've incorporated other histories, and pointed out counterhistories wherever I can. A critic might say that these are simply exceptions that prove the rule, but in defense I would say that the whole point of this history is to show the contingency of the state of affairs that liberal ideology wants to present as normative for the world. Though it would be fair to say that such a case would be more effective were I to write more about India or Brazil, this criticism still operates on the level of equity among nations. I make the attempt to tell the story as a transnational one, with the Anglo-American history as central to and exemplifying a world system. Still, national systems of government have exerted a strong gravitational pull.

Another criticism would point to the relative absence of subaltern voices in this history. Here I have to acknowledge an uncomfortable lack of fit between theory and practice. At several points in the book, I point to groups and movements outside the mainstream as being especially transformative, but the bulk of the narrative involves mainstream media. The book could be written without any white male protagonists, just to prove the point that media history has been made by outsiders. Instead, I've settled for showing the deep relationships between outsiders and insiders, and for pointing out mechanisms that kept outsiders outside. It's ironic that US journalists today owe so much to African Americans like Frederick Douglass and Ida B. Wells-Barnett – more than they do to their white counterparts like Thomas Ritchie or Thomas Cox – yet US newsrooms remain characterized by what Kevin Dolan calls "white incumbency" (Dolan, 2011). The durability of whiteness in the face of all of the work of people of color itself testifies to the hegemony of the mainstream media organizations that I focus on. I wish it weren't so; I hope that telling the story the way I do makes it easier to change things.

This book has been a long time in the making, and its agenda has evolved. It began by trying to address the dissatisfaction of my generation of teachers and scholars of the media system with the tools that were left to us 30 years ago. There had been a wave of criticism directed against histories that focused too narrowly on media in isolation from broader social and political histories. Beyond this critique of mediacentrism, I also wanted to disturb the tendency of media historians to invoke grand narratives, whether of the stages of media development (oral, literate, print-literate, electronic, as in Innis and McLuhan) or of the triumphal march of liberty in the world (as in the inevitable rise of freedom of the press in US journalism histories).

This is a history of media and public life, but it doesn't claim to be *the* history of media and public life. Like any history, it is very much a creature of its own time: histories aren't about the past, but about the relationship between the past and the present (Johnson, 1982). As a result, it is possible to write multiple true histories of any event or period; the number of true histories to be written about any complex subject approaches infinity. Historians of my generation had this drilled into us in grad school; we all have copies of Hayden White's *Metahistory* (1973) on our shelves, with the spine cracked and the underlinings diminishing by mid-book.

A decade and a half later, we all read Habermas's *Structural Transformation of the Public Sphere* (1989), an old book that became urgently relevant in the post-Berlin Wall and pre-9/11 west. At that point, a common sense emerged that said that history had ended with the triumph of market-oriented media systems, which provide a meaningful marketplace of ideas and allow journalism to be independent. If that were the case, why were democratic systems so manipulable? Why was public discourse so cynical? Why were voters so apathetic? This moment produced the public journalism movement. It also informed the development of the "blogosphere," so called out of an awareness of its potential as a public sphere. Bloggers picked pseudonyms like "Publius," in conscious imitation of eighteenth-century habits.

That moment had at its core a notion about legitimate government that has run through modern political theory in various forms but can be stated quite simply. For a government to be legitimate, it has to make it possible for the stronger argument to win on its merits. The political philosophers who recur in this book – Habermas, but also de Tocqueville, Gramsci, and Walter Lippmann – all express some version of the concern that the governing system make it possible for political action to be taken because it is the right thing to do. In democracies, this notion has a more particular form, in that voices representing ordinary citizens have to participate in public deliberation. Media systems are obviously implicated. A media system of a legitimate democracy must have the capacity to allow the public to participate in the kind of debate in which the stronger argument wins on its merits. This dream animated the "public-sphere" moment.

That moment has passed. The notion of the public sphere was an especially useful tool for deconstructing the mythology of the press system, but it had the disadvantage of inspiring a mythology of its own. Critics effectively pointed out that Habermas's historical account was partial and opportunistic. Then public-sphere fatigue set in.

After a few decades of this discussion, there remain two elements of liberal notions of public life that I have held on to as worthwhile. One is the notion of an intelligent supervising public as a regulative fiction. The fantasies of Internet enthusiasts about a new public of actually engaged, actually informed individuals have mostly evaporated, and it is tempting to just dismiss the public in general. But it seems to me that it is still worthwhile to try to find mechanisms by which to hold power accountable to something like an intelligent public, even as it's become increasingly apparent that professional journalism won't work as such a mechanism. The media system should be able to shame the people who run things into honoring basic truths and simple logic.

The second element – article of faith, really – that I hold on to is the worth of independent journalists. This may seem at first to contradict my criticism of professional journalism. The distinction is that professional journalism is an institution; independent journalists are citizens who engage in knowledge practices and discourse aimed at making public life more intelligent. What this looks like in practical terms is easy to explain. Just take the historical exemplars that professional journalists genuflect to – Lincoln Steffens, or I. F. Stone – and imagine what public life would look like if the media system made it possible for every ordinary journalist to work like them.

This is a history, but it's a curious one. It shuttles between two different kinds of voices. In parts it is abstract, while in other parts it lapses into concrete historical narrative that is often biographical in style. These concrete narratives are meant to carry the abstract parts forward. I believe that, if a history could be written in which every story is told, it would fully bear out the abstract arguments in this book. Put another way, I believe that the concrete lives of all the world's newsworkers have made the history that the abstractions try to sketch out. An argument like "objectivity came from the three-way battle between owners and workers, on the one hand, and owners and the public on the other" makes a promise, which is that, if one were to drill down into the everyday tensions and struggles in any news workplace, one would find that abstract narrative expressed. All the abstractions I've written in this book, I believe, would stand up to the test of microhistory. Let a thousand dissertations bloom!

1

The Printer's Newspaper and the National Public Sphere

We tend to approach the broad terrain of media, government, and public life with a set of concepts and habits of thought formed in the eighteenth and nineteenth centuries. Before that, thinkers considered both democracy and publicity generally bad ideas, which made it harder for a government to govern. At the time of the American and French Revolutions, there had been relatively little successful experience with free media and self-government. Half a century later, it was possible to not just philosophize about them but to empirically observe them.

In the 1830s, Alexis de Tocqueville visited the United States. He spent two years compiling the observations that would become *Democracy in America*, one of the foundational works of the eventual discipline of political science. De Tocqueville intended his book to be a scientific study of the strengths and weaknesses of democracy in general. He saw its strengths in achieving equality and freedom for people, whose heightened participation in government generated unprecedented energy while, surprisingly, also reinforcing stability. Its most striking weakness was the possibility of oppression and stagnation through the omnipotence of the majority, which governed not just the state but, because there was no other source of authority, also every area of social and cultural life. He saw the white majority subjugating minorities, especially African Americans. He saw the immense gravity of a middling mainstream propelling a tsunami of mediocre popular literature and fashions. So powerful was the majority that he concluded that he had never seen a society with so little real freedom of thought. Absolute freedom on the individual level led to absolute determinism on the collective level.

De Tocqueville devoted a number of long passages to describing the newspaper press of the Jacksonian era, an age of mass electoral politics. In his judgment, the press was one of the most powerful engines of democratic government, but it was also one of the most abused. If the largest danger in a democracy was the emergence of a tyranny of the majority, then the press was one of the key mechanisms by which tyrannical majority opinion could have expression. The entire political system as a result oscillated between stalemate and wild swings of popular enthusiasm.

It is easy to dwell on the criticisms in these still powerful chapters. On the other hand, it is also easy to poke holes in the analysis. The very generation that de Tocqueville observed was already producing the great writers who came to be known as key figures of the American Renaissance, as well as the great social reformers and political activists who would abolish slavery, fight for woman suffrage, and enact federal laws protecting minority rights. Moreover, they used the engines of the media system to drive these movements. Still, he had a point, didn't he? The system he observed seemed designed to make it hard for the public to be smart and make good choices.

What did de Tocqueville want from a democratic media system? Clearly, it was not simply the free expression of individual beliefs and interests – what would later come to be called the "marketplace of ideas," arguably the most powerful metaphor in common language for media democracy. Instead, he seemed to want the public to think straight. He wanted intelligence, in both senses of the word – the kind of information that early modern public folk used to make wise decisions, and the capacity to think clearly about the state of affairs and available policies.

In both the norm of intelligent discussion and the criticism of press abuse, de Tocqueville stood in a long line of theorists of political communication. Political leaders like Thomas Jefferson, activist intellectuals like John Milton, and numberless anonymous printers and editors had fantasized about a press system that would enable modern societies to govern themselves like ancient Greek city-states. Citizens, who would all be literate and economically independent, would all read newspapers, which would contain reliable, authoritative information, and also provide a platform through which they could discuss matters of common concern. Intelligent public opinion as formed and manifested in the press would then pilot the political process.

This set of concepts and expectations is now so obvious as to be taken for granted, not only in the west but also in the command economies of the Pacific Rim and the post-socialist countries of eastern Europe. But it would be hard to find sincere knowledgeable people anywhere who think that the media system is living up to this ideal. Why has the media system been saddled with responsibilities that it apparently lacks the capacity to perform? How did this strange situation come about?

This chapter begins an attempt to tell a coherent story about the history of media engagement with public affairs. Because this is so large a history, played out on a global scale over several millennia, the beginning of the story is necessarily presented as very abstract. But the story, at least as presented here, will become more specific in the years between the political crisis in Europe of the mid-seventeenth century and the period of the world wars of the twentieth century. After that, I'm afraid things become abstract again. The overall story looks something like an hourglass, wide at the top and bottom and narrowing toward the middle. So let's drop ourselves into the wide top.

Origins of News Systems

The capacity to govern requires communication. Governments always and everywhere develop systems of communication as tools of administration. Usually, they maintain some kind of news system for their administrators and try to limit access to it by those outside the bureaucracy.

The first formal news media were designed for use by governing elites. Imperial China and Korea, well ahead of western Europe in developing both paper and printing, circulated handwritten bulletins of court information, for instance. In Korea, which had developed a system of alphabetic printing with movable type before the European invention of printing, the court bulletins were printed for a short period beginning in 1577, giving Korea a claim to having produced the first printed newspaper (Kim, 2013). But these media were not produced for general circulation; rather, they were meant to circulate among a bureaucratic elite.

Any government also has a need to communicate to the public. Often this is done through spectacles, like the coronation of a monarch, and monuments, like the massive architecture of national capitals, which combine to produce a sort of official memory of how power has come to be exercised and why it is legitimate. On an everyday level, governments have to tell their subjects how to do things. The Roman Republic inscribed its laws in stone in the public forum, apparently not planning any major changes in those laws. The Roman Empire produced a daily news report, the *Acta Diurna*, informing the public of "vital statistics," like the numbers of births and deaths, and some affairs of state, like the outcomes of trials. (No copies survive, but the *Acta* is referred to by ancient authors, including a parody, set at Trimalchio's banquet, in Petronius's *Satyricon* (1959: 60).) This would become a common practice for many early modern governments, which established printed newspapers or "gazettes" as official organs of public information.

These two fairly timeless kinds of news media, the one for internal use and the other for public consumption, aren't very interesting. Historians of the news media sometimes mention examples of them as a way of clearing their throats before speaking about the real history of the media. But the history of news media becomes interesting at the point where governments lose their control over the uses of news, making it possible for unofficial actors to change the way states behave.

There also have been non-governmental uses for news in most societies. In every society, ordinary people have a use for tales of the novel or weird. There has always been some form of ballad culture or popular oral literature to tell stories that more recent generations would describe as "human interest," or "tabloid fare," or "infotainment." The stuff of such culture is often formulaic and timeless. In early modern European newsbooks, for instance, one finds fantastic stories being recycled from time to time (Stephens, 2007). Usually this type of news culture has been very moralistic as well. This is particularly true of crime reports, always a staple of popular news, whether oral or printed. There is a moral and a commercial logic to this. If one wraps a sordid tale inside a fine lesson of the evils of crime, then whatever titillation the story provokes can be rendered incidental and tolerable (Cohen, 2006). Popular culture often has needed a pro-social pretext.

Elite uses for news require less misdirection. Among the many kinds of specialized knowledge that news media have supported, commercial information has consistently been prominent. Handwritten newsletters containing financial information began to circulate in Renaissance Europe. The most famous of these were "avvisi" produced in Venice during its imperial years (Infelise, 2002, 2007; de Vivo 2007: 80–5; Kittler, 2009: 87–8). Mostly compiled from merchants' private letters, these circulated primarily among subscribers in trade centers, beginning in the first decade of the sixteenth century. They were meant to help a merchant elite make better-informed business decisions.

Modern news media developed out of this kind of "correspondence," a term that continues to inhabit the language of news.

Newsletter writers gathered news through the emerging postal networks that linked European cities, allowing them to correspond with government officials, commercial agents, and intellectuals (Wilke, 2008, 2013). Although it was possible for the wealthiest merchants to exchange correspondence through private couriers, any broader circulation would rely on publicly administered postal systems as essential infrastructure; these became formalized in the seventeenth century. The French system, for instance, was established in 1603 (Gough, 1988; Mattelart, 2006). It is difficult to overstate the impact of regular postal systems, which not only facilitated the work of merchants and printers but also allowed dispersed networks of intellectuals to correspond as they collaborated on the projects which produced the scientific revolution and built the Enlightenment Republic of Letters.

The more successful newsletter writers assembled material from their own correspondents and from newsletters and other documents into a summary of current affairs that had a certain coherence. The newsletter allowed its readers to update their already sophisticated maps of the flow of power and history, and thus to make strategic decisions regarding the conduct of their affairs. Because subscribers looked to newsletter writers for competitive advantage over other merchants, the less publicly familiar the news the better. In this, newsletters differed from later news media that tried to reach as large an audience as possible. The news in newsletters, at least in the original scheme, became public only by accident (Infelise, 2010).

But publicity had its uses too. The famously complex political machinations of the Italian city-states of the sixteenth and seventeenth centuries – in which, for instance, Venetian leaders sought ways to circumvent papal authority, or merchants in Genoa or Naples sought to undermine the influence of Spain in the western Mediterranean – encouraged newsletter writers to tactically publicize rumors and scandals, often with the support and patronage of political leaders. As Brendan Dooley has pointed out, simply by publishing such matters, newsletter writers changed the political environment by creating a kind of representation of public knowledge or public opinion (Dooley, 1996). The advent of printing intensified this kind of action by making publication seem universal. The power of the press has been imagined in many ways – as the power of truth, for example, or the power of reason – but one aspect of it has certainly been the power to represent public opinion.

News became a tool of competition among the powerful under specific circumstances: that's where the history gets interesting. In Renaissance Europe, partly at least because of the separation between the religious authority of the Roman Church and the emerging power of secular rulers, elites challenged each other across a range of issues. The divisiveness of European civilization seems to have been a key enabling factor for the growth of printed news.

Printing had been developed many times before its European invention. But its European history differed from, say, its earlier Chinese history in that, in Europe, no authority had both the geographical scope and administrative capacity to control it. Because the printing press happened to be introduced at a time when secular rulers sought to carve out a sphere of control separate from the Universal Church, it became a tool in the competition among different organized centers of power. It is because jurisdictions were so fragmented that it became common to talk about a "printing revolution" in Europe but not elsewhere (Eisenstein, 1979).

The argument that printing sparked a cultural revolution in Europe is most powerfully associated with Elizabeth Eisenstein. She argued that the printing revolution came from the "fixity" that was an essential affordance of print technology. Criticisms of the Catholic Church had sparked reform movements before printing, but, because Martin Luther printed his criticisms, they spread through space and lasted through time in a more powerful way. In the same way, printed astronomical observations helped overturn the Ptolemaic model of a geocentric universe. Eisenstein's argument about "typographical fixity" has been challenged by Adrian Johns (1998), who points out that print technology in its first century produced the same kinds of opportunities for forgeries and piracies that the Internet had in its early years. Only when state actors had codified property rights in printed products did typography become associated with fixity. This debate cannot be settled here. But it is interesting that the development of printed formats for news involved extensive dialog between the business interests of printers, the political interests of partisans, and the administrative interests of states, and so emerged only very gradually after the European invention of printing in 1450. The newspaper form did not emerge effortlessly from the technology of printing. In fact, it had to swim upstream.

Even when they fought with each other, elites could agree at least on the wisdom of keeping their affairs out of the reach of ordinary people. Then, as now, the powerful typically collaborated to create bodies that regulated the flow of information and punished those who used publication to weaken the authority of the state. All states do this, though democracies tend to adopt different policies and justify them on different grounds than monarchies or theocracies. Historically, every state has reacted to new communications technologies, from printing to the most recent digital technologies, with some form of regulation.

But in really interesting circumstances, competition among elites opened a space for ordinary people to change the way things happen. The conflicts that arose over Martin Luther's rebellion against papal authority in the sixteenth century are a prime example. Among other things, Luther produced a series of short texts that were commercially ideal for printers in places like Wittenberg. It has become something of a commonplace to argue that the printing press made the Reformation, but it is also true to say that the Reformation gave a tremendous impetus to the growth of printing in select areas (Pettegree, 2010: 91–129). Similarly, the European discovery of the Americas and the dynastic competitions in the early sixteenth century produced a swarm of cheap news pamphlets, written in a popular tone and intended for wide consumption; not that many of these survive (Pettegree, 2010: 130–41, Pettegree, 2014: 5–8). One particular genre of news pamphlet, which started appearing in Germany in 1509, used the title *Neue Zeitung*. These flourished especially in the 1530s, and were a reliable source of profit for printers. Of the 4,000 or so copies that survive – a surprisingly large number for relatively cheap ephemera – most deal with "high politics" (Pettegree, 2014: 74). The wars of religion that followed, especially the Thirty Years War (1618–48), produced a number of cases in which politics broke through the boundaries of class and privilege. The most famous involve Germany, the birthplace of European printing, the center of Luther's Reformation activities, and the home of the first regularly printed news periodicals; the Netherlands, where a rebellion against Spain produced a ferment of republican politics, and where the first English-language newsbook was published; and England, where a period of Civil War beginning in 1640 led to a flowering of news culture (Briggs and Burke, 2009; Raymond, 1996).

Histories of news usually cite German-language newsbooks, the first of which appeared in Strasbourg in 1605, as the first real newspapers. Scholars distinguish these newsbooks from news pamphlets because they were printed regularly, usually weekly; they distinguish them from avvisi because they contained information for a general public. In the seventeenth century, more newsbooks were published in Germany than in the rest of Europe combined (Baron and Dooley, 2001; Welke and Wilke, 2008). Other countries followed. The first Dutch newsbook appeared in 1618; the first English-language newsbook was printed in Amsterdam in 1620; the first French one in 1631; the first Spanish in 1641; the first Italian in 1643. These began appearing at the beginning of the seventeenth century partly because of dramatic political events, but also because of a general reorganization of postal services in western Europe. The postal system was an indispensable infrastructure for the news system, and could be considered a revolutionary technology in the same way as the printing press (Pettegree, 2014: 167–81).

These newsbooks – let's call them newspapers from here on – hewed to a common form. They were quarto or octavo in size, meaning they were made by printing four or eight pages on each side of a large sheet of paper and folding it two or three times. (The typical modern newspaper is a folio, made by printing two pages on each side of large sheets of paper and folding them once.) The make-up looked more like a book than a newspaper, often with something like a title page, and text not broken into columns. (Dutch newspapers were an exception; they were folio with two columns per page (Pettegree, 2014: 188–9).) Typically, the content consisted of a series of excerpts of other newspapers or of correspondence, not headlined but datelined with a place and date: "Amsterdam, 17 October," for instance. The events in that paragraph would not have taken place in Amsterdam on 17 October, however: that was the place and date of the written source of the information. Excerpts would flow, usually without commentary, in roughly chronological order. Sometimes a reader could detect a unifying narrative. Usually the reader would have to supply his or her own. These early newspapers typically lacked an editorial voice. Blandness kept the censors happy. Sometimes they included texts of state documents or transcripts of official addresses, which signaled a quiet political allegiance. In times of political conflict, however, the form could be readily adapted for propaganda purposes. But there was nothing in these newspapers that would qualify as "journalism" in the twentieth- or twenty-first-century sense of the term, which implies a professionalized newsgathering discipline.

Printed newsbooks had a complicated relationship with the handwritten newsletters that preceded them. They began as simply printed versions of handwritten newsletters, but, because they were more public, they avoided the confidential voice, strategic commentary, and implied political engagement found in the handwritten newsletters. Because of these features, the handwritten form remained useful to elite audiences long after printing had spread through Europe.

Printed news prompted states and churches to intensify their efforts to control the flow of information. The Vatican had long used forms of licensing to restrict publications; these efforts increased with the Protestant Reformation and the rise of printing (Pettegree, 2010: 204–8). Catholic states, like France, incorporated these techniques into their own systems of regulation.

Seventeenth-century France developed an effective system of press regulation based on grants of monopoly for particular kinds of printed matter. One printer, for instance, owned a monopoly for political news, another for scientific news, and a third for literary news, and each published a national title that dominated its field: the *Gazette*, the *Journal des Savants*, and the *Mercure Galant*, respectively. These patent holders paid for their rights, but were then permitted in turn to license other, especially regional, printers to copy their material. This system of intellectual property encouraged printers to work to keep the favor of the Crown, and hence to censor themselves, beyond the still existing requirements of formal censorship (Gough, 1988).

This system was not leakproof. A literary underground flourished, and has been studied most famously by Robert Darnton (1982, 1996). Much of what is known about these unlicensed publications and the news culture they helped sustain comes from police records. In other words, we know it existed because we know how it was surveilled and suppressed.

But even France, the most unified and powerful of the seventeenth-century nation-states, lacked the capacity to control printing beyond its borders. Printers in neighboring countries, such as the Netherlands and Switzerland, saw a business opportunity in producing French-language publications. Their governments, which would have prevented publications aimed at domestic audiences, tolerated and encouraged this sort of extraterritorial printing. Protestant states saw no problem in circulating literature that the Catholic French monarchy saw as subversive. Many of the famous works of the French Enlightenment were produced in Switzerland and circulated clandestinely in France (Darnton, 1979). This aspect of France's history points out the inescapably transnational nature of publication in a Europe divided by overlapping borders of politics, religion, and language. The porousness of political borders also allowed for cultural influence to spread outward. The influence of French salons was transmitted through both publication and correspondence, taking the form of a discussion without borders, known as the Republic of Letters (Eisenstein, 1992; Goodman, 1994).

Protestant powers also regulated printing. In England, the Tudor monarchs created an elaborate system of licensing that enfranchised not just the Crown but also the Church of England and the Stationers' Company, the private guild of printers and booksellers. The Crown granted the Stationers' Company a licensed monopoly on printing and bookselling; in return for the Crown's protection of its copyrights, the company policed its membership, limiting the number of legal printers and discouraging the publication of critical or destabilizing material.

The Tudor system also had its weaknesses. Printing was a relatively portable technology that could be deployed in small productive units, so it was difficult to control. There were always qualified printers who could not gain membership in the Stationers' Company and who were willing for the right price to print illegally. Printers tended above all else to follow business incentives. Dissidents (in England, Puritans and Catholics) with ready cash could beat the system (Siebert, 1952; Mendle, 1995; Clegg, 2001); Thompson (1998), on the other hand, finds censorship becoming more restrictive in the 1630s. So controversy found expression in newspapers and other printed forms. The forms and techniques of public debate in print developed early in the Elizabethan period, and members of the court used them to maneuver for advantage by invoking public opinion (Lake and Pincus, 2007). Conflict drove demand for news, which spurred the rise of both licensed and unlicensed printing in the seventeenth century, particularly during the Thirty Years War (1618–48).

The most dramatic outburst resulted from the revolution and Civil War of the 1640s. That conflict produced a total collapse of print regulation (Mendle, 1995; Raymond, 1996; McElligott, 2007). The revolution came from conflicts that had a lot to do with freedom of religion but, ironically, little to do with freedom of information or expression. Tensions between Puritan religious reformers and the established Church of England interacted with tensions between the Stuart monarchy, which needed revenue to wage an ambitious foreign policy, and the House of Commons, which balked at passing taxes. When the political system deadlocked, King Charles I retreated from London, raised an army, and went to war. When the Crown vacated the government, every factor in the system of press regulation – the King, his Privy Council, the Court of Star Chamber, the grant of monopoly that established the Stationers' Company, and the Bishops of the Church of England – lost its source of legitimacy and ceased to function. All of a sudden there was total freedom of the press. The result was a blossoming of pamphlets and newsbooks of every persuasion. Now all could see what an unrestrained press looked like.

With very few exceptions, elites did not like what they saw. Every leader, faction, or institution wanted freedom from regulation for itself, but none, or almost none, wanted freedom for everyone else. The revolutionary Parliament quickly restored licensing, substituting its authority for the authority of the Crown, setting up a licensing board and renewing the monopoly of the Stationers' Company. A few objected on principle.

John Milton made the most enduring argument against this renewal of censorship in his famous pamphlet, *Areopagitica*, later cited as the first mature formulation of a philosophy of freedom of the press. His justification rested on the notion of an emerging Truth, which he described in metaphorical terms: as a flowing brook, as a house under construction, as a tree or bush, with many branches growing out of a common root. Damming up or paring back Truth while it's flowing or growing would at best delay and at worst prevent its full emergence. It's what the Vatican had tried to do to Luther, and Milton wanted his fellow Puritans to be sickened by Parliament's misstep in imitating the Church of Rome. On the other hand, Milton had very large exceptions to his principle of free printing, most particularly "Popery, and open superstition." He urged freedom for various Protestant sects, whose "neighboring differences, or rather indifferences," could be seen as branches from the same root, but not for Catholicism, which was dedicated to undermining true religion and "civil supremacy."

The most often quoted of Milton's metaphors for free expression invoked athletic competition. He alluded to a wrestling match between Truth and Falsehood, and said: "Let her and falsehood grapple; who ever knew Truth put to the worse in a free and open encounter? For she is strong, next to the Almighty." The Divine power of Truth should always beat falsehood – in a free and open encounter. But what are the conditions for a "free and open encounter"? Clearly, Milton did not consider the Church of Rome's attempts to censor or purge Protestant arguments a free and open encounter. Even if the Roman Church were deprived of its power to censor, the very nature of its ideas and their authority, based on a corrupt hierarchy, meant that it could never engage in the kind of encounter Milton imagined.

To understand what Milton meant by a free and open encounter, we should look at the form his argument took. It was a pamphlet, printed in a run of about 500 copies and published in London. Rhetorically, it was structured as a speech to the Parliament – "Lords and Commons" – but its title, which invoked a similar speech by the Greek orator Isocrates, indicated that it was produced in writing for the larger public, as an open letter, and not to be orally delivered in the closed meeting space of the Parliament. Milton's argument was meant to be presented as a private citizen's petition to the government, with the condition that the entire citizenry could pay attention. The literary form of *Areopagitica* anticipated what Jürgen Habermas would later call the bourgeois or liberal model of the public sphere. I'll talk about that more later in this chapter.

Obviously, the whole citizenry, for Milton, did not include ordinary people. So much is obvious from even a superficial reading of the text. Milton expected his readers to know some Latin and Greek, to be familiar with the arguments of the Church Fathers, and to know the history of the early Church and of the Reformation. His imagined readership included only a highly educated fraction of the Protestant adult male population. In this he wasn't unusual. Most political pamphleteers would have assumed that their audience consisted of educated people who had been following public affairs, a small political class by later standards.

His argument and its publication put Milton toward the left end of the political spectrum, but not the far left. There were factions, like the Levellers and the Diggers, who believed in a far more expansive notion of rights, equality, and citizen participation. Milton included their leaders in the range of people who deserved to have a voice (Hill, 1978), unlike Catholics.

Milton drew boundaries around free expression because his core argument was based on the emergence of divine Truth, not the free flow of news. He seemed to flinch at unregulated publication of news, which would necessarily be mixed with rumor and falsehood, and might conceal all sorts of political agendas. One of his criticisms of the licensing board that Parliament had set up was that it lacked the capacity to prevent the publication of royalist newspapers, which turned up in the streets of London with the ink still damp from the press. Later, Milton would himself take on the job of licensing the official government newspaper.

Although modern liberals often criticize Milton as inconsistent, even hypocritical, there is a logical consistency to his thinking and to the media imaginary that informs it. His concern for the freedom of seekers after divine Truth sees freedom not as a natural right but as a moral one, conditioned by adherence to a reformed Christian faith. These seekers were a vanguard, whose learning and virtue earned them membership in a circle of privilege that should participate in the deliberations that would guide state policy. Free printing, properly used, would extend Parliamentary discussion outward to this circle – though not to everyone. *Areopagitica* itself, written in esoteric style and with an initial printing of perhaps 500 copies, was an example of this extension of privileged Parliamentary discussion.

Parliament continued to tighten its regulation of the news. After 1660, when the revolutionary government failed, and the Stuart monarchy was restored, Parliament continued to regulate the press, passing a very restrictive Printing Act in 1662, which created the powerful office of Surveyor of the Press. The man who was to become identified with this office, Roger L'Estrange, summarized the official attitude toward public communication when he said:

> Supposing the Press in order, the people in their right wits, and news or no news to be the question, a Public Mercury should not have my Vote, because I think it makes the Multitude too familiar with the actions and counsels of their superiors, too pragmatical and censorious, and gives them not only an itch but a kind of colourable right to be meddling with the government. (Roger L'Estrange, Intelligencer 1 (31 August 1663)) (Cowan, 2004)

This from a man who published compulsively, "perhaps three million words" in more than 1,000 titles (Kemp, 2006: 70).

England's experience dramatized the broader European history. Seventeenth-century eruptions of news culture did not prove durable in the short run. When order was restored, systems of regulation succeeded in largely suppressing news publications beyond intra-elite communication and official announcements. Serious people believed that public discussion should be regulated, even if they disagreed on who should do the regulating. From time to time, a practical incapacity to regulate opened a space for a "temporary public sphere" (Briggs and Burke 2009: 73).

Openness became normal only slowly and only by accident. In England, the rise of continuing party politics in the 1680s eventually made it impossible for Parliament to continue censorship (Lake and Pincus, 2007), and in 1695 the Printing Act lapsed. The breakdown of regulation produced another explosion of printing. Publications of all sorts appeared in London, many dealing with Parliamentary politics, and the first successful provincial newspapers were established, including one in the British North American colonial town of Boston. Still, elites could agree that news culture should be restricted on a class basis if not on an ideological one; a stamp tax enacted in 1712 effectively made a legal working-class press financially unsustainable.

The Public Sphere

Only in the eighteenth century did news culture come to seem to the leading classes in the west as a positive good. Gradually, they started to look upon it as an important feature of the mechanism by which people learned how to be good citizens. Only at the very end of the century was citizenship seen as the right of all "free men" (by which political thinkers meant males with the economic security to free them from the need to sell their labor to other men). These developments defined the norms associated with the modern notion of the "public sphere."

The public sphere is a term associated with Jürgen Habermas (1989), who defined it as the space where public opinion is formed through discussion and deliberation. Habermas argued that this abstract space has a specific history in the west. It appeared when a realm of private life (in "civil society," which included the marketplace, and in the "intimate sphere" of family relations) separated itself from the state. The space between civil society and the state became the public sphere. The bourgeois revolutions of the eighteenth century, especially in the US and France, formalized this formation, but it had appeared first in England. This social architecture explains the structure of the great eighteenth-century catalogs of rights, which protect liberty of conscience and expression alongside property rights from state interference. These rights formed a barricade to prevent state incursions into civil society; inside these fortifications, the public sphere would be a buffer zone between the state and the private realm of freedom.

But the public sphere was also supposed to operate as a steering mechanism for the state. It was the space in which private citizens (like Milton's persona in *Areopagitica*) could address matters of common concern. Ideally, citizens in public would be under universal supervision – anyone and everyone could witness the arguments they made. This made the public sphere different from both the courts of monarchs and the deliberations of legislatures, which operated as privileged spaces where argument could proceed freely because it was not supervised.

At the same time, speakers in the public sphere were supposed to honor the separation between their private interests and their status as citizens. When one addressed the public, one left behind one's economic interests, religious allegiances, and family status, and spoke only as a citizen speaking to other citizens. The ideal public speech situation, then, featured a citizen – a nobody – addressing all the other citizens: anybody and everybody.

In pragmatic or rhetorical terms, the speech of nobody addressing everybody could be called "rational." Pragmatically, when one makes an argument in which one forgoes any personal or charismatic authority, and honestly tries to speak to every other citizen, no matter what their political position, economic interests, or race or gender identity, one is forced to use only arguments that appeal to what ordinary people would call the common good, or reason. Any speaker who takes the abstract speech situation of the printed public sphere seriously would shy away from the sorts of things that today are called "special interest" appeals, or "dog whistle politics," or appeals to the social prejudices of segments of the public.

It happens that print was a good medium for making these kinds of arguments. It made it easy for a citizen to hide his (usually) identity behind a pseudonym (like "Publius," the author of the *Federalist Papers*). And it made it easy, and perhaps necessary, to pretend that the whole world could see whatever you wrote.

But surely, critics have pointed out, these arguments were never really so rational. Print may have broadened the sphere of public discussion, but not so much as to allow universal supervision. And many were still excluded: the unfree, the non-white, the non-Christian, and women (Goodman, 1994). A fantasy of equality concealed and reproduced privilege. Certainly these criticisms are correct.

Yet the discourse of the public sphere also produced a hegemonic notion of what a media system is supposed to do. Although it was at its heart a fantasy, it was a fantasy that drove the development of the press. The norms that it pretended to live by provided an arsenal for advocates of media freedom. Every democratic revolution since the eighteenth century has embraced some version of this fantasy.

For Habermas, the British experience was paradigmatic. There, because of the twin revolutions of 1640–1 and 1688–9, political turbulence invited a tradition of political debate that drew in a larger public. By 1702, this public's appetite for news had increased to the point where a daily newspaper was viable – the *Daily Courant*, which was to be the leading daily for the next few decades. This public in turn was cultivated by non-political or quasi-political periodicals to engage in polite deliberation and rational criticism on cultural affairs, producing a "literary" public sphere that developed the repertoire of habits of speech and thought for public politics. Habermas focuses particularly on two periodicals, the *Tatler* (1709–11) and *Spectator* (1711–14), edited by Joseph Addison and Richard Steele. They followed in an established tradition of moral criticism in print, most recently represented by Daniel Defoe's *Review* and Jonathan Swift's *Examiner*. But the *Tatler* and *Spectator* achieved unprecedented commercial success, selling several thousand copies and reaching an estimated 80,000 readers per issue. Influence radiated out from London through the entire English-speaking world.

The content of these papers consisted primarily of an essay published over a pseudonym – for the *Tatler*, "Isaac Bickerstaff." The fictionalized persona of the author, a device that allowed the actual authors to distance themselves from the particular judgments of the essay, made it easier to present the values championed in the paper as disinterested and rational. It is a gimmick that has been employed consistently in political criticism and satire, from the "Common Sense" of Tom Paine through the innumerable "Spys" and "Microscopes" of the next century and a half, to the "fake news" of Stephen Colbert's *The Colbert Report*. One of the more frequent targets of criticism was news culture itself. Bickerstaff mocked the content of most political newspapers as "imaginary entertainments in empty heads" (Cowan, 2004: 352, citing the *Tatler*, 18/1: 1490), a kind of manufactured spectacle letting its consumers believe in their own worldliness and civic engagement while actually driving them to distraction and agitation.

One reason for the success of the *Tatler* and *Spectator* was their integration into coffeehouse culture. Coffeehouses had become important points of social and political activity, and Habermas and others are keen to point out how they hosted and shaped public discussion (Pettegree, 2014: 230–48). Each coffeehouse served a habitual clientele identified with specific social, cultural, or political tendencies; one's coffeehouse provided a setting for casual conversation, spontaneous organization, and extensive reading in periodical literature. At the coffeehouse, one would browse the newspapers and discuss affairs with like-minded folk. Addicts were caricatured as "newsmongers," driven into an irksome irrationality by injudicious gossip and indiscriminate reading. Addison and Steele said they wanted to train more sober and polite patrons to displace the newsmongers (Cowan, 2004 Mackie, 1999: 2; Pollock, 2009: 2, 6)

While the *Tatler* and the *Spectator* were building a polite, middle-class public, the government was working to restrain the raucous undisciplined public that Addison and Steele satirized. One example of the kind of scandalous satirical sheet that provoked such alarm was the *Female Tatler*, published three times a week by Mrs Delarivier Manley. Mrs Manley's editorial persona was "Mrs Crackenthorpe, a lady that knows everything" (Williams, 2010: 62). Her essays in the *Female Tatler* and in other publications, like *Secret Memoirs from the New Atalantis* (1709), included thinly veiled attacks on prominent Whig politicians provocative enough to earn her an investigation for seditious libel and a payment – a bribe – from Lord High Treasurer Robert Harley, Queen Anne's leader in Parliament and an innovative manipulator of newspapers who subsidized both Swift and Defoe. It was Harley's idea for Parliament to pass its stamp tax on newspapers, periodicals, and advertisements in 1712. The stamp tax eliminated most popular publications by making them unprofitable. Printers would eventually find ways to circumvent the stamp tax, but these "unstamped" publications remained precarious.

The *Tatler* and *Spectator* didn't have a working-class readership. But the middle-class readership that supported Addison and Steele's efforts also became a market for political news, and grew in the course of the eighteenth century to be quite large. By the 1780s, to glance ahead, London collectively published 25,000 copies of newspapers daily, which, with the multiplying effect of sharing in large households and browsing in coffeehouses, could have served as many as 250,000 readers (Barker, 1998: 23–5), though a better estimate would be 100,000 habitual newspaper readers, and this in a city of fewer than a million.

By the 1720s this emerging readership had a recognized political philosophy. Its most influential formulation was in a series of essays written over the pseudonym "Cato" by Opposition Commonwealthmen John Trenchard and Thomas Gordon. Eighteenth-century political writers generally used pseudonyms because they provided some measure of anonymity and deniability in an age when prosecutions for seditious libel were common. But a pseudonym also served as a branding technique. "Cato" was a common pseudonym. It evoked the austere Republican virtue associated with the ancient Roman Cato the Censor, a hero of the Republic who opposed Julius Caesar, and indicated to the reader that the essay claimed to argue from the highest moral ground: the citizenship that called for sacrificing personal welfare for the public good.

Trenchard and Gordon argued that the press and public expression generally were important in a free state. Any stable republic contains competing interests, and needs to prevent any particular interest from gaining power and exercising tyranny over the rest. Since at least Plato, western political philosophers had seen the conflict of interests as the terminal illness of republics; eventually one interest or class would metastasize. The question that early modern political philosophers from Machiavelli on wrestled with was how to allow freedom while preventing instability and political opportunism. The answer revolved around the notion of virtue, understood as the commitment to putting the public good over private interest. Historians of political thought call this version of democratic theory "republican." Republican thought insisted that virtue was essential to free societies; for republicans, the real subject of liberty was the society and not the individual, whose freedom of action had to be kept in check by virtue. The historical Cato was a totem of this sort of virtuous self-denial.

For Trenchard and Gordon, the press was a key tool for promoting and enforcing virtue. By exposing corruption to the collective gaze of a supervising public, the press prevented abuse of power. Freedom of the press was thus the "palladium" of all liberties, the chief fortification that kept the hands of tyrants off free religion, free property, and every other form of personal freedom.

But the corollary to this argument was that the press, too, could be a tool of tyranny. The corrupt and powerful could also use the press to promote their own ends, to deceive and distract the citizenry, and to undermine the public good. So the republican version of the political philosophy of the press revolved around a notion of virtue that was embodied in an endlessly repeated distinction between liberty, or rational liberty, which was public-spirited and good, and licentiousness, which was selfish, dangerous, and not deserving of protection under the law. This was a philosophy that, like Milton's, had little confidence in the working of the marketplace, or the "marketplace of ideas" (a term which did not come into use until well into the twentieth century), as a bulwark against tyranny. Instead, it called for something more recognizable as a Habermasian public sphere, regulated by the principles of rational deliberation, with occasional assistance from the judiciary.

Part of the irony of *Cato's Letters* is that they were written as commentary on Acts of Parliament that were by law privileged, and not to be written about publicly. This privilege was traditional, and meant to protect the freedom of speech of members, who could rightly fear retribution by the monarch. Free deliberation required secrecy. During the upheavals in the middle of the seventeenth century, this prohibition relaxed, but it was reaffirmed by an Act of Parliament in 1660. Scrutiny of handwritten newsletters could be avoided, and those who printed newspapers also tried to evade the Act by waiting until Parliament was in recess and printing accounts as "history" rather than news. A subsequent Act in 1738 outlawed this practice, and instead magazines began publishing accounts that used fictional places and personae to portray Parliamentary debates. The absence of authoritative accounts of debates and votes meant that these fictionalized accounts could be very influential, a fact that would eventually lead Parliament to open its proceedings in self-defense, but only after an intense and extended campaign by the press in the 1760s. The ban was finally overturned in 1771. Among the heroes of that story is John Wilkes, a confidante of the powerful who became a Member of Parliament and then publisher of a newspaper called the *North Briton*. His criticisms of the administration of the Earl of Bute earned him prosecution for seditious libel and a period of exile in France, but he returned in glory, supported by the ordinary folk of London, to be re-elected to Parliament. Wilkes was a favorite symbol of the struggle against arbitrary authority in Britain's American colonies.

The British history of news formats and ideologies defined a North Atlantic system that included the English-language North American press. The American history began as a footnote to the British, and then in about a century reached parity in terms of quantity, became more advanced in terms of overcoming legal restrictions, and, by the end of the nineteenth century, assumed leadership, both within and outside of the English-speaking world.

British North America

The British colonies of North America were, first, British. Raw facts of geography reinforced this cultural identity. The overland routes between the colonies were rather difficult – interrupted by waterways and mountains, and spread out over considerable distances. But each colony was connected by a direct water route to London. The cost of shipping freight 3,000 miles to London in the eighteenth century was roughly equivalent to the cost of shipping it 20 miles inland; postage between Boston and London in the 1690s was a sixth of the cost of postage between Boston and New York (Johnson, 2009: 14–15).

The men and women who came to North America from Britain considered their culture, their institutions, and their identity to be British. Throughout the colonial era, they became increasingly British, and when they rebelled from Britain after a century and a half of colonial existence, they saw themselves as fighting to retain the rights and freedoms of Englishmen. As they became more British culturally, though, they became less British socially, mixing with the other cultures on the borders, and absorbing immigrants (free and unfree) from several continents. A wonderful example of the irony of this is provided by the Virginia gentry: perfectly imitating the habits of the English gentry, sending their sons to study law at the Inns of Court in London, buying their books and finery from London merchants, but drawing their wealth and prestige from African laborers, who brought their own food, music, and religion which continually seeped in to the gentry.

It's tempting to dismiss the Britishness of colonial society as superficial, a veneer, even comical. But this Britishness, which we might think of as a media culture, had a lot of work to do. Media are always expected to make meaning in a social world, a task which can be understood in many ways. Colonial media made sense by reinforcing and policing the values that separated the "civilized" from the "savage."

The various forms that conveyed news in Europe also appeared in the British colonies, including handwritten newsletters and pamphlet newsbooks. The networks that produced these resembled and were connected with European networks of commerce and officialdom. But in the seventeenth century the most important network was religious, and was rooted in the fact that through the seventeenth century the dominant impulse for colonization in the most literate provinces, in the northeast, was that of religious rebellion.

Ministers dominated the intellectual life of ordinary folk, particularly in New England, and were important nodes in the system of news circulation. Ministers gathered news for their sermons from letters circulated through a transatlantic network. Some of these newsletters survive. Handwritten and compiled out of a variety of sources, they are a curiously quasi-public vehicle of communication. Their contents were intended to be broadly shared, but the letters themselves were expected to be read by only a few, who would edit and augment the content to suit a general audience (McIntyre, 1998). The news was then incorporated into sermons. The sermon was itself an important medium. In most colonies, weekly attendance at church services was mandatory. In fact, the first publications that specifically recounted news were often sermons reprinted as pamphlets or newsbooks. These told the news, but did it explicitly to explain the working out of divine justice or providence in the world (Nord, 1990).

The first attempt at establishing a newspaper shared in this religious impulse, but was occasioned by the political upheavals that attended Britain's Glorious Revolution. On September 25, 1690, Benjamin Harris published the first issue of *Publick Occurrences, Both Forreign and Domestick*. The governing council of Massachusetts immediately suppressed it. In the centuries since, historians have disagreed on whether *Publick Occurrences* should count as the first American newspaper – because it published only one number, it might better be thought of as a pamphlet. Regardless, its story diagnoses the condition of public communication in English colonial North America.

Benjamin Harris had set up business in London as a publisher and bookseller in the 1670s. A religious radical and a political rebel, he had published pamphlets critical of the monarch Charles II, of his heir James II, and of the established Anglican Church. His media activities were serious enough to get him jailed twice before he fled the country in 1685. He followed the same path as other famous religious fugitives – from London to Holland, and then to Massachusetts. He arrived in Boston in 1686.

Massachusetts and the other New England colonies had been established by religious and political dissidents. For two generations these colonies had been largely free to set their own course, but, beginning in the 1660s and accelerating in the 1680s, the monarchy had become more concerned with streamlining colonial administration. The colonies expected a turn for the worse when James II assumed the throne in 1685. So momentous was that news that a printer in Boston, Samuel Green Jr, reprinted the edition of the *London Gazette* that contained the news – technically the first newspaper printed in the colonies (Clark, 1994: 69–70). In the same year that Harris arrived in Boston, James II erected the Dominion of New England, bypassing the traditional liberties of the colonies, and installed Sir Edmund Andros as its head. The appointment of Andros angered the colonists for religious as well as political reasons. He was an Anglican, and expected Puritan New Englanders to open their churches to Anglican services. Puritans had crossed the ocean to avoid the Anglican establishment. They began looking for an opportunity to send Andros back across the ocean.

In 1688, the opportunity came when James II was overthrown (Pincus, 2009). When James fell from power, all of the agencies and officers appointed by him lost their patron, including Edmund Andros. In a local version of the Glorious Revolution, in April 1689 Andros was thrown in jail and a provisional government set up to restore the old order.

Benjamin Harris wrote and published in support of the rebellion against Andros. *Publick Occurrences* was his most famous attempt. Clearly, he intended it to help promote the interests of the Puritan activists who had led the rebellion; he meant his paper to provide a resource for the provisional government. But that government forbade him to continue publishing. Why?

The reason reflected general principles. The order suppressing *Publick Occurrences* begins by pointing out that it had been printed "without the least privity or countenance of authority," that is, without the proper pre-publication licensing. In any good society, printing should be licensed by the governing authority. Arguments had been advanced for unlicensed printing, most famously by John Milton, but, between the decade of Civil War in England in the 1640s and the political restiveness of the 1720s, the notion of freedom of the press had receded from the forefront of British political thought. Benjamin Harris had endured punishment for violating this protocol twice under two different laws in England – once under the Printing Act and once under the common law of seditious libel (Clark, 1994: 71).

The specific content of the paper also offended council members. Contemporaries singled out two passages. One, referring to the French King Louis XIV, violated standards of decency by hinting at incest. The second criticized the colony's Mohawk allies for torturing prisoners and worshipping the devil.

You'd have to read the paper very carefully to be offended by these passages, I think. But, in a society in which printing was still scarce and in which reading practices remained intensive, politically active men would read the paper just that carefully, especially if they could further another agenda by doing so. In this case, William David Sloan and Julie Hedgepeth Williams have argued, *Publick Occurrences* gave the faction around Elisha Cooke a chance to embarrass the faction represented by Increase Mather (Sloan and Williams, 1994: 8–10). Mather's faction was trying to return control of the colony to a religious oligarchy, while Cooke's preferred a broader franchise. We don't need to go too deeply into the matter to recognize a common pattern. Controversies over the media often turn out to be proxies for some other kind of conflict. Aren't twenty-first-century arguments over "indecency" in popular culture really about gender or race?

It wasn't until 1704 that a successful newspaper began publishing regularly in the colonies. That paper was successful for practical reasons but also because of the gradual development of a culture of news. The practical reasons are easily identified: a regular clientele of government officials and merchants and a reliable infrastructure in printing supplies and most importantly in the expanding postal system (Smith, 1916: 267–8; John, 1995). The culture of news – the ways of doing things that saw publishing as good and useful – is harder to explain.

Most histories of colonial media begin with a remark by Virginia governor William Berkeley in 1671: "But, I thank God, there are no free schools nor printing, and I hope we shall not have these hundred years; for learning has brought disobedience, and heresy, and sects into the world, and printing has divulged them, and libels against the best government. God keep us from both!" (Hening, 1810–23, vol. 2: 517). Berkeley's outburst expressed the same attitude that had motivated Roger L'Estrange's surveyorship of the press in Restoration England. Elites viewed with suspicion popular interest in politics. The scarcity of printed matter and the difficulties of running a print shop in the colonies prevented this attitude from being tested until quite late in the colonial period. But this did not mean that colonial newspapers didn't matter.

Colonial newspapers had somewhat different uses from metropolitan ones. By the time the second newspaper appeared in British North

America in 1719, London already supported a flourishing printed public sphere, and reasonable people expected that news and public opinion would and should affect the conduct of government. Colonial newspapers seemed a pale imitation. The news in them focused almost entirely on European affairs, and concerned events that had occurred from a couple of months to a full year previously. When there was local news, it was either episodic – a report of a powerful storm or a dramatic crime – or dully official, like the text of the Governor's annual address to the provincial assembly. It remains difficult to decipher just why so much effort went into producing publications that seem of so little immediate use, particularly in a time and place where printing almost always was either devoted to religion, like sermons, or obviously practical, like schoolbooks and almanacs.

Charles Clark has proposed that colonial papers had important "ritual" uses (Clark, 1994), invoking a distinction between the "ritual" and "transmission" models of communication proposed by James Carey (Carey, 2009). In Carey's view, the conventional approach to understanding how communication media operate is to think of them as a way of transporting information, of moving data from point A to point B. While this captures an important dimension of what media do, it leaves out another perhaps more important dimension. The transmission model focuses on the conquest of space, but media are also a key part of the way that a society reproduces itself through time. So Carey calls attention to the ritual aspects of communication: the ways in which behaviors like reading a newspaper confirm and maintain a social order, even when the actual content of the newspaper is immediately forgotten. Reading the newspaper has the same ability to preserve a culture through time as attending religious services.

Clark argues that the importance of the newspaper in the colonies was ritual. Its readers were merchants and government officials, men (mostly) who identified strongly with their counterparts in the metropolis. These colonial gentlemen frequented coffeehouses, patterned on London models, where they read and discussed newspapers with like-minded gentlemen. Reading the newspapers in the presence of a tight community of fellows allowed them to preserve an identity with the metropolis, then, to see the world "with London eyes," as Clark puts it (Clark, 1994: 221).

Certainly newspaper reading did have important ritual uses. It was through the delayed circulation of the *Tatler* and *Spectator* that colonial men adopted habits of public comportment and expression. A young Benjamin Franklin, working as an unhappy apprentice in his brother's print shop in Boston, taught himself to write by reading essays from the *Spectator*, taking notes, then rewriting the essays from his notes. And it was through the republication of Trenchard and Gordon's *Cato's Letters* that a language of politics became widely shared among colonial citizens. This sort of intensive and repeated newspaper habit was an important mechanism for the preservation of a metropolitan identity in the distant provinces. (Colonial British North Americans mimicked the styles and forms of British prose – like Franklin and the *Spectator* – in a fashion common among provincials, who take metropolitan culture, queer it, and send it back. Repurposing, appropriation, and recombination were and remain key virtues in media life. One of the reasons why the US has been a successful media nation is that it has its own internal provincials – especially the south in literature and politics and African Americans in music and entertainment – who continually replenish its culture industries.)

But this analysis too easily dismisses the transmission uses of newspapers. The content of colonial newspapers arrived at the speed of colonial administration, after all. A three-month-old report on clashes between France and Spain would arrive at about the same time as orders for the French and Spanish fleets in the Caribbean, for instance, meaning that this old news was the key to understanding today's events nearby. But the reader had to have an already well-developed map of the way things worked to be able to use that key. Even a regular reader of a newspaper like the *Boston News-Letter* would not be able to acquire enough information from that paper to interpret the news that it reported. One would have to be deeply schooled through other means. And only a fraction of the population could boast such literacy. So these papers had transmission uses, but only for a mercantile and bureaucratic elite. Contrary to later ideology, news culture worked as another way of distinguishing gentlefolk from ordinary folk.

These elite readers usually were interested in maintaining the order of things. They largely shared the sentiment expressed by Governor Berkeley and Inspector L'Estrange in keeping politics away from the scrutiny of a larger public. But controversies inevitably arose, and found their way into print. Two are particularly well known in the eighteenth-century British colonies. One involved John Peter Zenger, in New York – we will discuss that one later.

The other involved a controversy over inoculation in Massachusetts. The *New England Courant*, published by James Franklin, printed letters criticizing an initiative to inoculate locals against smallpox. Underlying the debate over inoculation was a factional dispute between a relatively secular group, which patronized the *Courant*, and a group tied to a more traditional Puritan clerical leadership that included inoculation's champion, Cotton Mather. Because Franklin allowed the anti-inoculation faction to use his paper, he was jailed briefly for challenging the authority of the provincial government.

The inoculation controversy showed how unwise it was for a printer to ally himself with a political faction. James Franklin's younger brother Benjamin became wealthy and powerful, and joined the ranks of the political class, but very few printers were so successful. Most, like James Franklin, had to carefully navigate any competition between factions of the elite. They usually adopted a policy of neutrality, and claimed to be "open to all parties but influenced by none." Such printers tactically described themselves as "mere mechanics," using the generic term for an artisan. Stephen Botein (1975) argued that this humility was a business strategy, meant to appeal to the gentlemen in government and commerce who would be their main clients, without giving cause for offence. To work this strategy properly, printers needed to command a complicated bundle of skills and an extensive repertoire of social contacts, hardly the tools of a "mere" mechanic. Colonial printers were liminal figures, working the borders: the border between rival political factions, identifying with none because desiring the patronage of both; the border between literature and commerce; the border between gentlefolk and artisanal production.

This social position favored men, but a surprisingly large number of women ran print shops in the colonies. At James Franklin's *Rhode Island Gazette*, his wife, Ann, was actively involved in setting type and running the business. Many years later she established the *Newport Mercury* with her son James Jr. Anna Zenger ran the *New York Weekly Journal* while her husband was in jail. Elizabeth Timothy edited the *South Carolina Gazette* after her husband's death in 1738. Sarah Goddard and Mary Katherine Goddard, mother and sister of William Goddard, ran the *Providence Gazette and Country Journal*, and Mary Katherine later ran the *Pennsylvania Chronicle* and the *Maryland Journal* while William was busy running the continental postal system; she was hired by the continental Congress to print the "clean" copy of the Declaration of Independence. And Margaret Draper in Boston ran the *Massachusetts Gazette*. In every case, the woman had come to her position by virtue of her relationship to a man; still, women seemed freer to assume control of a print establishment in the colonial era than in the first decades after the revolution. Perhaps coincidentally, colonial printers did not make a big deal of their "manly" voices. They tended to defer to the elite, their readers, and to submerge their own voices; in Franklin's most famous publications, he assumed voices that were decidedly unmanly and unmasterful, like the spinsterly "Silence Do-Good" or the humble "Poor Richard."

The reluctance of printers to raise their own voices in a controversy was matched by a tendency to gather news passively. Unlike editors in the more developed London market, who would actively collect and compose the items in their papers to support a particular faction or movement, colonial printers took what news came to hand, from officials, regular sources like ship captains, and from other newspapers, putting it together so that the hypothetical reader, assumed to be a member of the elite, could believe that he (rarely she) would have selected the same material. The passivity of printers helped to dampen political controversies generally. James N. Green quips that William Bradford and his son Andrew, who published newspapers in New York and Philadelphia, "pretended to be open to all parties, but in fact they preserved their independence by being closed to all" (Green, 2000: 223).

Colonial Newspapers and the Public Sphere

Some scholars insist that colonial newspapers and the occasional controversies they engaged in marked the emerging power of public opinion and the appearance of a contested "public sphere" (Smith, 1988; Warner, 1990). Colonial politics never embraced "publicness," if by publicness we mean opening affairs of government to the scrutiny of anyone or everyone. Although colonial newspapers seemed to lay things out for all to see, they actually coded their material in such a way that only a few were likely to understand the action. An ordinary person could hardly have decoded them. In fact, the newspapers circulated in fairly restricted circles for most of the colonial period; even when they were available in taverns and coffeehouses, they were usually the places where gentlemen consorted. Richard D. Brown (1989) notes the restricted flow of information in colonial Boston by examining the diary of Samuel Sewall, a prominent merchant and officeholder. Sewall had access to information through privileged channels – from other officials, divines, and businessmen – and used newspapers to supplement this information. For men like Sewall, members of the political class whose personal contacts rivalled those of the postmaster and printer, newspapers had less importance as transmitters of information than as symbols of public life. But when

Sewall retired from active life, he lost his access. At that point, newspapers became more important but sadly inadequate; they could relate important facts, but carried little to explain the implications behind the facts. In other words, unless you were personally active in public affairs, a colonial newspaper wouldn't allow you to be in the know. Traces of public affairs appeared in the newspapers, but these didn't add up to either an adequate record or a full representation of public life.

So how should we understand the sometimes heated political debates that occasionally spiced the newspapers? Certainly the essays and letters that factional combatants published in newspapers were meant to appeal to something like "public opinion." What was the theory behind this practice?

I would argue that such controversies were extensions of legislative debate, and were considered "privileged" rather than public. It was one of the ancient rights of Parliament and, by extension, the colonial assemblies, to be free to speak, to criticize the government and remain immune from prosecution. We have already discussed Parliament's ancient right to speak free from supervision. Freedom of speech was a right of Parliament before it was a right of ordinary people. In fact, because the people's representatives exercised freedom of speech, there seemed to be no need for the people themselves to, and some felt that letting ordinary people participate in politics would interfere with public liberty by making it more difficult for Members of Parliament to do their business. In England, restrictions on Parliamentary reporting survived well into the eighteenth century and were asserted by the Commons in the 1740s to discourage newspaper discussions (Black, 1987).

This marriage of freedom to secrecy complicated the work of printed controversy. It meant that whatever appeared in print would have a double function – superficially, to tell the people what was up; on a deeper level, to tell the legislators that public attention was now a factor. In cases where one faction in a legislature silenced another, the losing faction would want to take its case to a broader public, and so into print. This would look like democracy. But the purpose of publicity was not to let ordinary people have a voice in government; rather, partisans publicized conflicts so that they could use the impression of publicity to maneuver for position within the legislature.

In the seventeenth- and eighteenth-century British Atlantic world, print remained limited. The audience for the printed arguments was not the people, the unrestricted body of citizens, but an elite somewhat larger than the legislature. Leaders feared the active attention of the masses, and would have kept printed news away from them if they could. But eventually censorship failed. Even the prohibition on printing actual Parliamentary debates led to thinly veiled fictionalized versions that were more mischievous than the real thing. Better than direct control were measures that simply made it more expensive to read the news, such as the 1712 stamp tax.

The political content of the colonial newspaper was an extension of legislative privilege. This applied to both the news content, which was intentionally fragmentary, and to opinion pieces, whose authorship was concealed behind pseudonyms and whose arguments often relied on misdirection and allusion. Printers happily worked this matter to make it difficult to unpack – eliding officials' names, encouraging elaborate satire, and reprinting British essays (most famously, *Cato's Letters*). For the most part, these techniques kept politics safely in the hands of gentlemen.

The Zenger Case

The most famous colonial controversy in print took place in New York and involved the jailing of a printer, John Peter Zenger. Usually remembered as a landmark in the history of freedom of the press, the Zenger case could also be read as an object lesson in the restrictions of provincial politics.

Although his name is firmly tied to the controversy, John Peter Zenger was perhaps the least important player in the whole affair. The controversy began when the Crown appointed William Cosby to be Governor of New York. It was ordinary for the Crown to appoint governors with little familiarity with colonial political realities, just as presidents today often appoint large donors to ambassadorships. Cosby displayed his ignorance of New York's power structure right away. A member of one of the clans that dominated the colony's government had been serving as acting governor, and Cosby was expected to allot him a fair share of the governor's salary. Cosby refused. The acting governor pursued his case to the province's Supreme Court, where Chief Justice William Morris, chieftain of another of the state's clans, butted heads with Cosby. Cosby fired Morris, who then organized a large Opposition faction among New York's elite. The Morrisites sought an outlet in print. The existing newspaper, loyal to the governor because of its government printing commission, shunned Opposition pieces. Instead, the Morrisites hired Zenger to establish the *New York Journal*.

Zenger was hardly politically astute. A German-speaking immigrant from Palatine, English was very much his second language. He acted as simply a hired printer for leaders of the Opposition faction, who actually composed his *Journal*. Much of the content consisted of reprints of British political essays. Most notable was *Cato's Letters*, especially the essays in which Trenchard and Gordon argued for the right of citizens to criticize a corrupt government. In the 1730s, this position remained controversial.

Cosby's administration quickly moved to try to silence Zenger's *Journal*. Cosby's newly appointed Chief Justice, James Delancey, tried twice in 1734 to have a grand jury indict it for sedition and failed. Finally, in November of that year, the administration sidestepped the grand jury by having the Governor's Council act in its stead. The Council in colonial governments was usually appointed by the governor, much like the President's Cabinet today, but also served as the Upper House of the legislature, like the US Senate. It did not usually hand down indictments. Cosby's Council found four issues of the *Journal* libellous, and ordered them to be publicly burned and Zenger arrested. Because Zenger was unable, and his backers unwilling, to raise the exorbitant bail of 400 pounds sterling (which would have been several times his annual revenue), he remained in jail for a judicial drama that was to last nine months.

Zenger's trial began with his patrons acting as attorneys for the defense. But Chief Justice Delancey debarred them because they continually raised questions about the legitimacy of his appointment. Then Andrew Hamilton came to Zenger's defense. Hamilton was at the time the most famous lawyer in the colonies, but his interest in Zenger's case is hard to explain. Hamilton was based in Philadelphia, and as a politico was not known as a champion of freedom of the press. In fact, he had earlier prosecuted Philadelphia printer Andrew Bradford for seditious libel. Some scholars suspect that he took Zenger's case in part to retaliate against Bradford's father William, who ran the *New York Gazette*, the colony's official paper (Katz, 1972).

Zenger's case finally came to trial on August 4, 1735. Hamilton's argument played on the sentiment that the whole proceeding was unfair. Cosby had not been a popular governor and it wasn't hard to make his actions seem tyrannical. He could not get a grand jury or the colony's elected assembly to act against Zenger, and so had turned to his appointed council to put him on trial before his appointed Chief Justice. But calling the prosecution unfair did not make it illegal.

Under the law of seditious libel, Zenger should have been convicted. The law clearly stated that a printer could be convicted simply for printing seditious material, and it was understood that even truthful material could be seditious. Moreover, by law the judge and not the jury should determine whether the material was seditious. Judge Delancey made that determination, and instructed the jury to consider only whether Zenger had in fact printed the material.

Hamilton did not dispute that Zenger had printed it. Even so, he urged the jury to acquit. He argued that it was proper and in fact a patriotic duty to truthfully and honestly criticize corrupt governments. He also argued that a jury had the power to interpret the law according to its own best judgment of fairness. Hamilton urged the jury to use its power to set Zenger free. And it did, without much deliberation.

The importance of this verdict remains unclear. To some, it was and remains a triumph for the freedom of public criticism of government. Many remember it as establishing truth as a defense in libel proceedings (Green, 2000). To others, it was a triumph for the right of juries to make broad-ranging judgments. But there are reasons to hedge on both these conclusions. Printers continued to be reined in by colonial governments; in New York, the assembly's threat of chastisement suitably intimidated printers. Zenger himself went from opposition to being the colony's official printer. And the law of seditious libel under which he was prosecuted remained unchanged.

The event itself might be best understood as a particular eruption of politics as usual. That is, a normal bout of factional rivalry ran its course, then passed from notice with a return to the status quo. A couple of key facts support this understanding. First, Governor Cosby and his appointees remained in power, despite Zenger's acquittal, and the Morrisites gradually reconciled themselves to his rule. Second, the other colonies took little notice of the trial and the drama surrounding it. In fact, Stephen Botein has pointed out that the greatest interest in the trial seems to have come from England. James Alexander's pamphlet about the trial was reprinted in London four or five times in 1738, which was also the year that Milton's *Areopagitica* was republished for the first time (Katz, 1972: 36). Botein argues that Zenger's *Journal* was patterned on the English newspaper *The Craftsman*, which had printed *Cato's Letters* and other pieces critical of Horace Walpole's government, and its printer had also been prosecuted. Zenger's paper reprinted pieces from *The Craftsman* and copied its general look. Botein suggests that the case was "a kind of libertarian drama, scripted in London and staged in one of the colonies – conceivably more for an audience (real or imaginary) back in the cultural capital than for New Yorkers" (Botein, 1985: 6).

Still, prosecutions for seditious libel became more difficult after the Zenger verdict. Zenger's trial inspired later arguments for a free press, and libertarian thinkers were able to distill a coherent philosophy from the verdict and pleadings (Levy, 1985; Rosenberg, 1986). This "Zengerian" theory of freedom of the press followed arguments earlier made in England – that a free press is needed to monitor corruption in government, and that a free press is the bulwark of all other liberties. After Zenger, such arguments carried greater authority.

But these arguments do not require a positive belief in wide-open politics. Under "Zengerian" principles, it is only when crooks run the government that free public discussion is needed. When public-spirited men [*sic*] sit in legislatures, and make determinations according to their honest sense of the public good, then the public doesn't really need to know the details. This philosophy is consistent with a belief on restrictions on public knowledge. It can sit comfortably with elite control, and then stand up and strike out when one faction feels aggrieved.

The Colonial Press, the Atlantic System, and the Revolution

London dominated the print culture of the English-speaking North Atlantic until the second half of the nineteenth century. But within the Atlantic system, the periphery experienced continual and dramatic growth. Newspapers became a normal part of the administration of the colonies that would become the United States by the middle of the eighteenth century. By the time the War for Independence began in 1775, there were around 45 weekly newspapers in the colonies, and, although most of them were based in the northeast, every colony had at least one.

The form and business model of these newspapers had been established early on. The form – snippets of news, copied from other newspapers and official documents, introduced with something like a dateline, involving a minimal editorial voice, and usually moving from the distant to the near – replicated the experience of a skilled newspaper reader in a well-stocked coffeehouse. Because the newspaper also occasionally contained correspondence discussing issues of the day, one can say that the entire product constituted a virtual coffeehouse (Barnhurst and Nerone, 2001).

The business model of colonial newspapers was most obvious in the print office, where the tangible work of production took place. There, a master printer directed the labor of family members, the occasional wage-earning journeyman, and apprentices, in an operation similar to other craft enterprises. But beyond the print shop, the colonial newspaper – like any media business – required a network of relationships to be set up. Any media enterprise will be based on a series of pipes. Some of those pipes retrieve content – news, say, or ads, or songs – from producing organizations such as governments, markets, and other media organizations. Other pipes deliver this content to readers or listeners or viewers. And other pipes carry money and other feedback back to the media organization. In commercial media, audiences themselves become a kind of content, and are sold to advertisers. In colonial newspapers, the key figure at the center of this network of relationships was the printer. The printer selected content from a range of documents, most importantly other newspapers, assembled it into printed form, and distributed the finished product to a client list which the printer recruited and maintained from among the leading members of the political class and social elite. Maintaining the steady patronage of the relatively small local elite, both for the newspaper and the print shop that produced

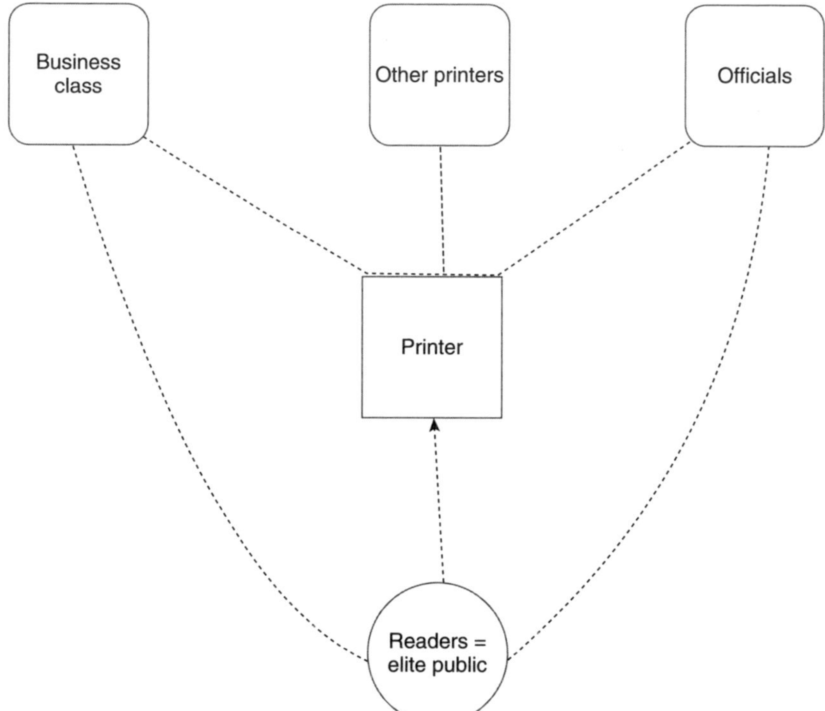

Figure 1.1: The printer's newspaper as a network of relationships

it, required social skill and maneuverability. In addition, to ensure a steady flow of content, printers needed to maintain a network of mutual exchange with other printers, with key players in the world of commerce and transportation (like ship captains), and especially with government officials. Government officials were sources not just of content, but also of printing contracts and other forms of patronage. In most colonies, the first printer was subsidized by the provincial government for the express purpose of printing the laws and performing other sorts of job-printing for the bureaucracy. That's why it was common for most newspapers to say that they were printed "By Authority" (Clark, 1994). That term also referred to the fact that provincial governments had the legal authority to license printers and to prosecute "unauthorized" publication for much of the colonial period.

The press of the eighteenth century did not feature what moderns would call "journalism." News was gathered out of a browsing of letters, government documents, and other newspapers, and assembled by practical printers with minimal editing (Clark 1994; Wilke 2003). The word "journalism" came into use in the wake of the eighteenth-century revolutions to describe political argumentation, not news-gathering. Journalists were controversialists. Ironically, because the press was supposed to be an instrument of public deliberation, such journalists were sometimes seen as a danger to the useful freedom of the press. Closer to the modern notion of the journalist in these newspapers was the "correspondent," a term which referred to a person loosely associated with a newspaper who sent in letters containing news from distant locations, like national capitals or commercial centers. Correspondents typically did this as an avocation, sometimes receiving pay per piece, but often writing for free, perhaps with the interest of a future literary career.

That mode of production and the formal appearance of newspapers did not change for many years. The print shop remained the key producing unit until well into the nineteenth century. But the appearance of a revolutionary movement in the 1760s fundamentally altered the uses of the newspaper, or, put another way, the existence of the newspaper as a network of relationships.

The revolutionary movement began as a series of ad hoc reactions to imperial legislation. It is fair to say that the history of anglophone North America from around 1760 to around 1820 was a subplot of the geopolitical struggle between France and Britain. A frontier war between the two powers began in 1754; called the French and Indian War in the British colonies and the Seven Years War in Europe, it ended in 1763 with Britain acquiring Canada and a massive debt.

Over the next dozen years, Parliament's attempts to administer Catholic Canada and to reduce the national debt would provoke increasingly violent responses from the predominantly Protestant population of the older British colonies.

US historians have long debated whether the revolutionary movement was a radical social movement, driven by class tensions, or a socially conservative political movement, aimed at a simple separation from formal Parliamentary authority. Despite attempts to portray the revolution as a tranquil, consensual process led by heroic Founding Fathers, historians continually rediscover deep social divisions within the colonies and a remarkable level of raw physical conflict and violence. Any number of other conflicts – between artisans and merchants, between mainline Protestants and evangelicals, between whites and red and black populations, between people who believed in monarchy and others who called themselves republicans and then democrats – straddled the one big conflict between the colonies and Britain (Young, 1976; Nash, 1979; Bouton, 2007).

Much of this complexity was repressed in the way the revolutionary movement presented itself. A leadership group, composed mostly of gentlemen – lawyers, merchants, clergymen – organized and debated, in many provinces struggling to triangulate between colonial administrators and more radical groups representing ordinary folk. The leadership produced a stream of correspondence, resolutions, public demonstrations, and print media that cloaked social struggles inside debates that pivoted on the interpretation of terms such as "rights" and "representation."

The media campaign was multiplatform and effectively orchestrated. The movement produced a broad range of media material, including broadsides meant for public display, often with a visual element; pamphlets of varying size and complexity, some relatively brief and comprised of a sermon or speech, others book-length expositions of political theory; and newspapers, which worked as an omnibus medium, digesting and collecting all the other print products while reporting on and amplifying the voices of demonstrations and committee meetings. The media activities of the revolutionaries expressed and framed a messy but effective organizational campaign.

The organizing impulse involved letting a thousand committees bloom. Beginning with the 1764 Sugar Act, which sought to enforce tariffs on a key commodity in the triangular trade between the Caribbean, the North American colonies, and Britain, "Committees of Correspondence" appeared, sharing information and coordinating responses. With the 1765 Stamp Act, which attempted to raise revenue in the colonies by taxing all printing and legal transactions by requiring them to use stamped paper, resistance appeared, organized at the grass roots and then networked with other groups throughout the colonies. The groups opposing the Stamp Act called themselves the Sons of Liberty. The name derived from a phrase used to describe the colonists in a widely reprinted speech in the House of Commons by Colonel Isaac Barre (Standiford, 2012). The name itself points to the importance of both the transatlantic media system and Parliamentary politics. The Sons of Liberty looked like a series of spontaneous and local clubs, but their branding suggests more calculation.

The committee movement simultaneously built a shadow government and performed a political philosophy. John Locke argued in his second treatise on government that all legitimate governments have been formed by the actual consent of free individuals in a state of nature. Once legitimate, governments could operate according to majority rule, and pass all sorts of laws, as long as those laws did not violate the fundamental rights of its citizens. If a government repeatedly invaded the rights of its citizens, it ceased to be legitimate, and the citizens were thrown back into a state of nature, where they could form a new government.

The resistance movement, in a conscious gesture toward Locke's philosophy, began to form committees that took on more of the work of governing. These Committees of Safety, as they were commonly called, presented themselves as the result of the "actual consent" of people thrown into a state of nature forming a new political contract. The committees worked on a local level much like the traditional legislative Assemblies, which became radicalized themselves, did on the provincial level. By 1774, this committee movement had matured to the point at which a Continental Congress, which might be thought of as the committee of committees, came into existence and started to act like a national legislature. By the spring of 1775, the Crown had declared the colonies to be in rebellion, and the War for Independence had begun.

The signal event, the rhetorical prodigy of the movement, was Tom Paine's *Common Sense*, the first real American bestseller, and a marker of the transatlantic nature of the resistance. Paine was a recent immigrant to the colonies, an artisan who had been relatively uninvolved in both politics and writing. He had come to Philadelphia after meeting Benjamin Franklin in London, and with Franklin as a reference had found work in Robert Aitken's bookstore, a meeting place for the politically engaged. He also began writing for Aitken's *Pennsylvania Magazine*. At the bookstore he met Dr. Benjamin Rush, a leader of the Pennsylvania patriots, who encouraged him to write a pamphlet arguing for independence. What he produced was a pamphlet that was reprinted over and over and excerpted in dozens of newspapers; Paine estimated that more than 120,000 copies were distributed within three months of its publication in January 1776, and within a short time it is likely that every American would have come into contact with its arguments – only 2.5 million people lived in the 13 colonies that would form the United States. Eric Foner argues that this pamphlet, in restating older arguments in new, plain, forceful terms, actually created a new language of politics that expressed and communicated with a newly politicized class of artisans (Foner, 1976; though Trish Loughran doubts that *Common Sense* actually circulated so broadly – 2009: ch.2.)

The Declaration of Independence was the climax of this performance of Locke's political philosophy. A second Continental Congress, already directing a military operation, called on the various provinces and localities to give their sense on the question of independence (Maier, 1997). The response was a wave of resolutions by local committees and public meetings calling for independence. At that point, the Continental Congress appointed a committee, whose chief members were Thomas Jefferson, John Adams, and Benjamin Franklin, to draft a declaration. The Declaration began with a condensed version of Locke's second treatise, which represented the ideological meeting grounds on which all the various revolutionary groups and positions could come together.

The Declaration was itself a media product. Because they recognized its propaganda value, the Congress encouraged the creation of a dramaturgy of Declaring Independence. This is exemplified by the signing of the document. Marshall Smelser remarks:

> Folklore says that scholarly William Ellery of Rhode Island (a man fond of reading Cicero, even on his deathbed) watched the expressions on the faces of the signers as they took quill in hand, for, after all, they might be signing their own death warrant. He reported, it is said, that all the signers showed "undaunted resolution." This is a regrettably impossible tale, because the signing went on for months. (1972: 141)

In fact, the names of the signatories were kept secret for some six months after the Declaration was passed.

Similarly iconic is the image of the embossed copy of the Declaration. This was created after the fact, as a kind of sacred relic of the Declaration. It was not the form in which the Declaration became public. Its first publication was in a Philadelphia newspaper printed on July 6, 1776. From that printed form, it was copied into other newspapers, issued as a broadside, read out loud at demonstrations, public meetings, and committee meetings, and promulgated through the vast and supple communications network of the revolution.

The myth of Declaring Independence obscures the real revolution that the Declaration effected. The revolutionaries had to pull off a double act of representation – representing the government to the people, and representing The People to the world. Notice that I'm distinguishing between "the people," by which I mean all of the individual people in the colonies, and "The People," by which I mean the collective body of the polity. The Declaration succeeded in representing The People, and making the people believe it. Framed as the Unanimous Declaration of the representatives of The People, and conveyed to the people through the many media of the revolution, it in effect re-constituted The People as a new political community. Declaring it made it so. (For a similar argument, see Warner, 1990.)

A similarly deep and quiet revolution took place in the media. The change in sovereignty that the Declaration effected was not necessarily apparent on the surface. The new state legislatures were actually the old provincial assemblies, and the new national leadership mostly came from old established elites – to all outward appearances, the revolution looked pretty conservative, and this was exactly what the leadership wanted, even though the revolution had already begun to effect a radical change in the social imaginary (Wood, 1991). Likewise, the forms of political communication didn't seem to change much. Newspapers looked pretty much the same, and the familiar genres – sermons, pamphlets, broadsides – remained in use. But a communications revolution also took place. Beneath their familiar forms, the media changed as networks of relationships. While they were changing individually, the media collectively also began to perform a new function. We might understand this new function as supporting a national public sphere. Although the leadership didn't seem to want to look like it was revolutionizing the government, it did seem to want to create a national public sphere. In doing so, it changed the relationship of the media to the distribution of power.

We like to think that information and communications are especially uncontainable forms of power, and we talk of the "power of the press" and the ways that ideas and information "want" to be free (Peters, 1999). In other words, our instinct is to think of information and communications as "spiritual," as different from land, dollars, public office, and other "material" forms of power. We like to think of the power of the press, for instance, as coming from the power of truth over a candid mind.

In any society, the media will work to distribute power. This work will be more significant in some societies than in others, and it will be more equitable in some than in others. In an ideal media system, the media will distribute power according to principles like truth and fairness. In an ideal media system, ordinary people will be able to direct social policy because the media system allows them to know and speak the truth. But only in such an ideal media system would we be able to claim that the power of the media is the power of truth. The actually existing media are sadly profane. Their content can be judged by standards of truth, but their power is like the power of land and dollars. Ideas may want to be free – who knows? – but media are properties that don't come free. In the history of the media, it has always been thus.

Colonial-era media patently worked to solidify the authority of elite groups. In new and turbulent societies characterized by significant social flux and political dissonance, the media, especially the print media, expressed a simplified and more homogeneous social world, one in which ordinary people recognized their social betters, left leadership in the hands of gentlemen, and rarely disturbed the sanctioned hierarchies of race, sex, class, and religion. To modern taste, the colonial world depicted in print culture was far less interesting than the facts on the ground, where sanctioned hierarchies were frequently challenged and occasionally overthrown. The placidity of print culture might be surprising. Colonial leaders like Governor Berkeley of Virginia feared and resisted the arrival of print because they thought it would destabilize the social order and encourage ordinary people to encroach on the turf reserved for their social betters. But their anxiety seems misplaced. Even though the "publicness" of print seemed uncontainable – after all, once it's in print *everyone* can see it – in reality the power of the press could be quite capably captured and channeled, as long as the relevant elite groups could agree on boundaries. The revolution, though, changed this calculus.

The American Revolution changed the way the media related to the distribution of power. Because the revolution demanded that its media bolster the legitimacy of contested governing powers, rather than primarily providing displays of power, the media also became battlegrounds of power. The revolutionary movement reconstructed the way power was conferred and confirmed. It initiated a change on a deep level that would continue to work itself out over the next generation. It began moving toward an unrestricted political arena. It proposed a national and "universal" public sphere.

The practicalities of revolution, which required mobilizing the general population, interacted with a tradition of political theory about government by consent to produce a norm of public deliberation as the source of legitimate government. An expanded press was both a cause and an effect of those revolutions. Revolutionaries rushed into print to represent the people giving consent to new governments; placing popular consent at the root of political authority in turn encouraged guarantees of freedom of the press, along with tremendous social investment in the infrastructure of the news system. In this moment of development, the mode of production combined with ideological and political factors to erect norms of news media conduct that centered on the master metaphor of the town meeting or the Fourth Estate. As we will see in the next chapter, most newspapers were produced by printers with a reliance on both state support and the patronage of local elites whom they were unwilling to offend. The ideology of the public sphere projected a neutral medium for information and deliberation, and the positive (subsidies) and negative (censorship) influence of the state tended to reinforce that.

But newspapers could also be used to promote a partisan interest, which made for continual tensions in the overall system. The post-revolutionary generation struggled to reconcile their idealized image of the press as a neutral forum for citizen deliberation with the activist use of newspapers for party interests. Only after much anguish did the next generation grow comfortable with a public sphere characterized by the permanent conflict of organized interests.

The French Revolution

France's experience with the rise of a print public sphere differed in both plot and tempo from developments in Britain and the US. The French monarchy had built the kind of stable system of monopolies that Britain's occasionally hoped for but never achieved. Even as the press expanded impressively in the eighteenth century (Chartier, 1993), the newer energies in print culture, including foreign publications aimed at the French public, continually were brought into the mainstream through the flexible adjustments of a fairly liberal administration. So even the ideas of the Encyclopedists and Physiocrats, initially treated as seditious and later seen as sources of revolutionary inspiration, managed to circulate through approved channels in the second half of the eighteenth century. News of the American Revolution, which the French monarchy supported in the interest of achieving geopolitical advantage over Britain, helped boost the circulation of both foreign and licensed newspapers in France.

So when the system of press regulation broke down, it was sudden and dramatic. Much like in the English Revolution of the 1640s, the monarchy lost its capacity to regulate the press when confronted with a competing power, the Estates General. In fact, the crucial moment in the collapse of the licensing system came in 1789 when activists like Mirabeau ignored the regulatory apparatus and published newspapers describing debates in the Estates General under the justification of reporting to their own constituents. Quickly political news and argument took over existing newspapers, which had previously focused on foreign news and commercial information. New newspapers appeared, attached to every sort of club or faction, so that by the end of 1789 there were 130 titles published in Paris alone, including 20 political dailies (Gough, 1988). According to Jeremy Popkin, circulation rose to as high as 300,000 a day, easily the highest penetration rate in the world, before falling back to around 30,000 in 1802 (Popkin, 1990: 82–6; Hallin and Mancini, 2004: 92).

In France, unlike in Britain or the US, the struggle to achieve freedom of the press became a key demand of the revolutionary movement. This had something to do with the suddenness with which the emergence of a free press occurred, but also with the fact that freedom of the press had become associated with political freedom through French observation of the British and American histories. When Mirabeau broke with the censorship regime, he also published a French translation of Milton's *Areopagitica*. The Declaration of the Rights of Man, which resembled in some ways the US Declaration of Independence and in other ways the Bill of Rights that the US Congress was debating at the same time, featured a call to freedom of the press as its eleventh Article. But the Bill of Rights had emerged at the end of the American Revolution, whereas the Declaration was the first grand product of the French. In the history of media systems, timing is important. It mattered that in the US history substantial freedom from formal regulation had preceded the revolution by half a century, whereas in France the two were simultaneous. It later mattered that in the US universal manhood suffrage had preceded the rise of a mass-circulation working-class press, whereas in Britain the two were simultaneous: Britain has ever since had a more powerful class dimension to its politics.

These apparently independent national histories were also entangled with each other. Political ideas circulated from one revolution to the next, although repurposed to each new situation. John Locke's "life, liberty, and estate" became Thomas Jefferson's "life, liberty, and the pursuit of happiness"; the French Declaration referred to "liberty, property, security, and resistance to oppression." The US First

Amendment in the Bill of Rights states "Congress shall make no law respecting an establishment of religion, or prohibiting the free exercise thereof; or abridging the freedom of speech, or of the press; or the right of the people peaceably to assemble, and to petition the government for a redress of grievances." The parallel text from the French Declaration, in Articles 10 and 11, reads: "No one shall be disquieted on account of his opinions, including his religious views, provided their manifestation does not disturb the public order established by law. The free communication of ideas and opinions is one of the most precious of the rights of man. Every citizen may, accordingly, speak, write, and print with freedom, but shall be responsible for such abuses of this freedom as shall be defined by law." The French made explicit expectations of social order that the US left implicit.

In each national history, the end of the eighteenth century saw attempts to reconcile professions of belief in natural rights with the need to maintain a stable and reasonable system of public life. Twenty-first-century liberals like to think that eighteenth-century revolutionaries believed in what the twentieth century came to call the marketplace of ideas: a notion that everyone pursuing self-interest in the political arena would automatically produce the common good, just as the pursuit of economic self-interest in a market is thought to produce economic growth. There is no evidence that eighteenth-century revolutionaries believed this. On the contrary, in both the US and France, revolutionaries were alert to the great damage to the common good that they thought could come from the expression of vicious, irrational, or self-interested opinion, and took direct action against printers whose work ran counter to the revolution. Well, revolutions are not markets. The coherent set of ideas behind these attitudes and actions held that free discussion could only be free if it was restrained by a virtuous consideration of the common good and a citizenly and brotherly [*sic*] refusal of self-interest.

These early experiments in democracy all labored under a burden of history. Common sense told thinking men and women that democratic governments were tremendously unstable, and that democratic publics were especially vulnerable to divisions caused by conflicts of interest. Democracies became fractious, and then ambitious leaders took advantage of ordinary people to achieve tyrannical control. Too much freedom leads to no freedom at all; so Plato taught us in his *Republic*, and so history from the fall of the Athenian democracy and of the Roman Republic onward confirmed. The English-speaking world thought the French Revolution proved this by birthing a Napoleonic empire that aped the styles of imperial Rome.

If the invisible hand of the marketplace would not save a free people from the ambitions of Caesar, what would? In the French Revolution, successive governments imposed ideological and political restrictions on the press; these did suppress publication but did not have the effect of supporting the kind of vivid public deliberation that could sustain a stable democracy. The British tactic was a tax scheme that walled off the voices of the lower classes from public life. This barrier decayed over the course of the first half of the nineteenth century, resulting in a political movement for universal manhood suffrage that worked with a radical "unstamped" press and intersected with a movement to end taxes on knowledge. In the US, a stable political order was built on a different kind of repression, with a foundation in racial supremacy. The end of this US system was the bloodiest of all.

2

The Editor's Newspaper and the Partisan Public Sphere

Two elements fueled the growth of the press in the early years of bourgeois democracy. One was the ideology of government by informed consent, which revolutions in key western countries had implanted. Thomas Jefferson formulated this notion, and the newspaper's role in it, memorably in a letter to another Virginian politician, Edward Carrington, in 1787. Jefferson was writing in the aftermath of Shays' Rebellion, a populist movement among farmers in Massachusetts, who shut down courts to prevent foreclosures, frightening bankers and the propertied classes. Jefferson was serene:

> The way to prevent these irregular interpositions of the people is to give them full information of their affairs thro' the channel of the public papers, and to contrive that those papers should penetrate the whole mass of the people. The basis of our governments being the opinion of the people, the very first object should be to keep that right; and were it left to me to decide whether we should have a government without newspapers, or newspapers without a government, I should not hesitate a moment to prefer the latter. But I should mean that every man should receive those papers and be capable of reading them. I am convinced that those societies (as the Indians) which live without government enjoy in their general mass an infinitely greater degree of happiness than those who live under European governments. Among the former, public opinion is in the place of law, and restrains morals as powerfully as laws ever did anywhere. Among the latter, under pretence of governing they have divided their nations into two classes, wolves and sheep. I do not exaggerate. This is a true picture of Europe.

Here he expresses a fantasy about public opinion and newspapers that has continued to animate media activism. He imagines a frictionless sphere of information and deliberation in which intelligent and public-spirited individuals can both steer the state and continually monitor the powerful. Each newspaper, and the system as a whole, will operate as a virtual town meeting, the master metaphor that guided thinking about the media, and a variant of the extended legislature metaphor that we saw in Milton. Informed public opinion, then, can "restrain morals." It can prevent the tyranny that naturally arises in and destroys democracies or republics.

The logical policy outcome of Jefferson's newspaper fantasy was social investment in the growth of the communications sector. In the US and elsewhere this did in fact occur. A number of tools were at hand, including the expansion of postal systems, the publicly funded construction of roads and schools, and the deployment of subsidies in the form of official advertising. Each of these initiatives had many other justifications, of course, but promoting the infrastructure of informed public opinion was always at least rhetorically prominent.

The second element, partisanism, grew from the first but also contradicted it. The tendency of political debate to coalesce into party conflict helped fuel the growth of the press and news culture in the eighteenth and nineteenth centuries. But thinkers were less comfortable about that dynamic, and were mindful that since ancient times political thinkers had always predicted that democracies fail when factionalism leads them to tyranny. Most countries designed systems of regulation aimed to slow down the viral growth of political division. The Anglo-American world was less concerned, and as a result became the leading region for press expansion. In the US, lax regulation, combined with infrastructural subsidies and dynamic politics, allowed newspaper growth to increase to the point of saturation in the first half of the nineteenth century.

This chapter will begin with a detailed look at US developments in the years between the American Revolution and the Civil War, the years in which the US took leadership in per capita newspaper circulation. Growth, enabled in part by infrastructure investment, sped ahead of what markets could support, providing an excess capacity that became available for mass political parties to exploit. At the same time, editors and politicians developed ways of thinking about a partisan public sphere, revolving around metaphors of military and courtroom competition. The result was a set of decentralized networks of party newspapers, promising something like the arena of public opinion dreamt about by Jefferson and others. But this public sphere turned out to be well policed even in the absence of formal censorship, as the case of the anti-slavery press shows.

After discussing the US case, I will pull the focus back to take in other places in the European world system. There were many paths to partisan journalism, but most western countries as well as many southern and eastern ones found their way there. Many stayed.

The Conflicted Revolutionary Legacy

The press was an important part of the machinery of the American Revolution, but the revolutionary movement itself did surprisingly little overt philosophizing about the press. British heroes of freedom of the press, like Cato and Wilkes, were also heroes of the revolution, but as general opponents of tyranny rather than specific proponents of a free press. Revolutionary leaders didn't worry about the tension between a profession of natural rights and the fact that Opposition printing was not allowed in territory that the revolutionaries controlled. Printers, who were at first reluctant to take sides in any controversy, mostly found a way to become eager patriots (Botein, 1980), but this involved accepting the proposition that the revolution had the actual consent of The People, meaning that allegiance to the Continental Congress, for instance, was beyond debate (Nerone, 1994: ch. 2). They could believe that they were "open to all sides" if they also believed that there was only one side.

The revolution, in other words, did not settle the question of the role of the press in the governing process. This became obvious when the Federal government began operating under the Federal Constitution ratified in 1788. That document did not include any mention of either the press or of political parties, and in fact the design of the Federal government seemed to assume that both elections and the governing process would be non-partisan, while the secrecy of the Constitution's drafting suggested that publicity was not a key value of the framers. They were more interested in reining in a disorderly social environment than in having another debate on mechanisms of governance (Holton, 2007).

But the process of ratifying the Constitution showed that both parties and the press would be features of governing. In most states, a vigorous "anti-Federalist" opposition appeared, producing a pamphlet literature similar in style to the revolutionary movement's media offensive (Cornell, 1999). Federalists controlled most of the newspapers, but, following the tradition of remaining open to all parties, many papers published both critics and supporters of the

Constitution. The most famous efforts of the supporters were newspaper essays published in New York State under the penname "Publius." Secretly written by James Madison, Alexander Hamilton, and John Jay, these essays became known collectively as *The Federalist Papers*. As rhetorical performances, *The Federalist Papers* reflected the "town hall" metaphor of newspaper publishing and intimated a Habermasian notion of the public sphere (Furtwangler, 1984). "Publius" invoked a hero of the Roman Republic, but also, literally translated, means "public man" or citizen. He is meant to stand in for everyman. Using calm legalistic reasoning, Publius makes arguments that suggest that the Federal Constitution is the best way to balance competing interests to achieve long-term stability, the protection of the rights of groups not in the majority, and ultimately the common good. Widely reprinted at the time, *The Federalist Papers* may have had an important influence on the outcome of the ratification process, especially in the key state of New York. Later collected as a book, they became a frequently cited authority for interpreting constitutional law.

One result of the debate over the Constitution was the recognition of a need for a Bill of Rights. This became a task for the first Congress, where James Madison negotiated a set of ten Amendments, a series of footnotes to the Constitution, clarifying the limits of federal authority. The First Amendment carved out a series of exceptions to congressional power, forbidding the establishment of a national religion or any interference with religious liberty, protecting the rights to assemble and petition, and forbidding Congress to enact any measure "abridging the freedom of speech, or of the press." Although it seems pretty simple, the wording of the First Amendment actually allows for a wide range of interpretation. "Abridging" is a weasel word, and generations of political leaders would argue that criminalizing speech and publication about things as disparate as anti-slavery arguments, hate speech, and military secrets does not "abridge" freedom of speech or the press. Moreover, the First Amendment applied only to the US Congress, and not to the many state and local governments within the national territory. These governments could "abridge" away. So why "abridge" and not some stronger or clearer word? Answering that question involves exploring the vision of free political discussion that animated the Bill of Rights: its "media imaginary," in other words.

The Bill of Rights, and especially the First Amendment, protected individual freedoms as a means for achieving popular self-government (Amar, 1998). The rights in the First Amendment sound very much like inalienable natural rights, but that's not exactly true: no one is born with a printing press, for instance, so freedom of the press is very much a social rather than a natural right. Why do I have freedom of the press? So *we* can govern ourselves. Implied in that rationale are reasonable limits to the free exercise of expression. It is harder for us to govern ourselves, for instance, if a single faction or interest monopolizes the news media. The system of freedom of expression will work best, in this media imaginary, if it combines robust argument in content with the kind of openness and impartiality associated with traditional print practice on the infrastructural level. Again: newspapers should operate like virtual town meetings. And citizens should operate like Publius. Any regulation that made their responsible behavior more difficult "abridged" freedom of the press, but policing bad actors didn't.

Around the same time that it was passing the Bill of Rights, the US Congress enacted a massive federal program to build the nation's information infrastructure (John, 1995: ch. 2). The Post Office Act of 1792 envisioned an expansion of service along a network of roads that would bind the nation together. It created what was easily the largest federal bureaucracy and charged it with producing a kind of geographic equality that would match the nation's political equality: just as each citizen would have equality in voting, each address would have equal access to the flow of information through the mail. In grandiose terms, the Act envisioned inscribing the logic of the Republic on to the land.

The Post Office Act intentionally and massively subsidized newspapers (McChesney and Nichols, 2011). It did this in two ways. First, it included a distribution subsidy. Newspapers could be mailed at a fraction of the cost of a personal letter. In fact, it was so much cheaper to mail a newspaper that ordinary families began writing personal letters in the margins of newspapers, a practice that was subsequently outlawed. Because many newspapers circulated to subscribers through the mail, cheap postage radically lowered their distribution costs. Moreover, the Act built in higher rates for longer distances for newspapers, though not for personal mail. This provision protected local publishing, making it more expensive for a resident of, say, Jacksonville, Illinois, to subscribe to a Philadelphia newspaper than to one printed within a hundred miles of one's address.

Second, and more importantly, the Act included an information subsidy in the form of free editorial exchange of newspapers. This provision meant that any printer or editor could send any other printer or editor a copy of one's newspaper for free: no postage required. Newspapers got almost all their content from other newspapers, and any successful newspaper maintained a large exchange list of other newspapers. In the first half of the nineteenth century in the US, a typical newspaper had a circulation of anywhere from a few hundred (the lowest viable circulation) to several thousand (the highest number of copies that the print machinery of the day could produce). Even the smallest newspapers would try to exchange with dozens or hundreds of other newspapers; the most prominent titles, like Baltimore's *Niles' Weekly Register*, found themselves inundated with requests for exchanges. My rough estimate, based on browsing newspaper office records, is that about 10 percent of the copies that a newspaper produced were exchanged with other newspapers. The exchange list was the equivalent of a membership in the Associated Press or a subscription to a wire service.

Editorial exchanges inflected the content of papers and structured the entire newspaper and media system. Any printer or editor composed the content of the paper with two audiences in mind: the local audience of paid subscribers, and the regional or national audience of "exchanges," fellow printers and editors with whom one exchanged. Local readers wanted primarily national and international news, and editors could clip that from their exchange papers, but the exchanges wanted something in return. Quoting with attribution was enough payback for some exchange editors, who were satisfied to see evidence of their growing influence. Most would expect to get some original content in return. Some newspapers would find that expectation hard to meet. Some localities produced a lot of news – state capitals and port cities, for instance, or scenes of warfare or natural disasters. Others lucked out with a gruesome murder. An ordinary printer might have to make do with the occasional human-interest story.

The system of postal exchange created an architecture for the media system that can be called a distributed network. Each printer created one's own network, but these all intersected with each other, forming a network of networks that could be said to host any particular newspaper. In theory, this postal Internet allowed any particular citizen to communicate through one's local newspaper to the entire national public. Any "Publius" could address everyone. And Congress made it that way on purpose, because that's how they thought a republic ought to communicate.

But this network architecture had some unforeseen affordances. The subsidies that it provided, along with the enthusiasm of a new generation of printers for political involvement, allowed local newspapers to increase in number to the point where many places hosted competing papers. Meanwhile, national political divisions radiated outward through the network of newspapers, where they found an environment that could host partisan printing. The growth of a partisan press was *not* an intended feature of the system, however.

The Press of the First Party System

During the revolution, printers had developed a repertoire of styles and tactics of agitation and advocacy, usually borrowed from eighteenth-century British party competition. After the revolution, factional divisions appeared around key national issues, like the extent of federal authority, the funding of a national debt, and the nation's posture in the great power conflict between Britain and France. It was natural for leaders to revive revolutionary press tactics as part of an arsenal of political warfare. Natural, but not easy.

For leaders and printers both, the turn to party conflict was traumatic. For leaders, it meant a rupture with former comrades in arms, and felt like the kind of division that had killed previous republics and could kill this new one. For printers, taking sides meant abandoning the tradition of political neutrality, violating the notion that a newspaper should be a virtual town meeting. This uneasiness added a great deal of heat to party conflict. It became very difficult for reluctant partisans to recognize their opponents as loyal citizens. Instead, contestants saw each other as corrupt agents of foreign powers or class interests, traitors of the common good (Smelser, 1958).

For most printers, there were solid material reasons not to go partisan. In the 1780s and 1790s, most printers outside of major cities still needed the patronage of the entire local political class to be commercially successful. These would shy away from taking a side on any issue on which local elites were divided. Now in many places local elites were *not* divided about the issues that drove national politics, and in these places printers could take sides. But even then, most local print shops did not have the capacity to produce a stream of partisan content, and could take sides only by copying from national papers. So the newspaper system was not yet a fully welcoming environment for press politics. A set of prominent national newspapers were highly partisan, particularly those based in the national capital (New York, then Philadelphia, then Washington). These papers exchanged nationally with all sorts of regional and local newspapers. Some of those tilted one way or another, while many others maintained a wobbly balance. And all of them accused the most partisan of being "licentious" rather than "free" (Levy, 1985; Nerone, 1989, 1993, 1994).

Political historians continue to debate the causes and nature of the party conflict that characterized the two decades following the adoption of the Federal Constitution. "Federalists" tended to favor a strong national government with a commitment to supporting national economic development through a funded national debt. "Republicans" preferred state sovereignty and an agrarian economy with minimal federal oversight. Federalists preferred Britain, Republicans France. Federalists clustered in the northeast, Republicans in the south. But the leaders of both parties had complicated personal loyalties and relationships. Republican Jefferson was Federalist Washington's Secretary of State and later Federalist John Adams's Vice President; Republican James Madison had co-authored *The Federalist Papers* with Federalist Alexander Hamilton. Family quarrels are the nastiest.

Journalism historians have tended to focus on the highly partisan national newspapers, both because these were the ones that were the most politically prominent and because they remain more interesting than their less partisan contemporaries. There is a conventional narrative that focuses on half a dozen editors and their papers. John Fenno's *Gazette of the United States* was the "court" newspaper of the Federalists from the beginning of the Federal government in New York (Pasley, 2001: 51–60). As a Republican Opposition appeared in Congress, Madison recruited a former college roommate, Philip Freneau, the "poet of the Revolution," to run a competing *National Gazette*; Jefferson subsidized the newspaper covertly by appointing Freneau to a state department job. Freneau's paper was short-lived; it yielded leadership to the *Aurora*, published in Philadelphia by Benjamin Franklin Bache, the grandson of Ben Franklin. (The elder Franklin had taught Bache the art of printing in Paris, when Franklin was ambassador to France during the revolution.) When Bache died of yellow fever in 1799, his assistant William Duane took over the *Aurora* and soon married Bache's widow, Margaret. Equally biting on the Federalist side was "Peter Porcupine," the pseudonym of William Cobbett. *Porcupine's Gazette* was perhaps the best embodiment of the satirical mode of partisan printing in the US.

The high-profile party editors were a remarkably international bunch. Bache spent most of his youth in school in Paris and Geneva, and in the company of his grandfather Ben Franklin, who himself spent much of the second half of his life in London or Paris. His partner William Duane was even more broadly traveled. Born to Irish immigrants in upstate New York in 1760, he was taken by his newly widowed mother back to Ireland in 1765. He apprenticed to a printer there, and then moved to London, where he worked on Parliamentary reporting for a politically connected newspaper. In 1786, he joined the East India Company as a soldier and left for India. Dismissed from his military post there, he instead operated a couple of newspapers, until the British governor expelled him in 1794 for being politically friendly to revolutionary France. In 1795 he was back in London, agitating as a printer and member of the London Corresponding Society against war with France; in 1796 he returned to the US (Phillips, 1989; Pasley, 2001: ch.8). Freneau had been a sea captain. Cobbett had been a British soldier, stationed in the Canadian maritimes, who left Britain for France and then the US in 1792, first disappointed in seeking a government job from Thomas Jefferson before becoming a teacher of English to French émigrés in Philadelphia, and then turning to Federalist politics. The migrations of these publicists followed the circulation of republican and revolutionary thinking from Britain to the US to France and back to the US.

The style of political argument in these papers was also international. The trunk of the literary culture ran from Addison and Steele, through Cato and the later controversialists of British politics, branching off into the pamphleteers of the revolution such as Tom Paine, with a successful graft from the journalism of the French Revolution. Cobbett's Peter Porcupine was probably the most successful stylist, with even his first target, Joseph Priestley, calling him "by far the most popular writer in this country, and, indeed, of the best in many respects" (Melville, 1913, vol I: 109). Here he is on Pennsylvania politician Thomas McKean: "His private character is infamous; he beats his wife, and she beats him" (Melville, 1913, vol 1: 110; Brewin, 2008: 50–3; Daniel, 2009). Not exactly Publius, but a modern reader immediately gets him. Cobbett left the country after being ruined by a libel suit brought by Benjamin Rush: Cobbett had ridiculed his treatment for yellow fever – bleeding and purging.

The partisan press war of the 1790s violated the norms of political discourse that newspapers were fond of announcing. Claiming to be "free but not licentious," they condemned partiality and "personalities," by which they meant attacks on personal character ("he beats his wife"). In spite of the attention they earned then and now, the national party papers were held in low esteem by rank-and-file printers who claimed to take impartiality and impersonality seriously. As in post-revolutionary situations in other places and times, serious people wanted to do something about it.

The major legislative attempt to deal with the partisan frenzy of the 1790s produced the Alien and Sedition Acts. The Alien Acts (there were three of them) were directed against the politicized immigration that sought the US as a refuge in the upheaval that followed the

French Revolution. These Acts tightened the borders, and gave the Federal government the authority to declare non-citizens "enemy aliens" and imprison and deport them. The Sedition Act addressed the press, and made it a federal crime to:

> write, print, utter or publish . . . any false, scandalous and malicious writing or writings against the government of the United States, or either house of the Congress of the United States, or the President of the United States, with intent to defame the said government, or either house of the said Congress, or the said President, or to bring them, or either of them, into contempt or disrepute; or to excite against them, or either or any of them, the hatred of the good people of the United States, or to stir up sedition within the United States.

The Act included the proviso that the accused could "give in evidence in his defence, the truth of the matter contained in the publication charged as a libel," and that "the jury who shall try the cause, shall have a right to determine the law and the fact." The Act also included a sunset clause: it would go out of force on March 3, 1801 – when the next Administration would be inaugurated.

The sunset clause clearly signals the partisan intention of this Act, which amounted to an attempt to suppress the Opposition press. Even though, on its face, the law seems to include the elements of the "actual malice" standard that defines modern libel law involving public figures, in practice it was possible, even easy, to find "false, scandalous, and malicious" material in any Opposition newspaper. Because of the time and distances involved in sending news, and the openness of the newspaper network, the exchanges that an editor received would almost certainly contain many unverifiable assertions that would later prove false. The effect of a falsehood could be presumed to be scandalous by legal standards of the time without proving any actual harm to the plaintiff. And the fact that a newspaper was partisan was itself evidence that its content was "malicious." In addition, trials were to be held in federal courts presided over by federal judges, who had all been appointed to lifetime positions by Federalist presidents. So this law made it possible to charge, convict, and imprison virtually any Opposition printer or editor. And in fact the leading Republican editors were all charged under this Act (Miller, 1951; Smith, 1956).

The laws, especially the Sedition Act, backfired. Not only did they energize the Republican Opposition, but they also radicalized a generation of printer-editors who had previously shied away from full partisan engagement (Pasley, 2001: ch. 5). Prior to the controversy over the Acts, the national press had tilted Federalist, and, outside of

Philadelphia, there were few full-throated Republican papers. After 1798, the momentum changed, and in 1800 the Opposition candidate Thomas Jefferson took the presidency.

At the same time, the Federal government moved from Philadelphia to Washington, DC. In so doing, it moved from the nation's largest and most dynamic city to a remote sleepy town, chosen specifically to insulate legislators from constant public agitation. Upon his inauguration, Jefferson pleaded for a cessation of party warfare, claiming that "we are all federalists; we are all republicans." And he made the most sedate and informative newspaper, the *National Intelligencer*, the new "court" newspaper. The *Intelligencer*'s authoritative congressional reporting would make it a newspaper of record for the next few decades, copied by editors of every political persuasion.

So did Jefferson try to live by the ideas he had set out in his letter to Carrington, quoted at the beginning of this chapter? Somewhat. Partisanship didn't disappear. Jefferson continued to come under personal attack, particularly for fathering mulatto children with one of his slaves (Reed, 2008), and, although he didn't try to re-enact the Sedition Act, he did encourage his supporters to use state laws regarding seditious libel to prosecute Federalist editors.

The Rise of the Second Party System

The competition between Federalists and Republicans, the First Party System, was different in key ways from the next generation of party conflict. Issues drove the competition, and the competition radiated out from disagreements among elites in the national capital. These issues did not necessarily map on to local political contests. More importantly, the competing sides lacked a notion of loyal opposition (Hofstadter, 1969). Federalists considered critics of John Adams's presidency seditious, and, because their criticism came in the context of geopolitical tensions with France, tools of an enemy power and traitors. This kind of party competition could not be considered normal or healthy. The First Party System did not end neatly at a specific moment, but the animus driving its rages faded, and a gradual consensus on key issues developed. By the end of the war of 1812, the Republican Party had achieved a near monopoly on key federal offices. It is too strong a judgment to call this a single-party revolutionary state, but it felt that way to some old Federalists.

But then the Republican Party itself broke into factions. For many election cycles, the congressional Republican caucus had serenely nominated a presidential ticket, but in the run-up to the 1824 election, the party failed to settle the competition among candidates. Instead, five viable Republican candidates ran in the general election, and none won a majority of the electoral vote. In the aftermath, the third-place candidate, Henry Clay, threw his support to the second-place candidate, John Quincy Adams, who became President and then appointed Clay as his Secretary of State and heir apparent. The first-place candidate, Andrew Jackson, did not take this well. He began a "campaign by continuation" that would win him the presidency in 1828 and inaugurate a new style of mass politics.

The Second Party System, in which Jacksonians or Democrats competed against, first, National Republicans and, later, Whigs, differed from the First in many ways. Both parties were truly national, for one thing, in that they competed meaningfully in every region and articulated local and state races with the national organizations. Partly as a result, voting mattered a great deal and, through the efforts of organizers and agitators, voter participation surged. Newspaper networks and party editors were key to the organizing efforts. And the organizing efforts worked best when the basis of organization concerned not primary issues but secondary or symbolic elements.

Jackson's campaigns – in 1824, 1828, and 1832 – are the best examples of how this sort of mass politics operated. First, Jackson, who had already become a national figure as a military leader and the hero of the Battle of New Orleans, set out to assemble a network of state-level supporters. In each state, several factions competed for favor, and each of these factions had a particular set of social concerns. In general terms, three types of social groups tended to support Jackson. In the south, he had a strong contingent of the planter class in his corner; in the south and midwest, independent farmers tended to favor him; and in midwestern and northern cities, artisans and laborers supported him. These three groups had obviously divergent economic and social interests. Jackson could harmonize leaders from these groups through traditional patronage – support me and I'll let you appoint a few postmasters – but harmonizing the broader electorate would be more complicated, and for this his communication network would prove decisive.

Although he was similar in many ways to most of the earlier presidents – a planter, a slaveholder, a military hero – Jackson's campaign presented him as a new type of leader. The first six presidents of the Union came from prominent families and were recognized as socially superior. Although many of them were famously earthy, none of them was ordinary, nor wanted to be thought of as ordinary. Washington, still the haughtiest president, set the tone; Jefferson made a display of democratic tendencies, and Federalists mocked his habit of wearing red breeches in sympathy with the French revolutionaries, but his very worldliness was a declaration of his elevation above the common sort. These presidents, all from Virginia or Massachusetts, were statesmen.

Beginning with Jackson (incidentally, the first president to wear long pants instead of knee breeches), the White House would be peopled with populists. No matter how extraordinary in real life, they would all insist that they emerged from the same mud as the rest of humanity. Jackson – who may have come from a lower position on the social scale than his predecessors but had ascended by the time he ran for president – pioneered the populist appeal. The new presidents were from such states as Ohio, Pennsylvania, and New York, states which, because of well-developed newspaper systems and heated factionalism, nurtured mass politics early. Few might be called statesmen. Virtually all of them claimed heroic military credentials. Jackson and Lincoln aside, none was much of a president. Nineteenth-century politics wasn't about Rushmore heads.

Jackson's defeat in the disputed election of 1824 allowed him to double down on his populism. He had been the people's choice, after all, and had been defeated by a "corrupt bargain" between Clay and Adams. Corruption was a protean vision that each group could see in its own fashion: planters could tie it to the bankers who held their debt, while artisans could associate it with downward pressure on journeyman wages forced by new owners; evangelicals could see in it the workings of hierarchical religious forces, while Irish and German Catholic immigrants could see it in the mainline Protestant clergy. All of these groups could be brought together under this symbolic umbrella to vote for Jackson, and this motley coalition swept him into office in 1828. Then, as president, he again found himself confronted with a powerful symbol, the Second Bank of the United States, which he refused to re-charter. In his re-election campaign, the "Monster Bank" took the place of the corrupt bargain, and paid all the same dividends.

Jackson's men combined his charismatic appeal with potent negative symbols to construct messages that mid-level leaders would use to knit together groups with diverse interests into a ruling coalition. The Italian political philosopher Antonio Gramsci called this kind of coalition a "historical bloc." Gramsci analyzed the ways in which Italian dictator Benito Mussolini assembled diverse interest groups such as traditional Catholics, northern industrialists, and southern peasants into a bloc that supported fascism. Jackson was not Mussolini, but the mechanics were not all that different. Both achieved power through the exercise of what Gramsci called ideological hegemony – leadership exercised through the work of "organic intellectuals," like priests, popular writers, and bureaucrats. For Jackson's era, the key organic intellectuals were newspaper editors.

Before the Tennessee legislature nominated Jackson for the presidency in 1822, formally kicking off his campaign, he had already lined up his chief newspapers. At the top of this network were a trio of dominant editors: Francis Preston Blair, Amos Kendall, and later Duff Green. Kendall, an easterner and Dartmouth grad, took over the *Frankfort (Kentucky) Argus of the Western World* in 1816; Francis Preston Blair took over the editorial chair when Kendall sold out a few years later. The two hooked up with Jackson early, and followed him throughout his political career. The *Argus* was the key organ for Jackson's first presidential run in the election of 1824. His second campaign was keyed by Duff Green's *United States Telegraph* in Washington, DC, founded in 1826.

This editorial trio signaled a grand change in the conduct of newspapers. Many of the leading political editors during the Age of Jackson, including Blair and Kendall, had no training as practical printers. Often they were lawyers, an occupation then plagued by low barriers to entry. Lawyers were plentiful, literate, and, as creatures of the courthouse, instinctively political: natural-born editors. They were also verbose and argumentative, and so were their newspapers. Lawyers became editors like generals became presidents.

To accomplish the feat of ideological hegemony, the rhetorical styles of Publius and even Tom Paine would not suffice. The complex debates of the First Party System offered too many openings and positions to be useful for mass organization. Among other things, their very complexity convinced many ordinary people either that they lacked the capacity to understand politics or that the privileged and wealthy were complicating matters intentionally to confuse and alienate ordinary voters (Manning, 1993). Mass politics wanted boxing instead of *nth*-dimensional chess. So party editors learned how to make a point in the space of a single paragraph.

Partisan papers adapted the format they'd inherited from the mid-eighteenth century. They were typically four pages long, or one sheet printed on both sides and folded once. Most were weeklies. The material printed on the outside – pages one and four – was durable stuff that could be printed earlier so the ink would be dry when the inside pages were printed. The most recent material appeared on pages two and three. This would be taken from exchanges and letters that had just come in the mail, along with whatever original material the editor composed. A regular reader would know to open the paper to the inside to read the most important content. The editor's own column appeared under a column-sized version of the newspaper's masthead and the local dateline, usually either at the top right on page two or on the top left of page two or three. There, the editor summarized what was to be found in the paper, presented paragraphs of his or sometimes her own news and commentary, and introduced the choicest items copied from the exchanges.

These columns became the sites of editorial combat. Opposing party editors in a city or region often matched up against each other and kept up a running debate. These were "gotcha" debates, in which an editor grabbed a line or a paragraph from another editor and refuted or ridiculed it. That tactic presumed that readers did not actually read the opposing paper's editorial material, unlike the prominent national papers of the First Party System. Gotcha editorial columns were not really intended to change anyone's mind. They presumed a like-minded readership, and aimed at reinforcing and mobilizing.

These editors and candidates built a truly modern political system. This system was fully secular: although it was shot full of appeals to divine plans and destiny, the real legitimacy of the governing party rested entirely on its claim to be the people's choice. People were expected to be selfish and somewhat rational, to compete with each other through politics. As a result, the political system was expected to be dynamic in the same way as the marketplace. Finally, politics was about interest, not truth. Political discourse, the public sphere, was about legitimating governance through the representation of public opinion, not about discovering truth through dialectic to steer governance.

Party editors represented public opinion not just by writing and printing but also by actively organizing party committees, public demonstrations, and the activities of public men and community leaders. Thurlow Weed, one of the most effective editors and an architect of the Whig Party, describes one particular burst of activity he orchestrated to influence New York's governor in the campaign leading up to the 1824 election:

> Governor Yates was furnished with the proceedings of well-attended village, town, and county meetings, deprecating the defeat of an electoral law, the removal of Mr. Clinton [DeWitt Clinton had been dismissed as an official of the Canal Commission], and the ingratitude of party leaders, etc., concluding with a resolution, respectfully appealing to the governor to convene an extra session of the legislature. Simultaneously, the governor received letters from prominent men in all those counties, reflecting the spirit of various popular demonstrations. (Weed, 1883–4: 114)

A hundred years before the invention of public-opinion polling, these methods of representing public opinion were as powerful, and as scientific, as any others.

"Hegemony" is the word that best describes the way modern politics represents "The People." Professional politicians know that their task – in hot pursuit of the 51st percent – is to take a complicated and diverse coalition and make it seem like a natural collection, to represent it as The People. The American Revolution may have invented this game, but the Age of Jackson perfected it. Jacksonian editors and politicos honed techniques of representing a political movement as the people's choice, of finding the symbols and myths that would make one party look like The People while driving wedges between the groups that composed the opposition.

The looming wedge issue in Jackson's coalition was slavery. Slavery lurked behind many of the apparent struggles of the early nineteenth century: much of the rhetoric in the fight over tariffs really coded disagreements over slavery. The Constitution had avoided using the word "slavery," leaving the legality of the system to individual states; but the Constitution also included a clause counting 3/5ths of the slave population in calculations apportioning congressional representatives. Because of this infamous "3/5ths clause," slave states were able to maintain disproportionate influence in Washington throughout the antebellum period (Richards, 2000). As a result, any successful national campaign would need to draw some support from the slave states. Leading up to the election of 1836, for example, Jackson's opponents tried to exploit the political power of the slave states by depicting his chosen successor, New Yorker and Vice President Martin Van Buren, as a friend of abolitionists. I'll return to this matter later in the chapter. This maneuver failed. Southern Democrats were leery of Van Buren, but their opponents couldn't unite behind a candidate.

By 1840 this had changed. The opposition, now taking the traditional name "Whig," came together behind William Henry Harrison of Ohio. Harrison was deutero-Jackson. A son of the Virginia gentry who had moved west, Harrison had achieved national fame around the same time as Jackson by leading a federal army in a rout of Native American forces under Tecumseh's brother at Prophet's Town on the Tippecanoe River in west central Indiana, near the present-day site of Purdue University. Harrison pursued a career as an officeholder, settling in a log house in North Bend, Ohio, which he later expanded into a considerable mansion.

Harrison gave the Whig press an opportunity to use Jackson's tool kit against his party. Led by editors like Charles Hammond of the

Cincinnati Gazette, Thurlow Weed of the *Albany Evening Journal*, and Weed's protégé Horace Greeley, who edited a campaign paper called the *Log Cabin*, the Whig press lionized Harrison's military prowess and democratic character, concentrating especially on the use of a log cabin for his home as a symbol of simplicity, virtue, and conviviality. The Democratic press objected early and often that Harrison's home had only the most remote resemblance to a log cabin, but that wasn't the point. The so-called Log Cabin Campaign successfully combined the invention of a mythic persona with canny exploitation of the economic troubles that followed on the Panic of 1837. Although the Whig press published long and learned essays on the nation's financial situation, and presented articulate proposals on the currency and banking, it was the staged campaign spectacles and overheated newspaper rhetoric that people noticed and that made the campaign extraordinary. To observers in 1840, it seemed obvious that the Log Cabin Campaign had set a new benchmark in popular enthusiasm and media effectiveness (Gunderson, 1977; Gasaway, 1999).

Hezekiah Niles, one of the nation's most influential editors, called the work of the new party press the "manufacture of public opinion." He described how party editors had been "arranged to 'wheel and fire,'" to "act together as if with the soul of one man, subservient to gangs of managers, dividing the spoils of victory, of which these editors also liberally partake – more than one hundred and fifteen of them being rewarded with offices, or fat jobs of printing, &c. This is a new state of things." He complained that "a falsehood manufactured or a calumny forged, runs through the whole line of hired presses" (*Niles' Weekly Register*, untitled editorial, 43 (September 15, 1832): 39). At another point he told how he'd detected a covert "opinion ring" in the state of New York during his normal editorial practice of clipping items for his own paper:

> in a period of eight or ten days, I cut out and laid aside nearly forty "EDITORIAL" articles, which all had the same "ear mark," and were evidently prepared by one hand; and these articles were afterwards collected in the "Albany Argus" and sent through the state as "PUBLIC SENTIMENT," and so "public indignation" has been more than once MANUFACTURED! ("The Organized Press, and the Case of Gales & Seaton," *Niles' Weekly Register*, 45 (January 4, 1834): 306–9)

The phrase "manufacturing public opinion" remained common in newspaper commentary through the century.

Niles's criticism reflects the way the press worked in the mid-nineteenth century. Editors and printers used the postal system both to gather news and to transmit their papers, sometimes to subscribers, but always to other editors and printers. Because editors could exchange papers with other editors at no cost, they eagerly solicited exchanges with as many editors as possible; they then clipped items of interest from those papers. This is how Hezekiah Niles composed his *Weekly Register*. He exchanged papers with hundreds of other printers, all of whom were eager both to read (at no cost) his definitive compilation of news and commentary, and to have their own remarks noticed in the *Register*. So the postal system and the press system were deeply integrated.

Niles worked as if this press–post system was non-partisan. He exchanged freely with editors from all parties, and, although he leaned toward being a Whig, he saw himself as communicating in a public space that accommodated a wide range of opinion. Hence his dismay at the manufacture of public opinion. Partisan editors deceived their readers – both their individual subscribers and the printers and editors who exchanged papers with them – and captured and spoiled a public resource in doing so.

Party editors didn't see it that way. They acknowledged that they were creating a partisan public sphere, but, they insisted, that was a *good* thing to do. They likened it to the court system. In a courtroom, lawyers argued on behalf of clients, presenting only information and commentary that would promote their clients' interests. True, this distorted the truth. But an opposing advocate also argued in the courtroom, distorting the truth the other way. This allowed the jury, representing the sovereign People, to make its own determination. Just as the courtroom promoted truth beyond the intentions of the actual antagonists in it, so the partisan public sphere would produce truth, no matter how party editors lied and misled. Remember that many of these editors were trained as lawyers. No wonder they pictured the press system as a courtroom rather than a town meeting.

But remember that the candidates were generals. A party newspaper was supposed to be also a tool of discipline, organizing voters into an army that would march in formation to the polls and vote the ticket. Party newspapers were full of the rhetoric of military discipline, and many of the editors were also officers in local partisan militia companies, mixing actual quasi-military exercises in public spaces with their virtual drills in newspaper space.

These two metaphors for the party press – courtroom and military – weren't really comfortable with each other. A jury in a courtroom was supposed to listen carefully to opposing arguments before rendering a verdict. A soldier in an army should be immunized against opposing ideas. The better an editor drilled his (usually) army, the less discussion and debate there would be between opposing positions.

In both models of party competition, the contestants were supposed to be manly. The editor of *Paul Pry*, a well-known Washington, DC, weekly, for instance, castigated fellow partisan Joseph Gales of the *National Intelligencer* in these fairly conventional manly terms:

> Joe is in fine spirits about the prospect. But while we were struggling hand to hand, against fearful odds, last summer, to save Georgia and Ohio, Joe was quietly looking on, with his arms folded, and descanting upon Spain – France – Texas – Beet sugar – Railroads – Liberia – and other fiddle faddle notions. Joe is a true Bladensburgh soldier [referring to the sacking of DC during the war of 1812]; when danger is, he is not to be found. Now and then he pokes his head out and cries "Whig, Whig." ("The Intelligencer", *Paul Pry*, October 22, 1836)

Gales is "skittish" and "womanly," full of "fiddle faddle" and "afraid of hurly burly." The irony here is that the editor of *Paul Pry* was a woman, Anne Royall.

Anne Royall founded *Paul Pry* in 1831, at age 61. She'd already had a long career in the public eye, having written a series of sketches, travel narratives, and autobiographies that played on her acquaintance with many prominent individuals. As the penniless widow of a revolutionary war veteran, she lobbied Congress for years to fund a pension for women like her, ostentatiously wearing a threadbare black dress which she claimed was the only dress she owned. She became something of a misery queen in Washington, of sufficient pedigree to be invited to social affairs, but apparently relying on the kindness of strangers and Masons for a living (James, 1972; Johnson, 2002; Bourdon, 2011).

Her marginal status gave her a kind of freedom that most women of her class rarely enjoyed. She was able to travel throughout the country gathering material for her sketches, which she marketed by selling subscriptions – a practice in which she imitated Parson Mason Locke Weems, the early biographer of Washington and a pioneering book marketer (Zboray, 1986). As a self-supporting author-entrepreneur, she was one of the nation's earliest literary professionals.

She was also a nuisance. She pestered public figures until she worked a subscription out of them. If they refused, she skewered them in her next collection. Some historians label her the original DC gossip columnist (Mott, 1950: 312). She showed an uncanny knack for working the press system too. In her travels around the country, the first stop in any town was likely to be the editorial office of one of the local papers, where she would expect to earn a paragraph in the editorial column; as these papers circulated through the exchanges, other papers with friendly editors would reprint the notice of her visit, creating a kind of buzz that would help her sell subscriptions.

Royall was quite good at creating buzz, but not as good as her contemporary feminist itinerant Frances Wright, who will enter our story later. Wright was a true radical, willing to jettison the bounds of polite womanhood by giving public lectures and socializing with African Americans; her local visits were always occasions of turbulent public interest. Where Royall rankled social conservatives and "blue-skins," Wright infuriated them, and was a true outcast, the object of violent hatred, and the target of mobs. Royall remained at the edge of but within the mainstream.

Royall was drawn to party politics. She met Andrew Jackson on one of her earliest travels, before he was a national candidate, and was enthralled. She was also, through her late husband, associated with the Freemasons and something of a free-thinker; she detested no one more than the evangelical Protestant reformers who opposed Jackson. They detested her right back. To moralists, Anne Royall was a woman of questionable character. In a famous incident, in July 1829, she was arrested and tried for being disorderly and a common scold on the complaint of a minister and his family. Despite warm and frequently jocular testimony from some of her famous Washington friends, Royall was found guilty, given a token fine ($10, which two reporters from the *National Intelligencer* put up for her), required to post a bond of $100, and put on probation for one year. In another incident, a bookstore clerk in Pittsburgh horsewhipped her for making disparaging remarks about anti-Masonry. He was fined $20.

Her earlier publications and subscription tours had already made Royall nationally famous when she established her *Paul Pry* (which was succeeded by a newspaper called the *Huntress*, which lasted until 1854). These papers didn't circulate broadly, but her notoriety and connections made editors copy them widely. Even if she had trouble selling newspapers, she could always make news. Partly this was because she was a woman. Famously labeled a "virago errant in enchanted armor" by John Quincy Adams (Adams, 1875: 312), she violated the bounds of womanhood, but also traded on the deference due her sex and age whenever it worked to her advantage. Her mastery at playing the gender game was matched by her skill in working the boundaries of politics and personality.

Royall's gossipy streak was not at all uncommon in the political journalism of her day. One of the grand strategies of party politics was the invention of personalities for the leading candidates. Television makes it comparatively easy to convey personality today, but then the printed word limited lionizers and detractors alike to heated prose and exaggerated stories. Davey Crockett is a good example. Remembered today as a frontiersman who fell at the Alamo, Crockett was also a pamphleteer who fictionalized himself through autobiographical sketches, much the way Anne Royall did. He also got himself elected to Congress. Anne Royall couldn't do that, being a woman. But it is unfair to single her out as a gossip when her male counterparts behaved in much the same fashion. Not only were there many other newspapers more gossip-oriented than *Paul Pry*, but there were partisan editors who eagerly retailed gossip on candidates. In the 1828 presidential election, for instance, Charles Hammond of the *Cincinnati Commercial Gazette* circulated rumors that Andrew Jackson's wife Rachel was a bigamist.

It is also unfair to accuse Anne Royall of calling attention to herself. Party editors typically made themselves the voices and faces of the party in their locality. They typically crafted literary personae in their columns. They eagerly promoted their own publications. And they typically took it personally when an opposing editor criticized them.

A good indicator that editors took things personally was the rise of dueling. As partisanship increased, and as the rhetoric of manly independence was applied more fulsomely, editors dueled more and more often (Nerone, 1994: ch. 3). Dueling had been the preserve of officers and gentlemen in the United States since the Civil War. As partisan passions heated in the early Republic, dueling became a familiar but controversial aspect of political struggle – Aaron Burr's duel with Alexander Hamilton being the most famous example. The partisan printers of the Federalist era rarely dueled, however, being of the mechanical sort and inferior in class to gentlemen, and therefore not worthy of the honor of the code duello. They did sometimes fistfight. William Duane was beat up by a gang of army officers, who refused him the privilege of dueling, though he demanded it.

The rise of mass politics democratized dueling just as it democratized other aspects of politics. Now it became more common, especially in the south and later in the west, for editors to shoot it out with other editors and with the political figures they criticized and lampooned in the press. Dueling among editors was common enough for Mark Twain to joke about it in the 1850s, when recounting his Nevada days.

The partisan public sphere worked through routinized combat, sometimes verbal, sometimes physical. The noise of politics signaled a kind of openness that had been lacking in the previous generation, when social superiors expected ordinary people to defer to their judgment. Many then, and many scholars now, hailed the collapse of deferential politics as marking a high point in participation. Many also argued that it marked a low point in public discourse. Both parties had mastered techniques of spectacle and misdirection, raising serious and permanent barriers to real debate on divisive issues.

How democratic was this system? A fair way to answer that question is to propose a test of capacity. In any system of political communication, there are issues or problems that need to be dealt with – failing to deal with them will ultimately challenge the viability of the political community itself. One might argue that twenty-first-century systems of political communication need to produce consensus on ways to deal with climate change, so that issue becomes a test of capacity. One might further argue that, because climate change is a global issue and systems of political communication remain primarily national, it is a test that will be failed. I contend that the proper test of capacity of the nineteenth-century party press in the US was the issue of slavery. And I think everyone can agree that it failed that test spectacularly, tragically, and grotesquely.

The Abolitionist Press

Slavery has a unique legacy in the US, but American slavery was an integral part of the eighteenth-century Atlantic economic and geopolitical system. The wealth of the Americas was produced by slaves, both in the extractive industries of the Spanish Empire and in the agricultural exports of the French and British colonies. Moreover, the trade in slaves was itself a major colonial industry, and wars were fought over participating in it. The anti-slavery movement also was Atlantic in scope. Activists collaborated across national boundaries, and understood their work to be truly transnational. The ocean could sometimes work as an amplifying device for any particular activist. An American traveling to England on a speaking tour would send correspondence and press clippings back to the US press, enhancing his or her notoriety and authority.

In the US, slavery eventually became a sectional issue, but until the second decade of the nineteenth century it did not seem such a point of contention between north and south. At some time, every one of the original 13 states had condoned slavery. After independence, the northern states gradually abolished slavery, but states like New York and New Jersey still allowed some slaveholding into the 1810s. Enlightened southerners, including Thomas Jefferson, had begun to assume at the time of the revolution that slavery would inevitably become extinct. Still, it was the southern states who insisted that the Constitution include a moratorium on abolishing the slave trade, and that slaves be counted toward congressional representation. And, if Jefferson disliked slavery in theory, he failed to abandon it in practice. Unlike some of his neighbors, he didn't emancipate many of his slaves; in fact, he freed only a few, mainly his own offspring (Reed, 2008). Jefferson also grimly assumed the master's duty of personally whipping his slaves from time to time.

The national contours of the slavery issue became much sharper in the late 1810s. What brought matters into focus was the question of national expansion. When the so-called Northwest Territory (the present-day states of Ohio, Indiana, Illinois, Wisconsin, and Minnesota) was organized in the 1780s, before passage of the Constitution, the ordinance that established territorial governance also outlawed slavery. But states to the south and west were admitted with slavery – Kentucky, Tennessee, Alabama, Mississippi – at roughly the same pace, preserving a careful balance in the Senate between slave and free states. A crisis came with Missouri. Missouri lies north of the usual line between slave and free states, but had been largely settled by southerners preferring a right to own slaves. Eventually the famous Missouri Compromise admitted it as a slave state. But by then the centrality of the slavery question to the future development of the nation had become obvious. In the decade that followed, the slavery question was the hidden agenda behind many of the compelling issues of the day.

Around 1830, the issue could no longer remain concealed. In rapid succession, the first spectacular anti-slavery weekly, *The Liberator*, was founded; an extraordinarily bloody slave revolt, led by Nat Turner, terrorized white Virginians; and the Virginia legislature debated, and voted down, a proposal for emancipation. Abolishing slavery would never again be a matter for political discussion for the southern states. Southern states outlawed anti-slavery activism, and tried to get northern legislatures to follow suit (Eaton, 1964; Nye, 1964). But in the north the anti-slavery movement became more vocal.

Anti-slavery activists cleverly exploited the resources that the press system had to offer. William Lloyd Garrison, the founder and editor of *The Liberator*, is a good case in point. Garrison's father, a ship's captain, took to drink and abandoned his family; Garrison was raised by his mother, an evangelical and lay preacher. They lived a hard-scrabble existence and were often separated; eventually, Garrison was apprenticed to a printer in Newburyport, Massachusetts, and his mother went to work in Baltimore. Garrison worked his way up the ranks in the office of the *Newburyport Herald*, starting as a printer's devil and becoming foreman. As the foreman, it was his responsibility to direct the work of the apprentices and journeymen in the office, to oversee the typesetting of the newspaper, and to make important decisions about style, design, and composition. After eight years in the *Herald* office, in 1826 he acquired control of the *Newburyport Free Press*, which he edited as a partisan paper for half a year, until he was forced to sell out (Thomas, 1963; Mayer, 1998). He retained a disdain for party papers and the compromises and prostitutions they were forced to accept.

Garrison nurtured his mother's evangelical faith, but used his newspaper expertise to promote it. Having turned his attention to slavery, he found backers for a newspaper that would advocate immediate abolition; his most important sponsors were free northern African Americans. Aspiring to middle-class opportunity in cities like Philadelphia and Boston, they had looked to the press as a sign of legitimacy; the first African American newspaper, *Freedom's Journal*, was established in New York in 1827 (a year before the first Native American newspaper, the *Cherokee Phoenix*). African Americans established about two dozen newspapers before the Civil War. Few of them were long-lived. The most enduring and important was the *North Star*, begun by Garrison's protégé Frederick Douglass in 1847; it survived as *Frederick Douglass's Paper* until 1860. Abolishing slavery was the overwhelming point of the African American press. Free blacks also offered support to white abolitionists and their publications. Garrison's *Liberator* needed this support in its early years. Critics argue that this hampered the development of an authentic black voice. On the other hand, Garrison was able to intrude on mainstream attention in a way that African Americans, even Frederick Douglass, never could.

This was because Garrison knew how the party press operated. Although he had few actual readers at first – three or four hundred – he quickly established a large national exchange list. He thus put his paper in the hands of all sorts of editors, some sympathetic, but many outright hostile, southerners and politicos who considered him the worst sort of subversive and agitator. But agitation was his point. Garrison's enemies eagerly copied inflammatory paragraphs from his paper, and wrote incendiary rebuttals; Garrison eagerly copied these rebuttals, proving to his readers and enemies alike that his paper was a force to be reckoned with.

The party press and the postal system worked like an echo chamber. A newspaper voice with an extensive exchange list that could be counted on to provide provocative copy would find itself a subject of national attention. Party editors understood the network and fit themselves and their papers into it. But the partisan newspaper networks also provided resource for other kinds of activists. In the 1820s and 1830s, all sorts of movements and groups began producing newspapers, exchanging with each other and with the mainstream press, hoping to have their voices heard in the national public sphere. The mainstream press noticed these only sporadically. The ones who got the most attention, like Garrison, were those who made the best news, or who provided material that could easily be turned to other uses. Garrison fed the echo chamber. He couldn't control what people made of the *Liberator*, but he knew how to force them to notice it.

From the outset, opponents threatened violent reprisals. Working from Boston, Garrison was relatively remote from actual slaveholders. But many of the politicians and merchants of Boston worked closely with southern planters and their representatives and considered Garrison's presence noxious. With the encouragement of some of the pillars of the establishment, a mob captured Garrison in 1835 and paraded him around the streets with a noose around his neck. He wasn't cowed; in fact, he trumpeted his martyrdom. But the goal of the mob wasn't to kill him. It was to make him ridiculous, to show the world that he was not "one of us." Garrison argued that the mob was politically motivated and directed, and he was correct. Mainstream politicians of both parties wanted to shut down the anti-slavery movement.

The movement to abolish slavery tested the limits of majoritarian politics. The goal of the parties being to construct a hegemonic bloc, the question of slavery figured as a loser. If the party embraced anti-slavery, it would lose the entire southern vote, which remained controlled by the planter class. If the party became loudly pro-slavery, then it might lose large chunks of the northern vote – the evangelical middle class, which opposed slavery on religious grounds, and much of the working class, which feared competition from unpaid labor. The canniest strategists in both parties tried to avoid a firm position, but neither side would forgo the advantage of accusing the other of being secretly anti-slavery, a game that quickly became violent.

The 1830s saw an epidemic of anti-abolitionist mobs like the one that attacked Garrison. These riots occurred in every part of the north; in fact, the first formation of an anti-slavery society or the first publication of an anti-slavery newspaper in any locale would be virtually guaranteed of prompting a riot (Richards, 1970). Some of these riots have become familiar to historians. Elijah Lovejoy, who re-established his *Alton (Illinois) Observer* three times after its press had been dumped into the Mississippi River by rioters, achieved fame as the first US martyr to freedom of the press when he died protecting his fourth press from a mob (Nerone, 1994: ch. 4).

Anti-abolitionist mobs represented themselves as simple and direct expressions of public opinion. Crowd actions from the colonial period onward did the same thing, with crowds declaring themselves "the people," assembled as a kind of unofficial legislature or judiciary, augmenting the laggard official institutions of government. But the anti-abolitionist riots were about hardball politics. Political chieftains cynically arranged many of them to send a message. The paradigm case was the Utica riot.

In 1835 rioters disrupted an anti-slavery convention in Utica, New York. The rioters gathered, conferred, passed resolutions, scattered the anti-slavery meeting, then attacked the office of a local newspaper with anti-slavery sympathies. Although this was a moderately destructive riot, its aim was not to destroy property or terrorize citizens but to make a political statement. The national media paid close attention to the goings on in Utica. The riot was one of the more momentous events in politics that year.

Why Utica? Utica was and is a mid-sized town in upstate New York, in a region sometimes called the "burned-over" district because of the waves of enthusiastic movements that had originated or flourished there – Mormonism, for instance, took off right nearby, and other evangelistic religions thrived there, as well as reform movements like temperance and anti-Masonry. That part of New York was also fertile ground for anti-slavery. But another factor came into play. Utica was within the home territory of Martin Van Buren, then the sitting vice president and the heir apparent to Andrew Jackson. Van Buren was rumored to be sympathetic to the anti-slavery movement, a fact that would scare off the southern wing of the Democratic Party and leave Van Buren's candidacy in jeopardy. Anti-slavery leaders chose Utica with the intention of using presidential politics as a platform.

Nor were they surprised when mob action was the result. In fact, by that point, the actions of anti-slavery mobs had become rather routine. The diaries and letters of anti-slavery activists are full of proud references to the angry crowds they encountered.

Mainstream political leaders, especially Jacksonians, often led these crowds. In Utica, the local anti-abolitionist leaders – Mayor Joseph Kirkland, US Representative Samuel Beardsley, and Augustine Dauby, editor of the local Democratic *Observer* – were all Van Buren loyalists. More remarkable are the ranks of those who defended the mob action. Among them was New York's Senator Silas Wright, who responded to South Carolina Senator John Calhoun's remark that New York was too tolerant of abolitionists by pointing to the Utica riot as "evidence of the correct state of public opinion." Van Buren himself in private was more blunt, remarking that "we have taken the Bull by the horns" (US Congress, 1836: 203–8; Van Buren, 1836; Morrison, 1981).

So political leaders raised anti-abolitionist mobs to placate their southern partners. The irony in the case of Utica is that both Van Buren and Silas Wright genuinely disliked slavery. Wright emerged as one of the most important leaders of the anti-slavery wing of the Democratic Party. But their personal beliefs could not stand in the way of what needed to be done to protect the party's strategic interests.

Eventually anti-abolitionist rioting became less ubiquitous, and finally a mainstream party embraced anti-slavery. Ultimately, the Republican Party was able to put John Fremont and then Abraham Lincoln forward as presidential candidates who were openly critical of slavery. And later anti-slavery agitators could speak and publish in northern states without expecting mob violence – though mobbings did not disappear from the north before the Civil War.

Because an anti-slavery president was eventually elected, and slavery ultimately abolished, one might argue that the party press system passed this test of capacity. The dwindling of anti-abolitionist violence itself is often told as a happy history. Russell B. Nye's (1964) account of this history credits an awakened public opinion: ordinary northern citizens heard and responded to the abolitionist argument that the threat to freedom of expression of anti-slavery agitators was a threat to the freedom of expression of everyone. Northerners who were not abolitionists came to believe in a slave-power conspiracy against the freedoms of northern farmers and laborers. In response, northerners adopted universal notions of rights that included protecting even abhorrent speech, like William Lloyd Garrison's.

But this can also be told as a sad history. In this account, the emerging tolerance of anti-slavery agitation occurred after the Mexican War, when the question of extending slavery into newly conquered territories replaced the abolition of slavery as the key anti-slavery issue. The argument against extension was widely popular, not out of sympathy with the suffering slaves and the moral corruption that slavery produced – Garrisonian arguments – but out of sympathy with the northern white worker and the threat to free soil and free labor in the expansion of the system of slavery. When westward expansion yielded a situation where a president could be elected without southern support, northern politicos began to construct a moderate anti-slavery party that would capture the allegiance of northern white workers and farmers. Lincoln won his election without being on the ballot in the south and without calling for the abolition of slavery. This version of the history sees only tactical maneuvers, with no embrace of a modern notion of free expression or an expansive view of African American rights and grievances. The party press failed to deal with slavery; the Union army abolished it first, and the political system legalized facts on the ground later.

The history of anti-slavery politics was replicated many times by other non-mainstream movements. Initially the tendency was to treat these movements as treasonous – as inherently threatening the integrity of the social fabric – and therefore as deserving to be put down, "lawfully if we can, forcibly if we must." (In the twentieth century, the need for mobs to stamp out radicalism declined as the Federal government took on that role, especially during and after World War I.) At some point many of these movements – Suffragism, Civil Rights – are taken up by mainstream political groups, or at least acknowledged as acceptable political positions. Such cooptation or acceptance occurs when the movement is de-radicalized and rendered useful in coalition-building.

The mainstream is tolerant, but only on its own terms, and usually at the expense of the political "other." In the final analysis, there is no question that the abolition of slavery became speakable in mainstream politics only when it was phrased as a white man's issue, only when it was made clear that it was the interests of the white worker and farmer that were at stake. Until that time, mainstream politicians refused to embrace abolition. No wonder it was war, and not politics, that ultimately freed the slaves.

The Gender Line

Also excluded from the game of politics were women. But this exclusion was more uncertain in practice than in theory. Certainly there was a virtually unpenetrated gender line where voting was concerned. Only in a couple of unusual constitutional situations – in the state of New Jersey, particularly – were women ever allowed to vote. But women were active in politics in many other ways. They read newspapers, they attended public events, and they formed church and civic organizations (Ryan, 1997; Zboray and Saracino Zboray, 2010).

The public activity of women shows their ambivalence to the dominant gender ideology of separate spheres. This ideology, especially suitable for the emerging middle class, divided the social world into man's sphere and woman's sphere, according to the supposed natural characteristics of men and women. Men, being vigorous but rude and insensitive, were well equipped to handle the boisterous and combative terrains of business and politics, realms where the necessity of endless conflict and compromise would continually outrage the finer moral sensibilities of women. Women were of course better suited to activities that required sensitivity, nurturance, and moral exactitude – childrearing, homemaking, and churchgoing.

This ideology of separate spheres cut two ways. It certainly endorsed the male monopoly in politics and the marketplace, but did so in a fashion that granted middle- and upper-class women enhanced domestic authority. If the proper woman had no business in Congress, she did rule the home, and even the congressman would have to answer to his wife on moral issues. And this was a central contradiction in the ideology. The moral superiority of women gave them the authority to pronounce on political issues as well, if not in the partisan forums where their fathers gathered, then in the shadow world of female associations. The anti-slavery movement especially nurtured such activity. Themselves marginalized from mainstream politics, and proclaiming a morally superior position, anti-slavery agitators were naturally more open to female activism. The anti-slavery movement provided the first sanctioned opportunities for women to speak in public on political matters, and was the launching pad for the first feminist movement.

Politics also generated a sentimental religious and literary press, which Ann Douglas has controversially characterized as "feminized" (Douglas, 1977). This literary public sphere was where exiles from (e.g., the clergy) and hopeful immigrants to (e.g., women) the political public sphere congregated. Defined in part by its otherness from the world of political partisanship, this realm produced both a highbrow literature and a populist reformism.

The literary sensation of its age, and the paradigm case of sentimental reformism, was *Uncle Tom's Cabin*. This novel is the best-known work of Harriet Beecher Stowe. The wife and the daughter of prominent ministers, she was involved in the great reform movements of the day from childhood on. And she also participated eagerly in the world of polite letters from her earliest years. She was already a seasoned writer and a savvy political thinker by the time she wrote her masterpiece (Headrick, 1994).

Appearing serially in the weekly anti-slavery magazine *The National Era*, *Uncle Tom's Cabin* crystallized and immortalized many of the motifs of sentimental women's religious and literary culture (Robbins, 1997). Among the book's chief characters are the Christ-like slave Uncle Tom, who ends his life tied to the whipping post in Louisiana, and the pure planter's daughter Eva, who dies from being too holy for this sinful world, but not before converting her once-dissolute father and many other one-dimensional figures. But what's important here is that this sentimental novel literally hijacked the stalemated political debate on slavery. In changing the terms of debate, and in establishing a new threshold in dissemination, it played the same role in the coming of the Civil War that Paine's *Common Sense* did in the coming of the revolution. It did so by insisting that moral sense trumped constitutional law. Moreover, it presented that coup in a neatly drawn scene early on in the story.

The setting is the happy domestic space of Senator John Bird of Ohio and his wife Mary. Senator Bird, who has just returned home exhausted from a legislative session, gets into an unwelcome discussion with Mary about the recently passed Fugitive Slave Law, which makes it a federal crime for anyone to not assist in the return of an escaped slave. Mary is convinced that the law is wrong because it contradicts simple human decency and simple Christian morality. She frames this objection in the language of woman's sphere: "Things have got to a pretty pass if a woman can't give a warm supper and a bed to poor, starving creatures, just because they are slaves . . . !" John responds in condescendingly patriarchal terms:

> "But Mary, just listen to me. Your feelings are all quite right, dear, and interesting, and I love you for them; but then, dear, we mustn't suffer our feelings to run away with our judgment; you must consider it's not a matter of private feeling, – there are great public interests involved, – there is such a state of public agitation rising, that we must put aside our private feelings."

John banishes Mary's feelings to private, domestic space. They are to have no impact on public policies, the proper domain of manly reason and manly duty. Mary, though, is a gifted feminine disputant, and volleys back:

> "Now, John, I don't know anything about politics, but I can read my Bible; and there I see that I must feed the hungry, clothe the naked, and comfort the desolate; and that Bible I mean to follow."
>
> "But in cases where your doing so would involve a great public evil –"
>
> "Obeying God never brings on public evils. I know it can't. It's always safest, all around, to do as He bids us."

Mary insists that private morality is a sound guide for public policy. Moreover, she insists that her intuition is a surer guide to morality, private or public, than John's reason. With simple feminine dignity she asserts: "I know it can't." Moreover, with her clear insight into human character, she knows for a certainty that John, in his heart, agrees with her. So she challenges him with the question, would you turn away a runaway slave?

> "Of course, it would be a very painful duty," began Mr. Bird, in a moderate tone.
>
> "Duty, John! Don't use that word! You know it isn't a duty – it can't be a duty!"

Obviously, it can't be a duty because it countermands the simple universal rules of human decency and Christian morality.

> "Mary! Mary! My dear, let me reason with you!"
>
> "I hate reasoning, John, – especially reasoning on such subjects. There's a way you political folks have of coming round and round a plain right thing; and you don't believe in it yourselves, when it comes to practice. I know you well enough, John. You don't believe it's right any more than I do; and you wouldn't do it any sooner than I." (Stowe, 1969: 121–3)

Does a "plain right thing" trump all the reasons of state and duties of public men? Stowe answers the question for us by having a runaway slave turn up at the door right at that moment. Of course John pleases Mary by answering his heart, by denying his head – by helping the slave. The moral intuitions of women, the domestic values of women, the Christian morality of women, conquer the reason, the will, and the political compromises of men.

Uncle Tom's Cabin asserts the primacy of woman's sphere. In that sense, it is a quasi-feminist text – quasi because its women are so womanish, so thoroughly imprisoned in the genteel routines and persuasions of the upper middle class. It is also a quasi-feminist communicative act. Its success as a novel and as a political tract signaled the triumph of sentiment over politics, and ultimately prefigured the triumph of warfare over politics. The early abolitionist periodicals – Garrison's *Liberator*, James G. Birney's *Philanthropist*, the *Anti-Slavery Standard* – all insisted on the value of traditional rational or critical political rhetoric. Though their arguments were often passionate, partisan, personal, and evangelical, they were still framed by the expectation that argument would convince the candid public mind, and that policy consequences would flow from public conviction. They were confident, then, that they were winning the argument. Every act of repression from the slave power was taken as testimony to the effectiveness of their manly rational discourse.

Uncle Tom's Cabin is the final and most dramatic evidence of the abandonment of that optimism. Rational/critical argument will never persuade the slave power. Individual men may be converted by individual acts of piety – as Arthur St Clare is converted by little Eva – but nothing is to be expected from the arena of political discourse, and nothing is to be expected from the mind of the south. Senator Bird's public life is a great obstacle to his private morality, not a vehicle for realizing it.

The sort of sentimental literature that *Uncle Tom's Cabin* epitomizes, then, rejects and infects politics at the same time. It dismisses the arena of political discourse – all that public men will ever do will be to reproduce the evils of the social order. But at the same time it inserts itself everywhere into that public discourse. *Uncle Tom's Cabin* was the political event of the 1850s, at least until its New Testament image of the suffering Christ was overtaken by John Brown's Old Testament angry Jehovah. And while the language of sentiment forced its way into the political stalemate, the bodies of women turned up more and more often in public settings – at rallies and speeches, and in auxiliary political organizations.

The Party Press in Europe

In the US, the disjuncture between the logic of the party press and the expectations of a non-partisan public sphere was especially striking. When partisan newspapering began, the US press was smaller and younger than the British press, the national government was newer and weaker, and the recent revolutionary experience had generated a clearer ideological mission for publication. When de Tocqueville explained his choice to study democracy by visiting the US, he asserted that it was the purest available example because of the absence of a feudal past and the broad social equality that characterized the white population. He may have been correct, though one can certainly find reasons to doubt the purity of democracy in America. But it is a good case for studying the dynamics of mass electoral democracy nonetheless. US mass politics did not spring from a protracted battle against suffrage restrictions, as in the UK, did not inhabit a dominant national capital city, like London or Paris, and did not revolve around the question of the role of the monarch or the problem of established religion, as in many other European countries. US parties tended as a result to be coalitional rather than ideological. Rather than being rooted in key ideas or philosophies, they tended to be loosely collected around symbols.

US parties used newspapers both as instruments of symbolic action and as organizational devices. It is easy to read the symbolic work of the newspaper in the paragraphs of the editorial columns. The organizational work of a party newspaper also left its traces in the textual content. Party editors were frequently listed as organizers of the public meetings that were reported in the paper. Typically they chaired or were important members of the local party committee. Often they were officers in a local militia company or other voluntary organizations. They were key figures in maintaining and extending a social network that could reliably produce core loyalists at election time.

The partisanship of nineteenth-century US newspapers was assisted by federal policy. The First Amendment tradition of lax federal regulation invited advocacy in the press, and the subsidies built into the US postal system, along with requirements that the federal and state governments publish the laws at advertising rates in newspapers (Smith, 1977), supported the creation of a newspaper system that could expand beyond market support. Excess newspaper capacity underwrote partisan affiliation. This was not what policymakers had intended. By all evidence, they had hoped for a non-partisan news system that would function like a virtual town meeting. But political divisions and contested elections quickly populated the press. The presidential focus especially encouraged party affiliation and the national networking of party editors.

The US press remained partisan until the end of the nineteenth century. Partisanship waned only when economies of scale caused newspapers to grow to the point where a party affiliation was no longer productive in achieving the largest possible audience. That is a long story for a later chapter.

Elsewhere, party politics and the party press developed in a fundamentally different manner. In Britain, party affiliations were typical for national newspapers printed in London, and canny politicians became quite sophisticated at maintaining networks of loyal editors and writers through various kinds of overt or covert subsidies. But these newspapers, which paid taxes and were printed on stamped paper, circulated among the more comfortable classes. A separate group of unstamped newspapers and pamphlets circulated to the working classes. The arch Federalist William Cobbett – Peter Porcupine – became one of the most effective writers for this unstamped press. As mass politics appeared in the nineteenth century, then, class divisions and the struggle for suffrage would be defining elements. The free play of symbols that would allow Jackson and William Henry Harrison to portray themselves as common men was less a feature of British partisanship. In most western countries, a party associated with the working classes formed around the issue of the right to vote, and a class valence would continue to be associated with popular politics. Britain's Labour Party and Germany's Social Democratic Party really had no parallel in the US.

Censorship was another key difference. In Britain, censorship was relatively weak; in France, it waxed and waned with the tides of revolution. In Germany censorship discouraged political agitation in the press until late in the nineteenth century.

But in the European world system, and most other places as well, every country's news system has experienced a period of partisanship. Scholars have been slow to study press partisanship comparatively or transnationally (Hallin and Mancini, 2004). Probably because "journalism" is understood normatively as impartial, journalism scholars tend to bracket off the partisan past. But some general points seem worth proposing.

Wherever there is political conflict, the combatants will seek to recruit the news media. For this reason, any modern nation will have had some history of partisan media, though the flavors differ from region to region. Latin American media have a particular history of partisanship, for instance, paralleling Europe and North America for much of the nineteenth century, with a strong class dynamic in the twentieth century that reflects recurring waves of authoritarianism and populism. At the end of the twentieth century a new kind of state-led populist news appeared and found admirers in many parts of the world (Fox and Waisbord, 2002; Waisbord, 2011).

Media are complex. As media became more commercial, the relationship between any particular media organization and political sponsors diminished compared with its relationships with commercial sponsors. In many market situations, however, party affiliation can enhance rather than contradict commercial appeal. This was true in nineteenth-century US cities, where large numbers of newspapers competed for readers. To be the organ of a party added value to a newspaper. Likewise, nationally circulated newspapers in Italy or France or Israel find political allegiances commercially useful.

If commercialization and industrialization tended to make partisanship less attractive for newspapers, an opposite trend seems to have taken place in broadcasting. In countries with well-financed national or public broadcasters, a commitment to political evenhandedness often was institutionalized by allotting chunks of spectrum or airtime to specific parties. In Italy, the "lottizzazione" of public broadcasting led to a proportional representation of the parties on the board of the national broadcasting authority, RAI, and an allotment of broadcasting resources. In the Netherlands, "pillarization" sanctioned the assignment of media resources to various organized social forces. These forms of "political parallelism" (Hallin and Mancini, 2004) might be thought of as secondary partisanship, to distinguish it from the form of partisanship that characterized early newspapers. Secondary partisanship exists in media organizations that have well-developed non-partisan domains. The newsworkers in these organizations embrace a kind of professionalism that moderates their partisanship also. Again, a long story for a later chapter.

Old-style partisanship has emerged again in the contemporary digital news environment. In the first generation of the blogosphere in the US and elsewhere, enthusiasts enacted a Habermasian moment. They wanted to be Publius. But this very brief generation of high-minded citizen deliberation was succeeded rapidly by a partisan approach. And then fairly quickly more professional media organizations began signing up the most successful bloggers, leading to a kind of domestication of unruly partisanship under the brand names of firms like Fox and the Guardian.

The new digital partisanship repeats an older pattern, in which expansions of capacity in the media system provide resources for party activities. Even within the digital revolution, waves of partisanship have accompanied new applications. Social media formats have intensified the partisan aspects of the blogosphere.

Media partisanship thrives in environments that encourage audiences to seek self-reinforcing messages. In a nineteenth-century marketplace flooded with party newspapers, readers naturally shied away from opposing points of view that would make them uncomfortable or would invalidate their attitudes or values. Likewise, in the twenty-first century, digital audiences cluster around their chosen voices and solidify their preconceptions (Stroud, 2011).

Partisanship has its virtues. It is instinctively popular, and invites ordinary people into the political spectacle, even if primarily as fans of a team, so to speak. It also keeps things moving. Party spirit disturbs political monopolies.

It is also corrosive. It encourages distrust. And, in mass electoral politics, it distracts people from fundamental problems and draws them toward movements and representations that can mystify and demobilize.

De Tocqueville thought partisanship didn't help democracies think straight. I tend to agree. In other moments, public media have subordinated politics to commerce or expertise. These moments have their own demons.

3

The Commercial Public Sphere

Historians like to write about revolutions. Some revolutions are more specific than others. The French Revolution, for instance, was something everyone at the time recognized as a concrete set of political and military events. The Industrial Revolution, however, was discovered after the fact, and is a rather abstract bundle of processes happening all over the world over many centuries. Revolutions like that may have a beginning, though it keeps getting pushed farther and farther back in time. They rarely have an end. The Communications Revolution is similar. So is the Market Revolution, which is the big process underlying this chapter.

Markets have existed throughout history but were usually tightly contained. At a certain point, however, the scope of social activity transacted through markets increased rapidly, and market logic came to be applied to more and more spheres of life. The contagious spread of markets through the social order is what some call the "Market Revolution." Of course, no one called it that when it was happening, and many scholars dispute that the word "revolution" really applies to the historical spread of markets. But no one disagrees that market forces have penetrated ever more areas of life.

I borrow the use of the term "Market Revolution" in the US context from Charles Sellers (Sellers, 1994). Sellers posits a particular timing for a Market Revolution in the US, and sees it unleashing disruptive forces in the 1810s, leading to social dislocations that provided the energy for Jacksonian democracy. In Sellers's account, the coming of markets was not a happy thing. His account has been controversial in two ways. First, scholars doubt that the coming of the market prompted the many diverse movements and events that Sellers ascribes to it. And, second, scholars think that the coming of the market was a more positive event, both in the eyes of contemporaries and in retrospect. These historians argue that US Americans who thought seriously about political economy in the years before the Civil War seemed to accept Adam Smith's *Wealth of Nations* as scriptural, and that this represents a broader laissez-faire consensus (Feller, 1997; Howe, 2007). But there was plenty of dissent – certainly those who thought humans could be chattel disagreed with an important element of the free market, and the fact that federal tariffs were the chosen symbolic issue for those who wished to promote states' rights signifies a deeper disagreement over Smithian economics. And there was no shortage of radical critics of free-market ideology among the northern working classes (Calvo, 2012).

But if we accept that there was broad disagreement among both experts and ordinary people on whether market forces ought to be contained and curtailed, we can still appreciate the productivity of markets and the delight that people took in the new goods that became available. Common sense should tell us that people viewed and continue to view the market with mixed emotions. There's a reason why you can't sell your vote or your children on eBay. People will continue to draw a line between the sacred and the profane, and want to drive the moneychangers out of the temple.

The same ambivalence has been evident in the history of the media, which claim to be both sacred (the flow of information that allows democracy to flourish) and profane (the sale of advertising that pays reporters' salaries). The influence of markets can be found everywhere in the development of newspapers, particularly from the 1820s on. And many people found the rise of more market-oriented publications to be liberating and exciting. A few key groups of people disagreed, however. The guardians of traditional culture – teachers, ministers, and community leaders – reacted as if the barbarians were at the city gate. Within media operations there were similar reservations and resistances. Printers feared that mechanization and divisions of labor would reduce them from skilled craftsmen to interchangeable unskilled wage slaves. And the politically oriented – not just editors but also candidates and voters – often viewed the influence of the market as insidious.

These fears make sense. Workers in areas where increasing market demand called for more efficient production saw lower career expectations: not all journeymen could hope to acquire their own businesses. Craft sociability also suffered as conflicting interests drove a wedge between workers and their employers, who had successfully followed a traditional path to independence (Rorabaugh, 1986; Baron, 1989; Hardt and Brennen, 1995). Print workers complained when owners who had climbed from their ranks pulled the ladder up after themselves, trying to unbundle the traditional tasks of the printer, and to hire less skilled children and women to do part of the work, making it harder for their workers to maintain an income that would allow them to eventually become independent. The same workers would resist new "labor-saving" technologies.

The unease of editors and correspondents and the political actors they served was less direct. While a majority took pride and satisfaction in the tremendous growth of the press, they considered the most commercial aspects of the rising newspaper industry as uncouth, unmanly, and perhaps undemocratic. It was crass to pander to money, and womanly to let the market tell you what to print; the old heads viewed the content of the most commercial newspapers as prostrated to the least common denominators of human interest – sex, gossip, frivolity. The more philosophical recognized a distinction between distributive principles in the domains of politics and the market. As Robert McChesney puts it, in politics the principle is supposed to be one person, one vote; in markets, it's one dollar, one vote (McChesney, 1999: 255).

This chapter will focus again on the US experience at the outset, with some attention to parallel developments in Britain. It will use this history to ponder the implications of commercialization as a moment of change for the media in public life. It will then pay some attention to the different histories of commercialization in other places and times. I begin with a story of personalities and media organizations and the unlikely connections among them.

A Tangled Story

In 1824, Robert Dale Owen, the son of the great industrialist Robert Owen, bought an abandoned religious commune and founded the New Harmony colony in the wild frontier of western Indiana. New Harmony was established as a socialist community, one of many such experiments in the new republic. Viewing the rising market economy as predatory and cannibalistic, its founders believed that, through enlightened cooperation, they could create a system that would be far more productive, and would gradually drive the old economy out of existence. Owen and the others recognized, though, that the competitive economy had important social and cultural defenses. Mainstream religion, for instance, buttressed it by justifying the enslavement of labor and women. Military and political establishments also had a stake in perpetuating the existing order of things. So the community became a magnet for a diverse group of radicals – feminists, labor activists, anti-clericalists, and free thinkers. One of the most famous was Frances Wright.

Fanny Wright had been born into a wealthy Scots family in 1795. Orphaned at age three and raised by her mother's sister and father in London, she became independently wealthy upon reaching her majority, and devoted herself to intense study and travel. (She learned economics at Glasgow, where her uncle had succeeded to Adam Smith's chair.) She sailed to the United States in 1818 – partly to see her anonymously written play *Altdorf* performed in New York – and wrote a travelog about the experience, which she published to some acclaim. Around this time she made the acquaintance of the Marquis de Lafayette, the French nobleman who, as a volunteer officer, had been a hero of the American Revolution. She became his "passionate friend," and lived for long stretches at his estate. When Lafayette returned to the US for a triumphal tour in 1824, Wright returned also, rendezvousing with Lafayette at many of his stops, and sojourning with him as Jefferson's guests at Monticello.

Although her acquaintance with Lafayette had given her entrée to the very center of political life in the States, Wright quickly found her way to the fringes. Dedicating herself to the abolition of slavery and the emancipation of women, she was attracted to the New Harmony experiment and to Robert Dale Owen. She pursued her own scheme for freeing the slaves by establishing a colony at Nashoba, in Tennessee, a community that would purchase slaves with the understanding that their work would eventually pay for their freedom. The long-term plan was to settle the liberated slaves outside the US, and replace them with free white laborers. Failing health forced Wright to abandon the Nashoba colony, but not before she sailed with freed slaves to Haiti (Eckhardt, 1984).

One of the early projects of the New Harmony colony was a weekly newspaper, the *New Harmony Gazette*. Devoting itself to the advocacy of a wide variety of reforms – anti-slavery, socialism, peace – the *Gazette* exemplified a simple philosophy of media effects. Truth, through reason, would conquer superstition. This Enlightenment faith in the power of truth over candid minds inspired a large segment of reform periodicals appearing alongside the party press.

In 1829, the *Gazette* changed its name to the *Free Enquirer* and, soon after, moved to New York. There it was printed in the office of George Henry Evans, who, along with Owen and Wright, became deeply involved in political organizing among artisan workers in New

York City. Evans and Owen soon founded another weekly newspaper, the *Workingmen's Advocate*, to be the voice of that prototypical labor movement. And soon the *Advocate* was announcing the start of the *Daily Sentinel*, which was to be a labor-friendly daily newspaper.

Among the printers associated with the *Free Enquirer*, the *Advocate*, and the *Sentinel* was Benjamin Day, then a 20-year-old journeyman printer. Day won a place in newspaper history a few years later when he established the first successful penny paper, the *New York Sun*. Three other partners in the publication of the *Sentinel* established a similar but less successful penny paper, the *Transcript*, in the same year (Saxton, 1984). The penny press, daily newspapers sold cheaply and available to a working-class readership, reached the readers that the *Free Enquirer* aimed at – the mass of the people – but sublimated radical content and political advocacy.

In 1825, Anne Royall, who figured in our last chapter, first met the editor and publisher Mordecai Noah. Noah, one of the less remembered pioneers of journalism in the state of New York, had been a Jacksonian politico and Tammany stalwart, founding the daily *National Advocate* in 1817, being appointed sheriff of New York City in 1822, and scheming to create a refuge in the Hudson Valley for Jews from around the world (Sarna, 1981). He proved helpful to Royall in 1825 and later by giving her publications favorable reviews and by trumpeting her visits in news columns; he also became a genuinely sympathetic friend, sharing both Royall's political attitudes and her marginal social status. It was Noah who labeled Royall "The Mrs. Walter Scott of America," a designation she reveled in for years. In 1825, he happened to have in his employ a recent Scots immigrant, James Gordon Bennett; Royall met Bennett then too, and they also became quite friendly (James, 1972: 133, 158). In 1829, Noah merged his *New York Enquirer* (not related to the later *Free Enquirer)* with the morning *Courier*, founded two years earlier by James Watson Webb, to form the *New York Courier and Enquirer*, which soon became perhaps the most successful daily newspaper in the States (Crouthamel, 1969). Webb and Noah continued to employ James Gordon Bennett, who was now their Washington correspondent, in which capacity he continued to associate closely with Royall. Bennett sat with Royall during her trial in Washington (mentioned last chapter), counseling and consoling her.

When Anne Royall undertook to establish her own newspaper, she solicited support from the network of editors who had given her favorable notice over the years. She did not, however, approach Noah and Webb. They had committed a cardinal offense. Along with a number of other prominent newspapers, their *Courier and Enquirer* had taken questionable loans from the Bank of the United States, the Monster Bank that Andrew Jackson demonized in his presidential campaign. Noah and Webb had borrowed $50,000, an extraordinary sum, more or less directly from the bank's wily president, Nicholas Biddle. Biddle had also made unusual loans to Duff Green of the *United States Telegraph*, one of Jackson's kitchen cabinet, who defected to support the Whig candidate Henry Clay in 1832, to Gales and Seaton of the *National Intelligencer*, still one of the nation's most powerful sources of political news, and to Thomas Ritchie, the leading southern editor and founder of the *Richmond Enquirer* (not related, of course, to either the *New York Courier and Enquirer* or the *Free Enquirer*). To savvy political observers, these loans seemed to have been tactically placed to bribe the nation's premier newspapers. Congressional investigations followed.

In the aftermath of this scandal, James Gordon Bennett quit the *Courier and Enquirer* and established his own newspaper, the *New York Herald*. Bennett copied Benjamin Day, and published the *Herald* as a penny paper. In short order, it was to displace the *Courier and Enquirer* as the nation's premier commercial paper. Bennett and James Watson Webb, his former employer, would remain bitter enemies. Bennett would repeat in print accusations that Webb had peddled influence in return for bank loans, and Webb would serially track him down on the streets of New York and beat him with his cane (Mindich, 1998: ch. 1).

Thurlow Weed, chief architect of the Whig Party and editorial strategist of the Republican Party, met Fanny Wright when he accompanied General Lafayette on a steamboat ride from New York City to Albany in 1825. The next year, Weed latched on to the anti-Masonic movement. Two years later, he founded the *Anti-Masonic Enquirer* – no relationship to the *Free Enquirer*, the *Courier and Enquirer*, or the *Richmond Enquirer*. And shortly afterward he would land in the editorial seat of the *Albany Evening Journal*, from which he would later help engineer the Whig electoral victories in the state of New York.

In 1837, with the Whigs newly installed as the governing party in the state of New York, Weed sought to amplify and diversify their media appeal. In particular, he wanted to establish a statewide weekly newspaper that would be sold for 50 cents a year – a penny an issue, more or less – and that would appeal specifically to working people. He got well-to-do Whig backers to open their wallets for this venture, and installed as its editor Horace Greeley. Greeley, who was to become the nation's most famous newspaperman in the years between

Benjamin Franklin and Joseph Pulitzer, was then a 26-year-old journeyman who was in the process of failing in his proprietorship of a weekly newspaper called the *New Yorker*. His new newspaper, the *Jeffersonian*, was to be considerably more successful (Van Deusen, 1947: 97).

Under Weed's tutelage, Greeley became an adept at the mysteries of partisan publishing. But he also sensed the magic of the marketplace. On a couple of occasions, he tried to conjure up a successful cheap daily, but failed. In 1840, he was tapped by the Whig leadership to publish a campaign newspaper called the *Log Cabin*. Printing 80,000 copies weekly, the *Log Cabin* circulated through the nation, acting like a bulletin board for the Harrison campaign. It clipped items from local Whig papers and gave them a national audience, and it produced detailed essays on policy matters that local editors could copy in turn. It functioned, before the age of the telegraph, like a kind of partisan wire service.

Greeley folded the *Log Cabin* after the campaign. Then, with the backing of Whig potentates, he began publishing the *New York Tribune*. The *Tribune* was, like Day's *Sun* and Bennett's *Herald*, a penny paper, smaller and much cheaper than conventional dailies like the *Courier and Enquirer*, and seeking to sell many more issues. Part of the success of penny dailies came from their stated aversion to partisanship, which they called irresponsible, but moreover stupid and boring. Greeley's *Tribune*, however, was also a partisan newspaper. And the Whig gentlemen who bankrolled it were willing to do so because they perceived, correctly, that the other penny papers in New York City were also partisan, but on behalf of the Democrats. In fact, the divide between the penny press and the party press, like the divide between the party press and the reform press, was never very clear (Nerone, 1987).

Commercialization and Newspapers

Commercialization refers to several interrelated developments in the media generally and in newspapers specifically. In the early and mid-nineteenth century, the most obvious impact of commercialization was the rise of mass-circulation media, which embraced and promoted popular culture. On a more infrastructural level, commercialization also describes the rising importance of advertising, which encouraged media producers to think of their audiences as a commodity to be sold in turn to advertisers. And again infrastructurally, the flow of news itself began to commercialize, as new forms of enterprise in news gathering and news transmission led to markets for news itself. Each of these developments deserves some extended discussion.

"Mass circulation" refers not just to the size of circulation but also to the quality of the audience and its engagement with media. In practice, mass-circulation media are intended to be put in the hands of anybody and everybody. Early newspapers were not intended for mass circulation; usually, their owners aimed for a politically active class that was set off from the general population by gender and income, as well as religion and race in various places. Occasionally events and activists overleapt these barriers. Tom Paine's *Common Sense* seemed to circulate so broadly that its argument and specific language reached almost everyone. Sustained efforts to put specific media into everyone's hands, though, evolved slowly and outside of the political realm. David Nord makes a sensible argument that tract societies and Bible societies were the first organizations to really attempt to put texts in the hands of virtually every reader (Nord, 2004). These organizations followed the logic of Protestant Christianity, which held that, because the fullness of revealed truth was contained in Scripture alone, all people should be able to read it for themselves. Politics in most places would lack such universalism through most of the nineteenth century, but with the achievement of universal white male suffrage in the US, and by around mid-century in Britain, political activists would have an incentive to reach all adult white men, regardless of wealth or creed. Mass electoral democracy, like religion, pushed for mass circulation. But newspapers remained relatively expensive. The cost of paper was high, and set limits that reined in newspaper production well after papermaking was mechanized (Smith, 1971). And the labor structure of print workshops was well suited to printing newspapers in runs of 500 to 5,000 copies, but, before the rise of steam-powered presses, there was little incentive in terms of economies of scale in expanding beyond that. In religious publishing, the calculus was different. The key incentive was spiritual, the temporality was eternal and not daily or weekly, and the subsidies that flowed from the faithful overcame scarcities of raw materials and limitations of productive capacities.

Underlying factors began to change in the 1810s and 1820s. Steam-powered presses became available, the first working model having been built by the German printer Friedrich Koenig in London in 1810. By 1827, patents had been issued in Britain for a steam-powered press with four cylinder platens that could produce over 4,000 impressions per hour – fast enough for a mass-circulation daily newspaper. Then, in the US, Richard Hoe designed a steam-powered cylinder press in 1832, and in 1844 a rotary press – in which paper could be printed continuously by running it between two rotating cylinders set with type. But these machines were quite expensive, and used only by the largest newspapers in London at first, and then in book-printing plants in the US and by the most successful metropolitan newspapers. Most newspapers, daily and weekly alike, continued to use hand presses through mid-century.

Factors besides technologies accounted for the increase in circulation of newspapers and other cheap print products. Popular fiction – large-circulation cheap novels, for instance – became common by the 1830s; in chapter 2 I mentioned the pamphlets that Anne Royall and Davy Crockett published. A broad popular literature spread through the US in the 1830s and 1840s, answering the demands and desires of ordinary people who could read for pleasure and afford to occasionally buy a cheap edition (Reynolds, 1988; Lehuu, 2000).

The desire to target these new readers led to a general rise in advertising expenditures. Newspapers had always featured advertising, and printers had always solicited it from merchants and shopkeepers as well as people looking to sell land, hire employees, or find runaway slaves. In the eighteenth century, columns of advertising usually occupied the front and back pages of four-page newspapers, daily or weekly, sharing those pages with poetry and essays and other material that could be printed in advance. The inside pages, pages 2 and 3, would be printed last, and contained the most recent material, including the main news items and the most important commentary. The advertising copy on the outside pages resembled the classified advertising that filled twentieth-century newspapers. Each ad was small and specific; even merchants and shopkeepers, who advertised on a regular basis, tended to run ads listing specific goods for sale that week. All but the most ambitious advertisers avoided design elements like logos, illustrations, or typographical variation.

As the market revolution produced new consumer goods, and as ordinary people acquired the money to purchase them, both the quantity and quality of advertising changed. Advertisers introduced design innovations in terms of type size, illustration, and white space into newspapers, innovations that newspapers would later use to enhance their news coverage. Headlines, for instance, first appeared in advertising and were then adopted for news stories (Barnhurst and Nerone, 2001). Newspaper ads stayed inside the column until the second half of the nineteenth century, for the most part. Larger-format display ads would appear in the next generation, produced by new kinds of advertisers like large department stores and nationally distributed consumer products. The most elaborate ads in that category in the first half of the century were for cultural goods like books and theater performances and for patent medicines. Each of these can be considered a "brand-name" product, with the brand name being the author, the star, and the physician – brand names that were also names of actual persons.

The desire to put ads before the eyeballs of consumers added an incentive to reach non-political readers. Party newspapers sought two kinds of readers above all others: voters and editors of other newspapers. Mobilizing local voters was obviously central to achieving the political ends that party editors aimed at. But just as important was the regional and national audience of other editors, who would constitute the network of exchange papers that provided most of the content of the party paper and would act like a chorus acclaiming the authority that an editor could command in the national public sphere. These two audiences intensified each other. A party editor like Thurlow Weed cared a great deal that local voters followed his advice and that other Whig editors followed his lead; his esteem among local voters grew because of his national reputation, which in turn rested solidly on his reliable ability to turn out the local vote for Whig candidates.

But advertisers did not necessarily share these priorities. They valued the attention of voters, of course, and, in any city that hosted more than one or two newspapers, the ability to deliver all of the, say, Whig readers made a newspaper very appealing. But they wanted to reach anyone with money to spend. This included many who did not or could not vote, like women. Women were interested in politics and did read party newspapers (Zboray and Saracino Zboray, 2010), but they did not subscribe under their own names, and very little of the content of a party newspaper needed to address them specifically. The market revolution encouraged newspapers to find different kinds of content that would draw more readers who weren't targeted by party papers, the readers who had already been drawn to sensational pamphlets or popular fiction.

Commercialization encouraged newspapers to pay more attention to content that has since come to be called "human interest." In the early nineteenth century, this meant gossip about prominent people, local, national, and international; stories about crime and punishment; and stories about the theater and show business – an emerging entertainment economy that was also a rising source of advertising revenue. Traditional morality considered this news vulgar, even evil. To fend off such criticism, published accounts always invoked a moral lesson, wrapping their excitements in the language of moral uplift. At the same time, they summoned a similar moral outrage toward the party press, which critics accused of selling out to the highest bidder, like the Second Bank of the United States or the "slave power," or being solely concerned with manufacturing public opinion.

These were the hallmarks of the so-called penny press. Penny papers appeared in the US in the 1830s. They got their name from their single-issue price, which was radically reduced from the six cents that dailies had conventionally charged for a single issue. Penny dailies sought readers that traditional dailies and many party weeklies had neglected, using content that critics would come to call "sensationalist." Penny papers were small and cheap. They circulated on the "cash system," in which the newspaper sold bundles to quasi-independent distributors, including newsboys, for a cash price (typically $0.67 per 100), who then delivered them to subscribers and hawked them on the streets. The business model aimed to dramatically increase circulation in order to dramatically increase advertising revenue. Unlike in the traditional model, subscriptions came nowhere near to covering production costs. In its first generation, the penny papers adopted a tone of sharp hostility toward party newspapers, and declared themselves politically neutral. This was somewhat disingenuous, as most of the personnel had some attachment to the party press. Within a few years, a second generation of penny papers, the most famous of which was Greeley's *Tribune*, had become openly partisan.

Historians like to see the appearance of the penny press as a revolution, a sharp divide between the era of the party press and the era of the commercial press. But in practice it was a tangled history. Politicization and commercialization went on simultaneously, and in many ways enhanced each other. The two processes are more easily separated analytically than historically.

And the characteristic content and tone of the penny press had a long pre-history in the appearance of alternative newspapers in the 1810s and 1820s. There was always a counterpoint to political newspapering, and, as partisan newspapers became increasingly single-minded, groups that felt left out started papers. Before 1830, US activists started three different kinds of newspapers that anticipated the later, famous penny papers. One was the gossip newspaper, a second was the mechanics' paper, and a third the "free presses" of the anti-Masons.

Gossip Papers

In the first three decades of the nineteenth century, gossip newspapers appeared in large and smaller cities in the northern states. Some of these focused on nationally known political figures, like the *Independent Balance* of Philadelphia; some focused on local politicians, dandies, and lowlifes, like the *Microscope* in Albany, the *Castigator* in Boston, and the *True Blue and Castigator* in Cincinnati, all of which drew inspiration from the *Tatler* and *Spectator* of the early eighteenth century. Before 1820, such papers concentrated on criticizing the moral lapses of conceited nouveaux, as the motto of the *Independent Balance* declares:

> Spare not the rod, says Solomon,
> But lustily the fool lay on;
> And well the wise man we obey,
> When any from decorum stray:
> – Our gun is pois'd, our aim is sure,
> Our wish is good, our end is pure;
> To virtue we are sworn allies,
> "And shoot at folly as it flies."

Gossip newspapers often were covertly partisan. Mostly, the partisan ones were founded by Federalists, who intended to retaliate against Republicans with a kind of reverse populism. Always they were socially conservative. The odd thing about them to a modern reader is how rarely anyone got named, including the people who produced the paper. An editorial persona is invented – in this case "Solomon," representing timeless, biblical values. These papers were also careful not to directly name the people they castigated, but one can safely assume that readers knew whom they referred to. Take this fairly typical item from the Albany *Microscope*: "If certain females could be convinced that Solomon spoke the truth when he said, 'the hand of the diligent maketh rich, but the path of the slothful leadeth to poverty,' they would discontinue their spunging [*sic*] visits to a family not a mile from the corner of Hudson and Pearl streets. D." Readers who lived in cities like Albany, then a town smaller and more compact than today's University of Iowa, would have been able to identify those "certain females."

These newspapers were only sporadically successful. The cost of ridiculing leading citizens was high. In some cases, gangs attacked gossip papers' offices and beat up editors; in other cases, repeated libel prosecutions crippled the publication (Nerone, 1989: 259–62; *Boston Castigator*, May 16, 1829). Circulations remained small and the appeal to advertisers was limited. The solution to these problems became clear when better-organized police courts began producing a steady stream of stories with the same moral punch whose protagonists could neither sue nor, because they ended up in jail, attack the editor.

Gossip papers always set themselves up in opposition to the mainstream press. They saw mainstream newspapers as the engines by which the less-than-virtuous maintained their reputations. The established papers (and especially the partisan ones) were just like the hypocrites the gossip papers castigated, claiming righteousness while actually following their most venal impulses.

The Workie Press

The same critique was voiced by the mechanics' papers. It had been common since the 1790s for some newspapers to make a show of appealing to the "producing classes," to those who worked with their hands. Hence papers with titles like the *Farmer's Museum*. Often these were very conventional weeklies. But by around 1820, amid the economic dislocations and political disaffections that were to produce Jacksonian democracy, papers with a more strident appeal to the interests of workers appeared (Schiller, 1981; Wilentz, 1984). Some of these were rural in focus, like James Gazlay's Cincinnati-based *Western Tiller*. Others – the more famous ones – were urban, like the *Workingmen's Advocate*.

The Workingmen's newspapers were part of a political movement that eventually formed the left wing of Jacksonianism. They shared an ideology based on an opposition between producers and the money power. Producers, like mechanics and farmers, sought to maintain a manly independence by the work of their hands; they formed the backbone not only of the economy but also of the Republic. But they were pitted in a losing battle against owners and managers who gained control of workplaces through financial maneuvering and technological innovations, reducing independent producers to wage-earners. In the process, the money power corrupted the political system and threatened all freedom. This ideology borrowed strands of Jeffersonian thought and revolutionary Republicanism, and in turn would inspire one brand of anti-slavery politics and much of the dissident journalism called "muckraking" later in the century.

The Workies' critique of mainstream politics and its press resembled that of the gossip papers but included a specifically class edge. The parties had become tools of the propertied classes. The partisan press did the work of the money power partly by openly propagandizing on behalf of candidates and partly by sowing confusion – creating a public arena so conflict-oriented, partial, and passionate that it concealed the deep sources of politics from the people.

Workie newspapers sought to revive politics by bringing rational public attention to it. Sometimes this meant a return to older notions of impartiality – papers like the Boston *Workingmen's Advocate*, while clearly partial, made it a habit to print the tickets and platforms of all political parties. Sometimes instead they directed attention away from elections and toward otherwise neglected issues – one special concern was imprisonment for debt, still legal in many states.

Anti-Masonry

More powerful than either the gossip papers or the workies, however, was the anti-Masonic movement. Often disregarded as antebellum craziness, anti-Masonry was actually one of the most momentous eruptions of reformist energy in US history. It was also one of the largest alternative press movements.

A largely middle-class movement operating most strongly in the reform-minded sections of the northeast and midwest, anti-Masonry claimed that many institutions, including the parties, the banks, and the press, were actually controlled by a secret organization with its own agenda (Formisano, 1983; Goodman, 1988). The cure for this cancer was exposé. But Masonry's control of the press prevented such exposé, even as it diverted attention with sham displays of partisan contest.

The solution was to establish alternative newspapers, like the early ones that Thurlow Weed edited. Many anti-Masonic newspapers emphasized that the mainstream press was controlled by Masons by calling themselves the *Free Press*. In the years bracketing 1830, over a hundred such newspapers were founded. Typically, like other movement newspapers, these were initially set up by an organizing committee, which circulated a prospectus and gathered subscribers who would underwrite the publication, and which also negotiated with a printer (*We the People*, 1830–6). Printers then compiled the newspaper by clipping items from other anti-Masonic newspapers and by printing readers' letters and notices of meetings.

The anti-Masonic excitement gradually wore off. In the meantime, smart operatives like Thurlow Weed found ways to channel its energies into new partisan coalitions like the Whigs. Many of the anti-Masonic newspapers assimilated to the mainstream partisan press – often the fate of successful alternative media.

From Alternative Presses to the Penny Press

The anti-Masons and the Workies – and the abolitionists and the temperance activists and vegetarians and free-lovers and peace advocates – who set up alternative presses in the antebellum period bore witness to a widespread perception. Along with a lot of other people, they were dismayed by the mainstream press. It was cynically partisan and anti-rational; it was controlled by the Few – a moneyed elite or a partisan elite or a Masonic elite – at the expense of The People.

These alternative presses also bear witness to the openness of the print system. Setting up a newspaper was not so daunting a task. Printing material and equipment was getting cheaper, and the postal system made it easy to get content. And many mainstream papers, particularly small-town weeklies, which were run on small but tight budgets, could be co-opted by anti-Masons in the 1830s or abolitionists in the 1840s for relatively small sums of money.

In any case, the backlash against partisan newspapering was already widespread before the appearance of the penny press, and the sensational content of the penny press had already been previewed in the gossip papers. In fact, mainstream party newspapers had been diversifying their content too. The typical newspaper became steadily more commercial and more news-oriented throughout the 1820s and 1830s, even as the partisan allegiances of most newspapers became more energetic (Baldasty, 1992). So the wave of urban penny dailies that appeared in the mid-1830s rode on a broad tide.

When Benjamin Day began the *New York Sun* in 1833, he drew on a Workie culture. When James Gordon Bennett founded the *New York Herald* in 1835, he applied the lessons he'd learned as a Washington correspondent at the side of the most celebrated of the gossip journalists, Anne Royall. Horace Greeley established the *New York Tribune* in 1841 with the backing of the same politicos who had bankrolled Thurlow Weed's anti-Masonic papers.

There is a recurring interpretation in the historiography of US journalism that sees the rise of a more commercial press marking the end of a political or partisan press. That is far too simple a story. Party papers commercialized while penny papers quickly became partisan. Likewise, there is no simple story to be had about reaching working-class readers. Party papers tried to reach all voters, and the penny papers that succeeded with working-class readers quickly sought to build more upscale readerships: James Gordon Bennett's *Herald* established its "money article" on financial matters as a prime point of appeal, alongside its coverage of show business and crime. Although there was in fact a dramatic outbreak at one moment, particularly in New York City, the changes that commercialization brought to the US press were more slow-moving and subtle. They involved changes in the mode of production of newspapers and in the shape and centers of gravity of the press system as a whole.

Commercialization Changes the Press

Earlier I suggested thinking of newspapers as networks of relationships. The printerly newspapers of the eighteenth century set up a fairly simple set of relationships, bringing a flow of content from officials, markets, and the postal system to a small and undifferentiated market of gentlemen. For all but the largest urban areas, these newspapers were monopolies, and they were run with a characteristic lack of interest in anything that would divide or alienate their audience. Newspapers with deeper political commitments had appeared during moments of political drama, like the English and French Revolutions, and aligned themselves with factions, parties, movements, or political clubs. Although less stable than most printerly newspapers, they remain more interesting, and have drawn a disproportionate amount of historians' attention. When mass politics appeared in the US, many of the habits and some of the content and personnel of these older revolutionary newspapers were adapted to a permanent political competition. This produced a set of relationships that looked like those shown in Figure 3.1. This is an oversimplification, of course. But it suggests a change in the network of relationships that was real, and that signals a shift in the dominant metaphor that governed newspapers: from coffeehouse or town meeting to courtroom or military. Most newspapers now competed in markets with newspapers that had differing political affiliations.

Commercialization produced a similar kind of shift in the network of relationships. In addition to the importance of a political party as a patron, source of news, and sponsor of a network of exchanges with other editors, commercial interests like shops, theaters, publishers, and producers of consumer goods became important as sources of advertising revenue and a market for readerships. Now, in addition to selling newspapers to readers, newspapers sold readers to advertisers. The new set of relationships looked like those shown in Figure 3.2. This new circuit of relationships was not wholly new – there had always been advertising in newspapers – but it achieved a quantitative reach that produced a qualitative change in the nature of the news business.

As I've already argued, commercialization did not require the elimination of partisanship. In fact, a party affiliation, in many markets, enhanced a newspaper's value to advertisers. It's better to think of the rising commercial relations as wrapping around the political ones. That wrapping around was embodied in the physical shape of a typical newspaper issue, in which the party paper – the

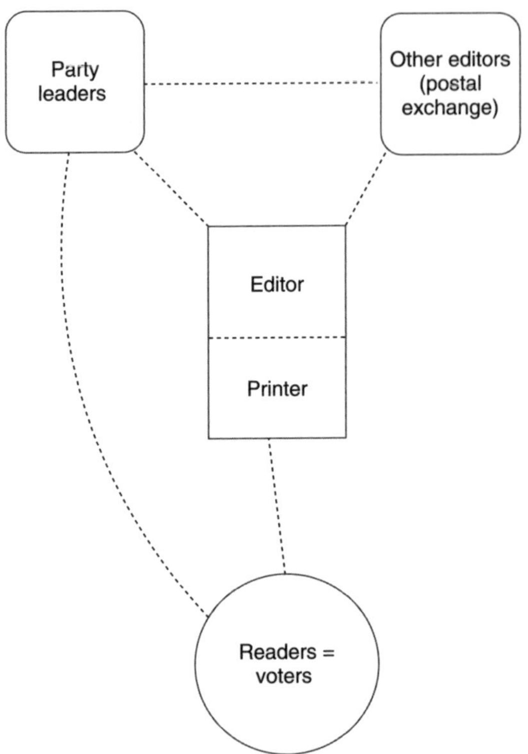

Figure 3.1: The partisan newspaper as a network of relationships

columns produced by the editor out of exchange papers – continued to sit in the middle, while commercial content, such as advertising, market information, and the kinds of content that attracted an ever larger readership, like local crime reporting, crowded around it. This commercial content would require an ever larger commitment of resources, to the point where one could argue it crowded out the politics (Baldasty, 1992).

The characteristic content of commercializing newspapers was gathered by beat reporters. The term "reporter" is an old one, with a fairly specific meaning, rooted in courtroom practices. A reporter was a stenographer, recording with fullness and fidelity the proceedings he witnessed. Reporters were not "correspondents," the letter writers who traditionally provided newspaper content. Correspondents were expected to have a point of view, and to give readers colorful impressions of distant places through their observations. "Correspondent" was an international term of art, and has endured, though with

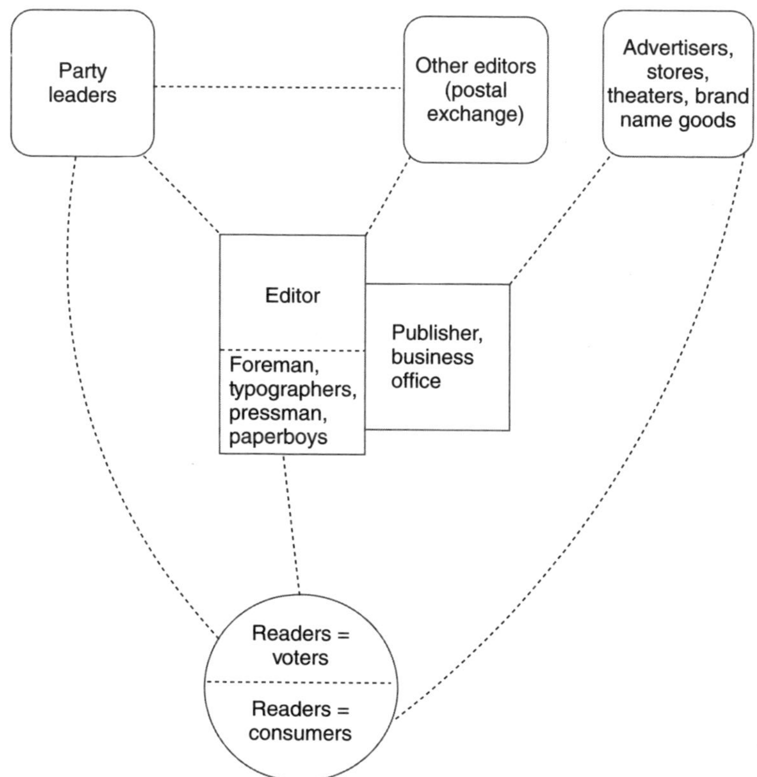

Figure 3.2: The commercial newspaper as a network of relationships

diminished meaning, applied to journalists covering wars, diplomacy, and national legislatures. In France, the most prestigious award for journalists is the Prix Albert Londres, named after a correspondent famed for his coverage of, first, the French Parliament, then World War I, the Soviet revolutionary government, and nationalist movements in China, India, and North Africa (Redfern, 2004).

Reporters, on the other hand, were supposed to be transparent and factual. Reporters should not have a persona. Reporters went out into the city and picked up information, often in the form of a digest or a transcript. Market information, like the current price of commodities in different cities, or lists of births and deaths and ships arriving in port and visitors arriving in hotels, often appeared in compact agate type, masking the large amount of reporting labor that went into compiling them. Transcripts of political meetings and speeches, of important sermons, and of proceedings of the police courts similarly strained the labor of reporters, although a friendly newspaper would gladly let a speaker edit the transcript of one's remarks. Abraham Lincoln made a habit of editing the copy of his speeches in the news office of the *Sangamo Journal* when he was a rising Whig politico in Springfield, Illinois (Harper, 1951: 2, 14–15, 30).

The rise of the reporter marked an important change in the mode of production of the news. In common sense, it indicated that newspapers were becoming more aggressive and competitive in newsgathering – a change from the habit of simply copying most of their news from other newspapers or official documents. In more economic terms, it meant that newspapers were adding value to the news they gathered, making some news items things they could hold more exclusively and even own. Newspapers began complaining loudly when they thought that a competitor had copied the content of their enterprise reporting. News that can be owned can be sold. The introduction of the telegraph at the end of the 1840s was the decisive moment for creating property in news, but we'll discuss that in a later chapter. Well before the telegraph, though, newspapers began investing in speeding up the news, using speedboats, carrier pigeons, and horse relays.

As the production of news became more like the production of other commodities, and as the production and distribution of newspapers became larger in scale, the productive firm itself became larger and more complex. Instead of a fairly undifferentiated set of apprentices and journeymen, each of which could be expected to acquire all of the skills involved in producing a newspaper, lines of demarcation began to appear between people who worked with text – reporters, editors, proofreaders – and people who worked with print machinery. And among the latter a line began to appear between the ones who set type and the ones who handled the printing presses.

And as this enterprise grew larger and more diversified, it also became a valuable business enterprise. It became more common for newspapers to be joint-stock operations. The first to reorganize itself as a joint-stock enterprise in Britain was the *London Gazetteer*, which did so in 1748 (Williams, 1965: 205–6). In the US, the *New York Tribune* is considered to be the first to distribute stock that could be publicly bought and sold, in 1848. Many had been set up as closely held joint-stock companies before that, but these were essentially partnerships among a few principals. And as individual enterprises grew larger and more complex, gaps grew between smaller and larger news establishments, and between metropolitan and provincial ones.

The commercialization of news redrew the map of the news system as a whole. The strongest influence on the geography of the news system in the generation after the revolution was the postal system, which tried to assert the total equality of all addresses. Within that egalitarian matrix, newspapers got special treatment. The combination of free newspaper exchanges and differential postage for local newspapers helped each individual town support its own newspaper. So the news system was a widely dispersed, decentralized network.

When the market directs the distribution of goods and services, it warps space in a different way. To the market, New York is closer to Chicago and Los Angeles than it is to many smaller towns in the northeast. Because markets tend to grow densely in cities, they come to constitute powerful gravitational centers. For commercial media, the largest cities attract attention and exert influence out of all proportion to the simple number of inhabitants. The metropoles became the centers of production of news, newspapers, periodicals, and media and fashion and ideas of all sorts. By the end of the nineteenth century, the largest cities, and especially New York, had become the gateways through which the nation's communications passed (Pred, 1973; Baldasty, 1992).

The new commercial media often had a populist tone or accent. Although they certainly had working-class readers, it is unclear to what extent they can be called working-class media, however. The US penny papers, for instance, appeared to have large middling-class readerships, and tended to code their class appeal, unlike, say, the unstamped radical press in the UK.

The Commercialization of the Press in Britain

Commercialization, as an international phenomenon, operated differently from country to country. Émile de Girardin, "France's first media mogul" (Benson, 2013: 28), was inspired by US penny papers to produce apolitical sensational newspapers that could evade the monarchy's censors. Although themselves commercially successful, these papers ironically reinforced the commitment of French intellectuals to a more committed political journalism.

The rise of a mass-circulation press in Britain shared some of the same chronology and technological and organizational innovations as the process in the US. But it was more complicated, made so by two features that didn't operate so strongly in the US. One was the class system, which had much sharper divisions than that in the US.

The other was the set of taxes on knowledge and related tools of press regulation. Together, they signaled a deep reluctance in the traditional culture to cultivate knowledge and action among the working classes. This reluctance was energized by the French Revolution.

The French Revolution sent shock waves through British politics and culture. Radicals, who drew their lineage back through John Wilkes to the seventeenth-century English Revolution, admired the ideological currents coming from France. Tom Paine, who circulated through the Atlantic world, was a particular inspiration. Paine's *Rights of Man* was published in 1791, and sold 200,000 copies in Britain before being judged seditious libel in 1793. More than two decades later, Radical publishers like Richard Carlile would spend time in jail for publishing Paine. Carlile made it a family affair: his wife and daughter also spent time in jail, along with many of the people who worked for him in publishing his newspaper, *Sherwin's Weekly Register*, which he renamed the *Republican* when it was ordered closed for its coverage of the Peterloo massacre, an assault on a peaceful demonstration of working-class activists that resulted in dozens of deaths (Wiener, 1983).

The most famous of the Radical publishers was William Cobbett, who entered our story as a Federalist propagandist in Philadelphia in the 1790s. Cobbett began publishing the *Political Register* as a pro-government newspaper in 1802 with the help of a grant from the Treasury. Always mercurial, he became incensed with inequities in the voting system, and within a couple of years had broken with the government to become a vocal critic of corruption in Parliament, the Church, and the system of financing for Britain's wars with France. In the process he identified himself as a champion of the exploited working class. When he broke with the government, he also began to take advantage of a loophole in the stamp duty. Newspapers were required to pay a stamp tax, but single-sheet, folded publications that carried opinion and not news were not subject to this duty. So Cobbett, like many others, began publishing unstamped. This allowed him to sell the paper for two pence (2*d*), making it affordable for ordinary folk, though more respectable citizens derided it as "two-penny trash" and "the pauper press." His circulation quickly increased to 44,000. Raymond Williams points out that because, like many working-class publications, the *Register* sold many of its copies to clubs and meeting rooms, where it was read aloud and debated, and because as a weekly opinion paper it did not lose currency as it passed hand to hand, it is reasonable to estimate that its actual readership was up to 20 times its circulation. This meant that potentially close to a million people encountered it – in a nation of 10 million (Williams, 1965: 209; Williams, 2010: 86–7).

The success of the Radical press prompted a two-pronged counteroffensive. One prong was repressive. The government increased the stamp duty, raising it 266 percent between 1789 and 1815, the years of the French Revolution and its Napoleonic aftermath. This proved counterproductive. Working-class publications found the tax unaffordable, and chose to evade it. The result was a tremendous increase in the number of unstamped publications, especially during periods of high tension (Curran and Seaton, 2009: 8). Perhaps more discouraging was the use of the law of seditious libel. It was a fear of imprisonment that finally hobbled Cobbett, who fled to the US in 1817 in response to a suspension of the right of habeas corpus. But others, like Carlile, found imprisonment a kind of martyrdom that enhanced their popularity and success.

The other line of attack was more positive and more successful. Middle-class reformers established cheap publications meant to satisfy working-class appetites for print media with wholesome fare. Hannah Moore's monthly cheap tracts were the first to achieve real success. Perhaps the most famous sponsor of this sort of material was the Society for the Diffusion of Useful Knowledge, established in 1826. One of its members, Charles Knight, established the *Penny Magazine* in 1832; before it ceased publication in 1845, it regularly achieved circulations of 200,000. Note how closely its career matched the chronology of the most famous US penny papers, which might be thought of as a meld of the unstamped Radical press and this more conventional press of upwardly oriented respectability. In Britain, a similar hybrid appeared in the Sunday papers, about which more below.

The campaign against the unstampeds was at best marginally effective. The combination of class tension and political grievance led to continual upsurges of Radical press activism. The most effective attempt at reining them in was, ironically, a deep cut in the stamp duty in 1836. By then the circulation of unstampeds had risen to two million, rivaling that of the legitimate press. Daily newspapers began to make noises about themselves refusing to pay the stamp tax, and the government bowed to the pressure, cutting the duty by 75 percent, which, coupled with strengthened enforcement measures, made compliance much more attractive (Curran and Seaton, 2009: 8).

The 1836 reduction in the stamp duty, like the 1832 Reform Act that had expanded the franchise among the lower middle classes, underscored the rising independence of the middle-class daily press. From the early eighteenth century on, the London dailies had all enjoyed some measure of political subsidy, usually covert. As advertising became a more important source of revenue, newspapers began to find it advantageous to declare independence from political interests. *The Times* is the most famous example. By 1817, its commitment to a business model based on advertising supported its ability to give comprehensive balanced reporting of the Peterloo massacre. *The Times* editorial in criticism of the government is considered a landmark on the road to press independence. Gradually dailies began turning down covert grants. By 1840, none of the dailies took them. In 1834, a year after the establishment of the *New York Sun* and a year before the *Herald*, *The Times* announced that it would no longer use the advance reports of actions that the government produced – a kind of information subsidy – and would instead rely on its own reporting (Curran and Seaton, 2009: 6).

The populist impulse of the unstamped press and the commercial success of the middle-class dailies merged in the rising Sunday press. Sunday papers first appeared in the 1780s, but found their successful formula in the first decade of the nineteenth century. By 1810, the most successful circulated 10,000 copies weekly with content focused on crime and sports. Raymond Williams argued that the Sunday papers fulfilled part of the promise of the radical weeklies:

> These attempts [to establish a working-class press], in their direct form, were beaten down, but a press with a popular public was in fact established, in another way. This was through the institution of the Sunday paper, which, particularly from the 1820s, took on a wholly different character and function from the daily press. Politically, these newspapers were radical, but their emphasis was not political, but a miscellany of material basically similar in type to the older forms of popular literature: ballads, chapbooks, almanacs, stories of murders and executions. (Williams, 1965: 197–8)

Especially after the 1820s, these papers achieved massive circulations, even at seven pence (7*d*) per copy, which was quite high compared with the two pence (2*d*) that Cobbett had charged and the penny (1*d*) that the *Penny Magazine* sold for. Obviously, the content of a copy of a Sunday paper reached more than a single reader.

The appearance of a depoliticized Sunday press did not mark the end of political working-class papers. There was a great upsurge in the 1830s, which tapered off with the stamp tax reforms of 1836, but resumed with the rise of Chartism. The *Chartist Northern Star*, established at Leeds in 1837, circulated 50,000 copies a week by the end of the decade, in spite of its relatively dull appearance and content (Williams, 2010: 91–2). But it was the Sunday press that established the recipe for appealing to working-class readers that later cheap papers would follow, including the cheap dailies that appeared after the abolition of the stamp tax in 1855, and the evening papers that followed in the 1870s and 1880s.

Conclusion

The class divide in the press and in politics remained more salient in Britain than in the US. But in both countries commercialization had ambivalent implications for working-class readers. On the one hand, mass circulation, and the advertising revenue that came with it, could not be easily achieved without selling to working-class readers. On the other hand, the political and economic interests of the working class had no special appeal to advertisers. In Britain and in the US, it became common for mass-circulation media to simultaneously attract working-class audiences and promote reactionary politics. In both countries, working-class media with working-class politics, even those with immense audiences, have had to swim upstream in attracting advertising support.

The depoliticizing effect of commercialization should have come as a pleasant surprise to those who feared, with Plato, that democracy would bring class warfare. With politics mediated first by the electoral system and then by the press, the direct expression of class interests receded. Many would argue that the sphere of mass consumption and popular culture had become classless. Rich and poor alike followed sports, thrilled to tales of celebrity and crime, enjoyed mass-produced consumer goods, and recognized themselves in popular song. People may remain working class in their production while achieving middle-class consumption, as long as they earn (or borrow) enough to pay for it.

In its nineteenth-century form, then, commercialization exerted a centripetal force, drawing diverse social elements into an increasingly powerful mainstream center of gravity. There were forces that resisted the homogenizing effect of mass culture. In Britain, the class system stubbornly asserted itself. In the US, race created a subaltern class while conferring an element of equality on white folk whether rich or poor. Immigration also threw up a barrier to class assimilation in the form of language – in fact, the most enduring working-class media in the US would be circulated in languages other than English, like the Yiddish-language socialist press and theater in New York (Dolber, 2011). But the chief line of force was the pull of consumer culture emanating from the largest cities.

Commercialization disturbed observers who thought that the essence of democracy was public intelligence. De Tocqueville's analysis of the democratic public anticipated a more general critique of consumer culture. The ways that free and equal political actors argued and voted seemed to him to betray the best hopes of democracy and free expression, bending public life toward an intolerant and tyrannical mass opinion. A quarter-century later, his admirer and correspondent John Stuart Mill contemplated the threat to individuality coming from a mass-commercialized public:

> Those whose opinions go by the name of public opinion, are not always the same sort of public: in America, they are the whole white population; in England, chiefly the middle class. But they are always a mass, that is to say, collective mediocrity. And what is still greater novelty, the mass do not now take their opinions from dignitaries in Church or State, from ostensible leaders, or from books. Their thinking is done for them by men much like themselves, addressing them or speaking in their name, on the spur of the moment, through the newspapers. I am not complaining of all this. I do not assert that anything better is compatible, as a general rule, with the present low state of the human mind. But that does not hinder the government of mediocrity from being mediocre government. (Mill, 1859: 118–19)

Both de Tocqueville and Mill had come to the conclusion that the conditions of actually existing democratic societies worked against the power of truth over candid minds.

We could argue simply that these men were aristocrats who failed to respect the intelligence and creativity of people who didn't belong to their social set. Fair enough. But didn't they have a point? Left critics also viewed the rise of commercial culture with suspicion. To them, the flood of efficiently produced cheap media made it more and more difficult for working-class publics to recognize their own interests. Members of the Frankfurt School famously saw the industrial media as having inherent characteristics of fascism, and every generation since has thought of some new media practice as a threat to free government.

4

The Industrial Media and the Culture Industries

As the market revolution was transforming the distribution and reception of the media, the Industrial Revolution began to transform their production. Media of all sorts, beginning with books and especially the cheap fiction known as "dime novels," adopted techniques from sectors like textiles. News, and the newspapers and magazines that reported it, came to be mass-produced by industrializing workforces in both the pressroom and the newsroom. The larger industrializing society produced a new agenda for news and governance. The news industry addressed itself to the symptoms of social strain produced by new styles of production and transportation – the new industrial cities, the new workplace struggles, the new waves of working-class migration, the new mass-produced amusements. But the industrializing news industry itself became a target of social and political criticism, and found itself defensively redefining journalism.

Industrialization is a sprawling concept. It usually calls to mind mechanization and mass production, though it can be used in a more diffuse way to refer to any kind of rationalization of production. It's helpful to start by clarifying the term.

The Industrial Revolution

In most accounts, the Industrial Revolution began in the English textile industry when a few new machines accelerated production, in the process upending the classic craft-based system of bundled skills and privileges. US manufacturers copied these machines, hooking them up to mills powered by streams located along a geological fall line in New England. The most famous of these mill towns was Lowell, Massachusetts, where genteel young ladies played the piano and edited a periodical called the *Lowell Offering*. The idyllic image of Lowell conceals the inner dynamic of the process, which involved the deployment and concentration of capital. By 1850, a group calling itself the Boston Associates dominated the textile towns of New England. Their kept lawyer and politician was Daniel Webster, the great Senator from Massachusetts. Webster had become famous in 1818 for his defense of Dartmouth College's Articles of Incorporation before the US Supreme Court. Chief Justice John Marshall's decision affirming Dartmouth's rights laid the foundation for what would become the doctrine of corporate personhood – the notion that corporations are "fictitious persons" with all the rights under the law that natural persons have. This doctrine, coupled with an opportune interpretation of the Fourteenth Amendment's guarantee of due process, would be crucial in defeating attempts to regulate industry later in the nineteenth century.

So what is industrialization? Two elements are crucial to industrial production: power and organization (Stearns, 1993). In common sense, most of the transformative influence of industrial production is credited to power. For instance, much is made of the importance of the steam engine, especially when it was hooked up to railroads and ships and printing presses, or of electricity, especially when hooked up to light bulbs and computers. Certainly power was crucial. But the organizational innovations of the Industrial Revolution were, I think, even more important and more contagious than its machines.

The new power and organizational techniques enabled a system of mass standardized production that was rationally managed, and this is what we usually mean by the term "industrialization." Obviously, this is not an exhaustive and exclusive definition. There are other aspects of industrialization, and there are other systems of production that might be described by this definition (for example, certain types of plantation agriculture). But it will do for our purposes.

Mass production often means mechanized production. Industrialization transformed textile production in England when entrepreneurs installed machines that multiplied the output of individual workers. The machine was crucial in this case. But, in other cases, industrialization proceeded without machines when complex tasks were divided into simpler ones. This happened in printing. The first print factories used presses that were not much different from the ones that Gutenberg and Ben Franklin had used, but instead of having a single (journeyman) printer to compose, press, and do allied tasks, they divided these tasks (Baron, 1989; Rorabaugh, 1986; Wilentz, 1984). In 1850, Harper & Brothers, the largest book publisher, employed 100 women to fold and sew pages (Munsell, 1850: 56). As each worker specialized in the task at which he or she was most efficient, overall production increased. This required no new machine, at least as we generally understand the term "machine." On the other hand, if we think broadly, we can see that in fact there was a new machine here: a machine that consisted of the workers themselves. This is the machine we call "the factory."

Factory production enhanced mass production in several ways. First, it allowed for easier standardization. When a product was manufactured and assembled in a factory, its production was broken down into discrete steps, and each particular execution of any step had to be identical so it could fit with any particular execution of any other step. All table legs had to be identical so they could fit with all table tops. So the production of table legs became routinized in furniture factories. This meant that worker A's table legs had to be identical to worker B's table legs, and the workers themselves had to be interchangeable. (It doesn't take much imagination to understand how worker A making table legs might be wistful about the days when he or she was carpenter A making tables, and chairs and doors and so forth.)

Second, by gathering many workers in one place and setting them to specialized tasks, the factory allowed for centralized control. At first, owners exercised control sporadically and hesitantly. This is because the first factory owners and workers alike had come from a craft tradition. The first owners of print factories were likely to be printers – master printers who had accumulated significant capital and were able to attract more business than they could handle through a traditional shop. The first print workers were likely to be journeymen who had done an apprenticeship in a traditional craft shop. At first, the craft culture that owners and workers shared tended to retard the rationalization of production. But more aggressive owners took advantage of the opportunities that factory production offered. By continually dividing labor into smaller and smaller tasks, it was possible to "de-skill" them. In printing, it was no longer necessary to hire a skilled journeyman printer to compose type. Instead, an owner could train women or (in the case of Duff Green) orphan boys to perform this single task. After all, it was work that didn't require the strength of a grown man; rather, it required the dexterity that it was assumed women and children excelled in (Baron,

1989; Pretzer, 1985). Over time, new machines allowed tasks to be even further de-skilled. Composing with type case and stick required more skill than composing with linotype, which in turn required more skill than composing with a desktop computer. Printers, however, organized effectively in the face of new technologies, both to maintain high-skill levels and to retain some measure of control over their own work.

Factory divisions of labor produced endless battles over control. A skilled task requires a skilled worker, and a skilled worker achieves a certain level of control over the production process. So workers preferred their jobs to consist of complex bundles of tasks with high-skill levels. Owners preferred reducing tasks to simpler and simpler skill levels, which in turn would allow them to relocate control to management (Braverman, 1974; Montgomery, 1989). As long as workers retained some control, it was impossible for owners and managers to exercise that control. In this way, factory production incorporates a never-ending struggle for control between workers and managers.

So far I've used the word "control" and not "power" when describing these struggles. The two words are similar but not identical in meaning. Control is something a director exercises over a process or a system. Power is something a person or group exercises over another person or group. The same person, obviously, may have power and control at the same time. This became true of factory owners, whose claim to control over their property, that is, the production process, came to mean power over their employees. So what was at root an economic transformation also became a political one. Both workers and owners knew this.

Both control and power required new disciplines. That is, both the desire to maximize output and the desire to subordinate workers called for machine discipline and time discipline. By machine discipline I mean that factories were understood to be machines, and workers were understood to be their moving parts. Like the cogs and gears of a giant clock, workers had to move with regularity and predictability. This required that workers internalize a new sense of time – what sociologists have called time-discipline (Thompson, 1967; Rodgers, 1977). The new sense of time is another profound aspect of industrialization.

Generations of watch-wearing have inured us to the obviously false notion that all time is the same. On the contrary, the universal experience of humanity is that time is all very different. In terms of quality, some time is brisk and other time is torpid – an hour in a classroom is usually longer than an hour in a bar. Likewise, time moves in different directions. Some kinds of time move in a cycle – daily time and seasonal time, for instance. In non-industrialized societies, cyclical kinds of time organize the life-world. Industrial production believes in none of these distinctions. In industrial production, there is only one kind of time. It is measured in standard units, and it marches in a straight line to infinity, without ever turning around or slowing down. Workers must punch the clock. Industrial time is relentless, perpetual, and uniform, and asserts its primacy over all other varieties of time.

Industrial production also demanded the annihilation of space. The market revolution of the early nineteenth century worked through the creation of a city system that was connected by a network of ever-improving transportation and communication corridors. Industrialization intensified this process. And the most emblematic development was the creation of a railroad/telegraph system.

It is a commonplace among scholars of industrialization in the US that the railroad industry was the "take-off" sector for the process, just as the textile industry was in England (Taylor, 1951). The importance of the railroad was not just transportational, of course. Railroads in the US were the largest consumers of steel (thus sparking the steel industry) and among the largest consumers of coal (ditto); they were also crucial to the commercialization of agriculture – not just in transporting goods to market, but in taking land in grant from state and federal governments and selling it to farmers. Perhaps the most important function of the railroads was in helping to create a new space–time grid for the national market. By reducing transportation costs, railroads greatly diminished space as an economic factor. Corn and cattle and steel came to be pretty much the same price in any market in the US at any given time. The declining economic importance of space is paralleled by the increasing homogenization of time. It was the railroads that created the standard time zones of the US (Carey, 1983; Schivelbusch, 1986).

The expansion of the railroad system depended on and at the same time made possible the expansion of the telegraph system. Railroads needed telegraphs. To control a railroad system, you need some means of communication that moves faster than a train. Telegraphs also needed railroads. Telegraphs used long lines that required actual physical construction and maintenance, and there was no more convenient place to build a telegraph line than along a railroad track. So on this level it's useful to think of the railroad and the telegraph as a system. (The newspaper and the telegraph constituted another system, as we shall see; it gradually replaced the older, and more egalitarian, newspaper-and-post system.)

Industrialization decreased the importance of space. Distance became a less important economic fact – less of the price of a commodity was related to transportation costs. Distance also became less important culturally. Mass production, transportation, and new systems of retailing and communications allowed for a far greater homogenization of the material life of a nation. Cultural and consumer products from the cities penetrated with ever more ease into the countryside, a process that continues to this day (Pred, 1973). The age of industrialization was the age of the department store and the Sears catalogue (Leach, 1993). Even more important than the shrinking of national space was the conquest of global space. The middle third of the nineteenth century saw the building of railroads worldwide, the acceleration of water transportation – though in many cases sailing ships were still faster than steamships – and the creation of a global system of telegraphic communication through the laying of underwater cables. As Eric Hobsbawm noted, a truly global economy with global business cycles and financial crises came into being through industrialized transportation and electrified communication:

> the business-cycle crisis became genuinely worldwide. That of 1857, which began with a bank collapse in New York, was probably the first world slump of the modern type . . . From the United States, the crisis passed to Britain, thence to north Germany, thence to Scandinavia and back to Hamburg, leaving a trail of bankruptcies and unemployment, meanwhile leaping the oceans to South America. The slump of 1873, which began in Vienna, spread in the opposite direction and more widely. (Hobsbawm, 1977: 69–70)

But the waning of one hierarchical system of social geography did not mean the disappearance of social geographies. While the distance between consumers in Chicago and San Francisco steadily declined, the distance between wage earners and professionals in those same places steadily increased. This was both an economic and a spatial process. In the rising industrial cities, vast internal cities appeared, institutionally complete, virtually walled off from the "public" city by class or race or language. It was much less of a journey for a middle-class Chicagoan to visit counterparts in New York than to stroll through sections of the south and southwest sides of Chicago itself. This was because the evolving middle class had begun to generate a single national culture for itself (Zunz, 1990: 9).

The link between the Industrial Revolution and this kind of urbanization is perhaps not an essential one. The early textile factories in New England were located in mill towns remote from the larger urban centers – put there because of the use of falling water as a power source. As the power source for mass production shifted to coal and then to electricity, it became more convenient to locate factories in cities, which were already transportation hubs. Coincidentally, cities were also good locations for a renewable supply of cheap labor. In the US, excess population from the countryside and immigration from Europe (and, in the west, Asia) found its way into the larger cities, swelling the ranks of available workers and at the same time reducing the level of pay they could command. By the early twenty-first century, of course, these factors had shifted again. For a variety of reasons, often it became more convenient to locate factories in the countryside or in smaller urban areas. Japanese automakers have been attracted to towns like Marysville, Ohio, and Spring Hill, Tennessee, where land and labor are cheap again.

The industrial city was not just an economic creature – it was also a social and cultural phenomenon. Its rapid growth seemed to represent an entirely new social and cultural order, one where heterogeneity ruled, where struggles for power were constant and untameable, and where the forces of disintegration were always on the march. The city of Chicago was the nation's most explosive exemplar of industrial urban growth. There, railroads met water, connecting the livestock and grain and timber of the midwest, the plains, and the northwest with the coal and iron of the mideast and the labor that poured from eastern and southern Europe through the Great Lakes (Cronon, 1992). Spreading over a terrain made homogeneous by the engineers who erased its swamps and streams, this motley population carved out a jigsaw puzzle of reinvented "old countries" – Little Lithuania, Chinatown – insular communities set off not by geography so much as by language and religion. The urban landscape, with its odd collection of strange cultures, looked like the bleeding edge of civilization, and took its place next to the frontier as a location of national identity (Denning, 1987; Slotkin, 1992).

If frontier mythology remained strong culturally, it came to rely economically on city institutions. Dime novels that celebrated frontier heroes and outlaws were produced in cities by industrialized firms. There were other ways in which city culture came to dominate the countryside. Improved delivery systems allowed metropolitan newspapers to reach rural markets, and reduced to marginality traditional country papers. Not just news, but also clothes, books, music, sporting teams, and other features of city life achieved everyday importance in the countryside. Naturally, this produced a series of culture wars between the city and the country. Perhaps the most powerful political force in the US at the end of the century was the rebellion of the backcountry against the financial institutions of the cities – a rebellion that targeted the gold standard for currency and demanded a freer supply of paper money (the "Greenback" movement) and the free coinage of silver. In the populist movement of the 1890s, the most important third-party movement in US history, this currency agitation melded with other social, cultural, and economic currents to present the image of a general rebellion against urban industrialization and the "money power."

These culture wars masked the real interdependence of city and country. Even while the corn and wheat farmers, the cattle ranchers, and the lumbermen of the midwest and west decried the ethnic debasement and moral corrosion and economic domination of Chicago, it was the existence of Chicago's railroads and factories and slaughterhouses and commodities exchanges that allowed all of those rural occupations to flourish. This is not to say that the typical farmer flourished. On the contrary, the industrialization of agriculture, while it was great for farming in terms of increased yields and productivity with lowered prices for the consumer, was very hard on the average farmer. As a way of life, family farming, in step with artisanal production, began the long march to quaintness.

The impulse to rationalization that informed industrialization worked on farms as well as factories. It introduced a logic of efficiency that seemed ready to revolutionize every aspect of life – including health and politics. Rationalization in the hands of properly trained experts, it was claimed, would wipe away encrustations of tradition and yield pure machine-like efficiency.

The central players in these dramas of rationalization would be the managers. They would compose a new middle class of professionals. Often university-trained specialists, they would be responsible for running the factories and the newly formed corporations that owned the factories. The same sort of person was also placed in charge of city government and the federal bureaucracy, as powerful reform movements replaced elected officials and patronage appointees with permanent civil servants. The new professionals acquired tremendous authority, and justified this authority on the basis of a notion of value-free expertise. Their power, in short, derived from science.

The age of industrialization was pre-eminently an age of science. Much of what was called science at the time seems hardly distinguishable from antique superstition now – "scientific" racism is the classic example. Much energy was devoted to mapping the particular physical causes of racial "character," under the assumption that cultural patterns must be biologically determined (Stocking, 1968). Science in this instance is just a new idiom for old notions. But it is more than a little interesting that a new idiom was called for, and it speaks volumes about the spirit of the age. For the rising class of managers and experts, legitimacy had to come through science, just as for earlier classes legitimacy was expected to come from religion. Unfortunately, science proved to be just as pliable as religion in justifying whatever was required.

In the years following the Civil War in the United States the best way to seem scientific was to phrase things in evolutionary terms. Charles Darwin's notion of natural selection, which exploded into public discussion with the publication of the *Origin of Species* in 1859, offered a supple metaphor for the pseudoscientific framing of social and economic problems. Social Darwinism soon acquired hegemonic force in public discussions. There is an irony to this.

Darwin's argument in the *Origin* involves more than just change over time. The important point is the sheer randomness of the process. There is no guiding intelligence in this universe, no moral reason why some survive and others die. Outcomes are determined only by how well an organism adjusts to its environment, and the environment consists entirely of the sum total of all the creatures and features in a given place, all of which are themselves products of random events. This nature is not only irrational and random; it is also cruel, a nature "red in tooth and claw."

Darwin's vision is of a messy world. But to some this world seemed to be progressive and harmonious – a model for social policy. This was the Social Darwinism of William Graham Sumner, for whom natural selection was something like the invisible hand in Adam Smith's marketplace – another apparently messy place that turned out to be really pretty spiffy after all. Just as the laws of the market produced growth and fairness, so did natural selection produce increasingly stronger and more complex societies – if left to operate without interference. It was unfortunate, to Sumner et al., that government attempts to ameliorate the dislocations produced by industrialization were actually sabotaging the necessary operation of natural selection. The end result would be the production of a weakened race through the artificial protection and subsidized reproduction of the weaker elements. This version of Social Darwinism did not shrink from a society red in tooth and claw. It was a happy ideology for late nineteenth-century industrialists – call them captains of industry or robber barons.

But Sumner's version of Social Darwinism is hardly faithful to Darwin. In fact, natural selection doesn't operate in society, because society is itself an artificial environment, made by humans for human purposes and subject to conscious direction. This doesn't mean that evolutionary processes are non-existent in society, but it does mean that they don't have to operate randomly, as they do in nature. On the contrary, it is possible to engineer an environment so that a stronger society with healthier and more self-reliant individuals is produced. This Reform Darwinist position promoted intelligently directed social change through "environmental" reforms like public schooling and industrial planning.

While not as well suited to industrialists, this ideology was nevertheless handy for the managerial class. In Reform Darwinism, the heroes are not the wealthy and powerful but the technicians and social engineers, the ones whose expertise allows them to direct social progress. Reform Darwinism was an ideology for the bureaucrat, both in government and in business.

In fact, the triumphant business organizations of the latter nineteenth century were the managerial ones. The firms that emerged from the wild competition of the Industrial Revolution were the extensive vertically integrated ones, the ones that could manage with some precision the vagaries of supply and demand by owning their own suppliers and to some extent producing their own demand through marketing and advertising strategies. These firms freed themselves from dependence on the invisible hand of market forces (Chandler, 1977; Beniger, 1986).

This kind of large-scale organization is part of what it means to refer to industrial production as a system. Industrialization by its very nature led to increases in scale and scope for manufacturing and transportation firms, which then became national bureaucratically organized corporations. And none of these companies existed in isolation – they were interdependent, as we've already seen in the case of the railroads. In fact, if you look at any particular industrial product, you can pretty much see that an entire industrial society is involved. Take an automobile, for example. By its very composition, it tells you that it comes from a society with a steel industry and a rubber industry and a machine tool industry and an electronics industry. If you think beyond these immediate implications, though, and consider the uses of an automobile, it will also tell you that there is an infrastructure – roads, gas stations, and so forth, which are themselves industries. It also has a radio in it, and perhaps a phone, which tell you that the society has a communications system. One might also suppose that the automobile indicates a certain lifestyle. It means that the individual or family that owns it has reason to use private transportation on a regular basis and has the disposable income to afford it. So this single industrial product diagnoses an entire industrial society.

Industrial production is a system that tends to spread to every aspect of a society. The rise of industrialization in the British textile industry was hardly containable; industrial production spread to other sectors of the economy not just because of the specific economies of scale achievable in that new sector, but because the mass production of one article demands the mass production of other things. And the industrial system spread its tendrils out into the entire world. Tires for automobiles in France required rubber plantations in Indonesia. Copper for wires in Manchester required mines in Chile. And the proper management of any large enterprise anywhere required a flow of information about global economic trends and conditions. As industrial capitalism globalized, of course, there were winners and losers. As many have noted, rising tides lift those in boats; the others drown.

As the industrial economy became ever more complexly interdependent, the logic of laissez-faire Social Darwinism came to seem as quaint as the old Puritan ethic of hard work and self-denial. An economy peopled with national corporations needed a higher level of coordination and direction than either the marketplace or any one firm could manage. More and more the logic of social engineering pointed toward government action.

The age of industrialization was also the age of the birth of the state regulatory agency. Again railroads were in the fore. In the US, a series of scandals in railroad finance and a litany of complaints about unfair pricing produced a public animus that neatly coincided with the industry's own fatigue with wasteful competition to push for the creation of the Interstate Commerce Commission, the first federal regulatory agency, in 1887. From that point on, the Federal government would come to assume more and more responsibility for assuring economic coordination in specific industries.

The social fact of industrialization required forms of rational management in the economy. The political system provided some, and other sorts of national bureaucracies appeared in the private sector, like the National Association of Manufacturers and other trade associations and labor unions that were more industry-specific. This sort of national management structure was facilitated by the growth of a new industrial communications system.

The Industrial Communication Infrastructure

Industrialization enabled and entailed changes in the environment in which news media were produced. Railroads needed to be incorporated across many states in the US, and so did telegraph companies, wire services, features syndicates, and advertising agencies. Together, these innovations brought major changes to the networks of relationships that constituted newspapers.

The telegraph is perhaps the most familiar part of this story among journalism historians. Its arrival meant the "annihilation of space and time," to use the common term from the 1840s. Carey (1983) and others pointed out that it marked the decisive separation of communication from transportation (Packer and Robertson, 2006). It is true that the telegraph marked a dramatic change in the way information traveled. But it did not eliminate distance; rather it reorganized space. It reinforced an emerging network of information-producing places and institutions – major cities, markets, stock exchanges, political capitals, and bureaucracies of all sorts, from police systems to professional sports leagues.

The invention of the telegraph is credited to Samuel F. B. Morse in the United States, to William Fothergill Cooke and Charles Wheatstone in Britain. The near simultaneous independent invention of electric telegraphy indicates that science and engineering had arrived at a point where they were ready to produce practical answers to social and economic needs. Cooke and Wheatstone designed their telegraph specifically for a British railroad.

But before the electric telegraph, there were other kinds of telegraphs. These were mostly visual telegraphs, signaling systems using flags or lights placed on high points that could be seen from a distance of perhaps 10 miles. That's why places were named "Telegraph Hill" or "Beacon Hill" well before Morse's invention, and why newspapers were named "Telegraph" earlier too. The first "revolutionary" telegraph system was not Morse's, but a visual telegraph network built in Napoleonic France (Mattelart, 1996; Starr, 2004: 156–7).

The electric telegraph represented an obvious improvement over other systems of communicating at a distance. Nevertheless, it was not immediately adopted. Even after Morse demonstrated its practicality in 1837, it was many years before a working line was funded and built. By 1844 it began to be used to transmit news to newspapers, and gradually became something more than a novelty, its development sped along by the Mexican War. One of the reasons for the delay was the difficulty of building out a network. Individual lines were built between specific cities by partnerships or companies that were put together on an ad-hoc basis, and arrangements to link these lines up had to be worked out over time. Newspaper owners participated prominently in this process: Morse's two most important partners were William Swain of the *Philadelphia Public Ledger* and Amos

Kendall, Andrew Jackson's early editorial booster and later Postmaster General. Newspapers would be the first significant clientele for the new telegraph companies, with railroads and financial markets emerging as more important within a few years (Blondheim, 1994).

The rise of the telegraph gave a significant boost to cooperative newsgathering in the US and elsewhere. Commercial competition between newspapers had already produced investments in speeding up news transmission. In the US, the chief items targeted for acceleration were news reports from Europe, political news from Washington, and news from any theater of war. Before the electric telegraph, the ways to speed transmission involved faster modes of transportation – speedboats to meet incoming ships, visual telegraphs to relay headline items, horse relays from Washington to New York. One of the most successful entrepreneurs was Daniel Craig, who used carrier pigeons. Craig became a founder of the pioneering telegraphic news service, the New York Associated Press, and remained a dominant figure in telegraph news for decades (Hochfelder, 2012). Founded to speed news from the Mexican War, the New York Associated Press, later the Associated Press, became powerful because of its capture of the European news through a collusive arrangement with the telegraph line from Halifax, the first port of call in North America for ships from Britain. The Associated Press leveraged that resource into a virtual monopoly on national and international wire service news in the US by the end of the 1860s, and then expanded into global news markets, where it competed and eventually colluded with the leading European agencies.

In Europe, Reuters in Britain, Havas in France, and Wolff in Germany had begun dividing the world into exclusive territories as early as 1859 (Rantanen, 1997: 615). The expansion of the news agencies rode on the expansion of European commercial and then imperial interests. Reuters, for instance, which established an office in India in the 1860s and then expanded to other important locales, enjoyed privileged status on government-owned underwater cables as well as informal subsidies, even while maintaining an appearance of independence that allowed it to also market its news services to local newspapers in countries like Egypt and China (Nalbach, 2003). The global expansion of western news through the wire services was an important support in the emergence of a hegemonic notion of journalism (Nerone, 2013).

News services treated news as a commodity to be sold to news media – newspapers, especially – but also to financial agencies, governments, and other clients. As in any business, players angled for advantage through any available means. Aspects of telegraphic communication offered some new opportunities for deranging the playing field.

Any telegraph line was a "natural monopoly," a term economists invented to describe a situation in which competition would be prohibitively wasteful. Most natural monopolies involve some kind of public service: a sewage system for a city, for instance, or a fire department. (In fact, there was a time when private firefighting companies competed; bad things happened.) A telegraph line between any two cities was expensive enough to build and maintain that no firm would waste its capital building a second, competing line. All the more so with international cables, which required government backing. Even though a telegraph line is a natural monopoly, it doesn't follow that a telegraph system should be a natural monopoly; certainly it is possible for various independently operated lines to interconnect without all becoming jointly owned and operated. But in fact in most countries telegraph systems did become monopolies, albeit through tactics that would later be made illegal. Once they became monopolies, it was usually the case that governments would take them over and run them as part of the postal system. Furthermore, in most places, this treatment of telegraphy would set a precedent for treatment of broadcasting technology, which tended to be operated by a dominant state authority – the BBC in Britain, RAI in Italy, and so forth. This did not happen in the US, which would become the most important case of a predominantly privatized media system.

Telegraph companies and news services in every country introduced new aspects of industrial control in the news system. In the US, a dominant telegraph company emerged – Western Union, which by 1865 controlled the majority of lines, though it still had to fight off competitors. The Associated Press (AP) allied with Western Union, and by 1867 controlled the flow of European news and was the biggest player in national news as well (Schwarzlose, 1989, 1990). Both Western Union and the AP became attractive takeover targets. The notorious railroad magnate Jay Gould acquired a controlling interest in Western Union in 1881 (John, 2010: 156–94), spurring reformers to campaign for public ownership through congressional action. In Britain, the situation was a bit more complicated, as the news system was divided between London, where the powerful political dailies, led by *The Times*, fielded correspondents throughout the empire and the world, and the provincial press, which occupied a subordinate position in the news system. With the advent of telegraphic news, Reuters began to dominate the flow of international news, which freed provincial papers from dependence on London dailies and reoriented the foreign correspondents of the London dailies toward providing interpretation and color rather than information. And provincial newspapers began to support the Press Association (PA), which provided access to national news (Williams, 2010: 116–17). But the advantages that telegraphic news offered for provincial papers were temporary. Eventually improvements in transportation and printing technology allowed London papers to circulate nationally, leading provincial papers to focus more and more on local news.

Other agencies sprang up to serve the content needs of news media. Features syndicates became wholesalers of soft news and fiction, especially for weeklies and the Sunday editions of metropolitan newspapers (Harter, 1991; Johanningsmeier, 2002). One especially successful syndicator was Samuel S. McClure, who later converted his service into his own magazine, which became a chief organ of the new critical enterprise journalism known as "muckraking."

Advertising agencies were another type of wholesaler. Initially agencies dealt in space, buying chunks from newspapers and magazines and selling them to advertisers. Later, they expanded their service to clients by engaging in creative consulting on ad style and content (Fox, 1984). Advertising styles spread in part because of a seemingly simple printing innovation called "stereoptyping."

The term "stereotyping" referred to casting replicas of printing plates. Typesetters would set a page of type, or woodcutters would produce an engraving, and then a negative form would be molded from which identical copies could be made. Though it seems an obvious technique, stereotyping would have far-reaching effects. For book printers, it meant that copies of pages could be cast, and then the type broken down and reused. Because type did not have to be tied up, it became possible to vastly expand the catalog of available texts. Eventually this produced economies of scale for the largest publishers. For newspapers, stereotyping encouraged the use of multiple presses, making it possible to mass-produce copies in a time-sensitive way. This became even more important with the advent of multiple-cylinder rotary presses. For advertisers, stereotyping allowed the reproduction of woodcuts and other illustrations. An ad could be cut in an engraving shop, reproduced, and sent to newspapers and magazines across the country. By mid-century, advertisers were copying the graphic techniques of handbills, with ornate circus type and dramatic pictures. Eventually these techniques found their way into news columns in the form of banner headlines and illustrations.

One logical development of the rise of these various wholesale agencies involved patent insides. Printers of patent insides assembled advertising and other paid content, printed it on one side of a standard-sized sheet, then distributed them at a reduced rate to publishers of local weeklies, who printed their own copy on the other side of the sheet and folded it to yield the typical four-page edition (Rogers, 1942). Patent insides remain common in some backwaters of publication, like church bulletins.

Industrializing the Newspaper

At the same time as the infrastructure of the media business industrialized, with the appearance of telegraphic wire services, features syndicates, advertising agencies and so forth, media firms themselves became more industrial in organization. Helped by new printing technologies and a changing business environment, daily newspapers especially embraced mass production. They set about rationalizing and maximizing capacity in their production of copies of newspapers and, at the same time, in their production of the news that filled it.

The appearance of new printing presses has already been mentioned. First steam, then cylinders, then rotary presses that could continually print, then machines that could fold newspapers, and trains and trucks to carry them to customers, increased the capacity of the newspapers that could afford to invest in the ever-improving equipment. The new machines also de-skilled some of the work of making newspapers. A couple of highly skilled engineers could lead a team of unskilled workers in running the more advanced presses. On the typesetting side, stereotyping meant that the work of a single compositor could be multiplied in house, even as more and more content was set outside the shop by other agencies. The print trades – unlike the newsroom staff – had formed unions early in the nineteenth century in the US and other countries, and resisted these economies. They fought long battles against "dead-heading" (the use of boilerplate copy, more or less) and insisted that new machines like the Linotype (which mechanized much of the work of typesetting) be staffed by union members being paid union rates (Nerone, 2008). Because the entire industry was expanding rapidly through the second half of the nineteenth century, it was possible to maintain industrial peace for the most part, though the process of industrialization was marked by a series of dramatic strikes in specific cities.

The newsroom labor situation also industrialized, but mostly without the worker activism of the pressroom. As newspapers hired reporters to cover local news, routines and mechanisms developed that mimicked the discipline and rationalization of industrial workplaces. Reporters became attached to particular "beats," a term that apparently migrated from the jargon of newly professionalized police forces. Reporting beats, like city hall, the courthouse, the docks, and the markets, provided reliable flows of news. By the 1840s, the city editor had emerged on metropolitan dailies as the manager who orchestrated the movements of reporters around these beats and other events, such as rallies and speeches (Solomon, 1995). These reporters were the foot soldiers of the newswork army, producing material that was meant to be a raw collection of facts and transcripts. The city editor enforced discipline by controlling compensation for reporters. Reporters, unlike correspondents, were not independent voices or observing personae with apparent attitudes; they were workers, usually paid by the line, and required to keep their voices out of their copy. Should a reporter fail to produce good copy, the copy would be cut, cutting the reporter's income in turn. Reporters in industrial newspapers engaged in a life-and-death struggle with copy-editors, who had the power to, more or less, edit a reporter's income (Smythe, 1980; Wilson, 1985, ch. 2).

The workplace organization of the newsroom cultivated a particular approach to reporting the world outside. Michael Schudson writes of reporters of the late nineteenth century, "They were, to the extent that they were interested in facts, naive empiricists; they believed that facts are not human statements about the world but aspects of the world itself" (1978: 19). Reporters were supposed to mechanically record facts with the same fidelity as a photograph or a phonograph, two of the technological marvels of the age. Kevin Williams notes the importance of Isaac Pitman's shorthand system, introduced in Britain in 1837, for the work of Parliamentary reporters and others, comparing it to telegraphy and photography in the arsenal of fact-gathering (Williams, 2010: 101–3).

By the 1850s, then, the typical daily newspaper had three streams of news content occupying different spaces in the day's paper. The editor's news came through the mail. Still clipped from other publications or written by one of the editorial staff, it remained the heart of the paper, and appeared in the center of the newspaper – pages 2 or 3 of a four-page paper, or pages 4–5 of an eight-page paper. It was sandwiched between the other two streams, the telegraphic news and the reporters' news. Both of these newer streams of content were industrialized, mass-produced by rational factory-like systems and then owned and sold as commodities. The telegraphic news was produced by wire services which, like the railroads, were highly articulated national or international organizations run by professional managers. The reporters' news was produced in newsrooms

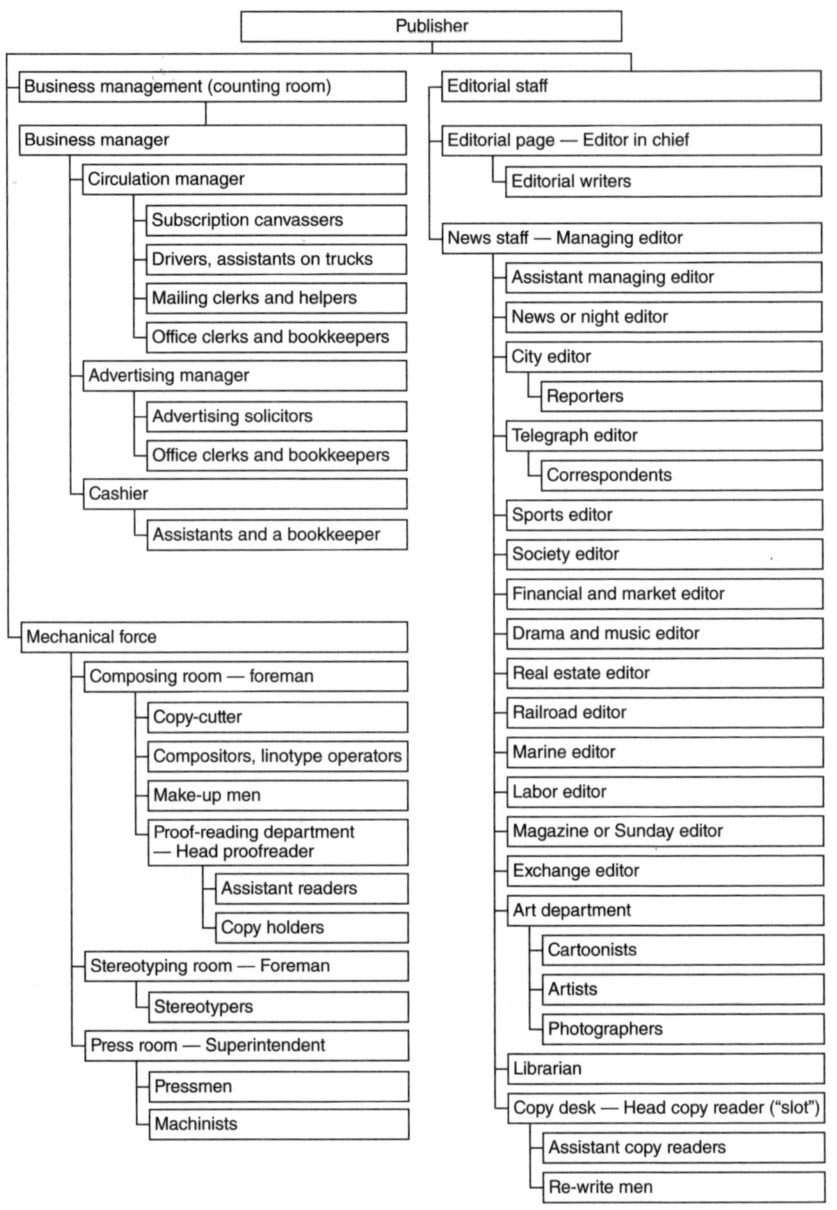

Figure 4.1: The industrial newspaper's division of labor
Source: Typical Metropolitan Daily, *c.*1913. Willard Bleyer, *Newspaper Writing and Editing* (Boston: Houghton Mifflin 1913), pp. 2–6.

which were run like small factories or, perhaps, sweatshops: after the introduction of typewriters in the 1880s and 1890s, newsrooms looked like garment shops, with workers at long tables fixed on their machines.

The Reinvention of Journalism

In the second half of the nineteenth century, the word "journalism" came to be used in a new way. In the age of revolution, a journalist was a propagandist, a pundit, a polemicist. In the age of the Industrial Revolution, "journalist" became the covering term for the very different occupations of editor, reporter, and correspondent. That's what is implied in the title of the first important US trade journal for the newspaper industry, *The Journalist* (est. 1884). Over the next few decades, a positive sense of the meaning of journalism developed. It involved a mixture of the fact-gathering work of the reporter, of the dialogic and correlational work of the editor, and of the subject-grounded observation of the correspondent.

The new meaning of journalism can be found first in news practices that have usually not been considered central to "journalism history." One of these was illustrated news.

Illustrated news had a pretty precise international history (Martin, 2006). The *Illustrated London News* appeared in 1842; its techniques and personnel traveled to other countries, including the US, where two national illustrated weeklies, *Frank Leslie's Illustrated Newspaper* and *Harper's Weekly*, dominated the field. In the years between 1842 and 1890, a particular kind of illustrated news prevailed in the various western countries. This was not photojournalism. Photojournalism promises to offer traces of events recorded with mechanical fidelity. The point of illustrated news was quite different. An illustration was meant to provide the mental image that one would have retained had one been present at an event. It was emphatically a processed image. It was intentionally rendered in a way that would convey narrative, character, and moral values. For the major national illustrated papers, the news pictures were consciously deployed to create a national civic culture. For the *Illustrated London News*, whose career began shortly after the ascendance of Queen Victoria, this meant providing a particular kind of imagery of the royal family (McKendry, 1994). For *Leslie's* and *Harper's*, it involved presenting a particular anthropology of the national population by race and class (Brown, 2002).

The procedures of illustrated journalism differed from reporting just as the uses of illustrations differed from the uses of photojournalism. Reporting, like photojournalism, was meant to gather traces of social life and present them to the reader. Illustrated news constructed accounts of scenes and events out of multiple sources. The best examples are the large-scale illustrations of grand events such as coronations, assassinations, and natural disasters, which filled the two-page center of each issue. For these, correspondents and sketch artists would gather graphic details by visiting scenes and talking with eyewitnesses. Then a master illustrator would assemble this diverse material into a coherent picture. After that, a team of engravers would take pieces of the final drawing and work them into a woodblock. So illustrated news was a collective process on the way in and the way out, and the master illustrator worked as the mediator.

The master illustrator thus did something quite different from what the classic correspondent or the reporter did. His (usually) work involved sorting through overlapping traces and accounts to construct a unifying account, one that included a range of points of view, therefore, and entailed an awareness of the subjective element in social knowledge. Illustrated news was interpretive and explanatory in a way that reporting and correspondence was not. It prefigured what modern news professionals would mean by journalism (Barnhurst and Nerone, 2001: ch. 5).

Journalism in its modern sense is an "ism," a kind of philosophy. It is the set of ideas and values that grew up around professionalizing news practices. News organizations sought to guarantee the public that they deserved credibility even as they struggled with government and their own owners for independence and autonomy. The struggles for autonomy and independence were intensified by the industrialization of the press, and the credibility problem became more severe as news organizations came to look more and more like other big businesses.

Credibility was hardly a new problem. Party newspapers had gleefully challenged opponents' credibility, and, as partisan readers were likely to choose media that reinforced their own attitudes, they would naturally think of the opposing party's editors as liars and opportunists. But the credibility problem entered a new register with industrialization.

Party newspapers cared about making money, but industrialized newspapers seemed to care about nothing else. From the point of view of traditional morality, newspapers seemed increasingly to pander to the worst instincts of the multitude. In Britain, the great poet and cultural thinker Matthew Arnold voiced this critique in his characterization of the "new journalism" as "feather-brained" (Arnold, 1887). For Arnold, the new journalism was the journalism of exposé pioneered by William T. Stead, the energetic editor of London's *Pall Mall Gazette* and author of the sensational exposé of Victorian prostitution, *The Maiden Tribute of Modern Babylon*. Published in 1885, this series of articles leapt the oceans via the underseas cables, appeared in newspapers throughout the world, and sparked an international panic over "white slavery" (Soderlund, 2011; Brake et al., 2012). Stead was in fact on the serious end of the new mass-circulation cheap press which might be said to have begun in Britain with the penny dailies of the 1860s (*The Daily News*, est. 1868; the *Telegraph*, which had been established just after the stamp tax was rescinded in 1855, cut its price to a penny also and remained the circulation leader for many years) (Williams, 2010: 112–13). A second wave of popularization began in 1881 with the establishment of *Tit-Bits* (Jackson, 1997), which was the breeding ground for a generation of editors and publishers, including Alfred Harmsworth, Lord Northcliffe, who started a series of imitators, beginning with *Answers to Correspondents* in 1888, then bought the *Evening News* in 1894 and established the *Daily Mail* in 1896 (Williams, 1965: 225–7). This version of the "new journalism" emphasized short items, miscellany, human interest, and large headlines; it offered easily digested and endlessly engaging news for the busy lower-middle-class and working-class reader. Its critics considered it "American."

The new journalism was clearly a transatlantic phenomenon. Paris newspapers, which boasted the largest circulations in the world at the beginning of the twentieth century, felt the influence of the US new journalism too (Benson, 2013). Stead was fascinated by US news entrepreneurs like Joseph Pulitzer and William Randolph Hearst, who had pioneered a similar populist style in the years following the Civil War. Pulitzer, an Austrian immigrant, had learned the newspaper business as a party editor for German-language newspapers in St Louis, then crossed over into the English-language press there, buying the *Post* and merging it with the *Dispatch* to form his signature newspaper. In 1883, he brought his style of journalism to New York City when he purchased the *World*. The *World* became the training ground for US journalists, and inspired Hearst, who had turned his family's *San Francisco Examiner* into an example of the new journalism on the west coast, to establish the *New York Journal* as a competitor. In one of history's most famous circulation wars, Pulitzer and Hearst competed for New York's readers by investing heavily in talent and producing ever more alarming front pages, culminating in the sensationalist coverage that many contemporaries believed prompted the Spanish–American War (Campbell, 2006). Such newspapering seemed to traditional elites to be entirely mercenary. It mocked accepted morality. It trampled respectable concerns for personal privacy (Warren and Brandeis, 1890). Columnists in the new trade journal, *The Journalist*, reinforced Pulitzer's outsider status by referring to him repeatedly as "Jewseph," and insinuated that there was something unmanly about his lust for market share.

Pulitzer's outsider status points to the continual dialog between mainstream and periphery in the history of the media. The industrialization of the press was a complicated set of processes, and it's easy to oversimplify, implying by omission that the emerging mainstream news industry was a product of upwardly mobile white men. In fact, ethnic and gender dynamics break through this veneer at every point. The growing mass market for cheap newspapers was composed largely of women, and part of the cultural work of the new journalism involved policing women's desires and bodies, which had been made newly visible as women entered industrial workforces (Soderlund, 2013). Many of the innovators in the news business and in journalism came out of ethnic enclaves – like Pulitzer himself, whose career path began with the German-language press.

Others came out of the growing black press. After the US Civil War, black Republicans in the south began producing newspapers aiming to give newly enfranchised African American voters a voice in public debates. The southern white press typically refused to recognize these newspapers, except when a pretext was needed for violent repression. The most famous case in the late nineteenth century was the violent overthrow of an elected African American administration in Wilmington, North Carolina (Prather, 1984; Cecelski and Tyson, 1998). Here white agitators, who had never acknowledged the local black newspaper, cited an editorial arguing that alleged cases of black-on-white rape were often consensual romantic liaisons. It was a similar debating point that provided the justification for the mob attack that drove Ida B. Wells out of Memphis. Wells went north, and became the nation's most important voice in the movement to make the Federal government take action against lynching (Wells-Barnett, 1972).

Contemporaries often seemed blind to the importance of the work of reform journalists like Wells-Barnett (the name she preferred after her marriage). Because she published her most remarkable work in the black press or in self-published pamphlets, white critics could easily dismiss her. But, like abolitionists before her, she was able to use the Atlantic Ocean as an amplifier by traveling to Britain, where her public addresses were considered quite newsworthy (Bederman, 1992). As both a transatlantic celebrity and a pioneer of the journalism of exposé, she deserves a larger place in the collective memory of journalism. Like other advocates in the black press, she deserves to be considered a founder of the new form of journalism that would come to be called "muckraking." The fact that their work went unrecognized by white journalists points to the ideological work needed to make the new journalism acceptable to both elites and ordinary white folk.

Ordinary people had reasons to be suspicious of the industrialized press. Party papers had been explicit about their agendas, but the owners of the industrial newspapers often concealed their business and political interests. The very content produced by the news industry encouraged readers to question its motives. Much of the news of the age of industrialization – from the bizarre financing schemes for railroads to the baroque tales of working conditions in mines and mills to the scandalous revelations of dealings between political officials and aspiring monopolists – cumulatively portrayed an age in which appearances always deceived and no one with power could be trusted, an age when the "money power" was puppetmaster in the political spectacle. A public that had been schooled by the news to be wary of the nexus between money and politics could not help but become cynical about the nexus between big business and the newspapers that had themselves become big businesses. In the US, newspaper chains run by entrepreneurs like Edward W. Scripps (Baldasty, 1999) and William Randolph Hearst demonstrated the real possibility of industrial control of the news of the day. Examples abounded of the ability of the "money power" to manipulate publicity by secretly owning newspapers or by controlling infrastructure, like the controlling interest in Western Union held by Jay Gould, for whom the title "robber baron" seems not exaggerated. In Britain, similar enterprises appeared around the same time. By 1884, Andrew Carnegie, the Scots-American founder of US Steel, controlled a chain of 8 dailies and 10 weeklies. By 1910, Northcliffe, along with two other press barons, Cadbury and Pearson, controlled two thirds of the circulation of national dailies (Curran and Seaton, 2009: 39–40).

Inside newspapers, meanwhile, newsworkers fought for wages and control just like their counterparts in steel or textile mills. The people who sought careers in newsrooms were a curious mix of political enthusiasts, aspiring writers, ambitious workers who rose from the ranks of newsboys and copyboys, college graduates and autodidacts, and crossovers from business, show business, religious publishing, reform newspapers, and the foreign-language press. The newsroom workforce was socially and culturally diverse, then, and lacked the unifying experience of the print trades in the pressroom. Print workers formed unions and retained some control over wage scales and work routines. Reporters aired their grievances over low pay and low prestige, but unionized more slowly. In Britain, the National Union of Journalists formed in 1907; in the US, attempts by the International Typographical Union to organize newsrooms around the same time failed, and it wasn't until the Great Depression of the 1930s that the American Newspaper Guild gained traction. Instead of unionizing, newsroom workers sought to professionalize – a topic taken up in the next chapter. But already by the end of the nineteenth century a journalistic persona had developed that the professionalization project would claim as its ideal.

The Muckraker as Proto-Professional

If the most famous newspapers of the Industrial Revolution were the yellow papers of Pulitzer and Hearst, the most famous journalists of the era were the muckrakers. Practicing a journalism of exposé designed to provoke outrage by unveiling the corruption behind the power that the wealthy enjoyed, the muckrakers developed the scrupulous standards and middle-class respectability that professional journalists since have aspired to. Often conflated with yellow journalism, they're better thought of as its antithesis.

Muckraking was not native to newspapers. In fact, one reason that muckraking took hold was that a place had been made for it in a new medium – the cheap national magazine. Beginning in the 1880s, magazines underwent a transformation similar to the new popular newspapers in the 1870s. The great leader of this transformation in the US was the *Ladies' Home Journal* under the editorship of Edward Bok, whose autobiography is one of the most revealing cultural documents of the age. Bok mixed traditional women's fare, like homemaking and fashion advice, with the sorts of civic information that more progressive women were interested in. He attracted a broad middle-class audience of women and some men that could then be sold to national product advertisers. Other innovators in magazines worked similar veins. The most important to our interest was Samuel S. McClure.

Sam McClure, like Pulitzer and Scripps, came out of the midwest. Coming from a hardscrabble background – his mother was widowed twice – he made his way from Valparaiso, Indiana (where he worked as a printer's devil on the *Valparaiso Vidette* after having to drop out of school), to Galesburg, Illinois, where he enrolled at Knox College. His experience at Knox would shape his approach to both the media business and reform journalism.

Knox was founded by evangelical reformers before the Civil War and was a strong regional presence in the anti-slavery movement. Edward Beecher, Harriet Beecher Stowe's brother, was a stalwart on its faculty, William Lloyd Garrison was a visiting professor, and many relatives of the great abolitionist orator Wendell Phillips were McClure's classmates and future collaborators. Knox College also had two other notable features. It was open to women, both as faculty and students, and it had an interest in journalism. Both these features were embodied in Ellen Browning Scripps, sister of E. W. Scripps, who taught for many years before going off to join her brothers in establishing their newspaper chains. One notable female student, Mary Hatton, moved on to Kansas, where she gave birth to William Allen White, one of the leading progressive journalists and a long-time writer for *McClure's Magazine*.

McClure flourished at Knox. He had to work his way through school by selling products door-to-door, experience that made him intimately familiar with the sorts of national marketing that his magazine would service. He took over the student magazine and professionalized it, recruiting advertisers, adding features, and making it the basis for a collegiate news service that he ran, collecting stories from campuses, putting together a digest, and selling it to student newspapers at other colleges. By the time he graduated in 1882, a year before Pulitzer bought the *World* and three years before Stead's *Maiden Tribute* series, he had acquired all the skills he would later put to use. He had also met many of the men and women who would work with and for him, most of them Knox graduates (Wilson, 1970: 4–30).

In 1884, McClure moved to New York and set up a feature syndicate for magazines and newspapers. McClure's chief stock-in-trade consisted of stories from well-known writers – William Dean Howells, Arthur Conan Doyle, Rudyard Kipling. His best clients were Sunday papers, a relatively new phenomenon in the US news industry. The step from the syndicate to running a magazine was a natural one.

McClure's Magazine appeared in 1893 at a moment of transformation in the magazine business. Since before the Civil War, the nation's leading magazines had been either polite, genteel women's magazines, like *Godey's Lady's Book*, or serious literary periodicals, often run by publishing houses to promote their authors, like *Harper's Monthly*. These magazines were pricey – 35 cents per monthly issue. *McClure's*, by contrast, started at 15 cents. The trick in lowering the price was to attract plentiful advertising from national retailers and manufacturers, like bicycle companies, who wanted to reach new middle-class consumers. The business model for the new cheap magazines appeared before the content, opening a space for experimentation. Some magazines, like *Munsey's*, produced by the innovative Frank Munsey, aimed downscale, toward sensational fiction and features – closer to the successful formula of the British Sunday newspapers and *Tit-Bits* and its successors. Others, like the *Ladies' Home Journal*, used more conventional self-improvement features and practical advice to reach a traditional audience segment. *McClure's* advanced a new kind of journalism.

There had been earlier examples of the journalism of exposure in print. The *New York Times* had exposed the corrupt city government of William Marcy Tweed, and cartoonist Thomas Nast had dramatized the excesses of the Tweed Ring in the pages of *Harper's Weekly* (Leonard, 1986). But these exposés were also features of partisan competition. William T. Stead had done his exposé of prostitution in Victorian London, which was closer to the mark. He followed that dramatic success with book-length reports on the corruptions of Chicago and New York City (Nerone and Barnhurst, 2012). While doing the research for his Chicago exposé, Stead met and formed a longstanding relationship with Henry Demarest Lloyd, whose *Wealth Against Commonwealth*, which appeared in 1894, denounced the rise of Standard Oil as the most important US monopoly (Digby-Junger, 1996). Lloyd and others went beyond party politics to a systemic critique of industrial power. And Ida B. Wells-Barnett's exposés of racial violence pointed to a system of white supremacy that had similarly infected and distorted political life.

The muckraking magazines turned this critique into a genre. From about 1900 to 1912, muckraking reports filled the pages of a large number of national magazines. Two famous series that ran in *McClure's* were paradigmatic – Ida Tarbell's *History of Standard Oil* and Lincoln Steffens's *Shame of the Cities*. Both also show the way muckraking combined elements of evangelical reformism with labor politics and scientific rationality.

Ida Tarbell grew up in the coal and oil region of Pennsylvania, the daughter of an oilman. She entered journalism through religion, working with Methodist Church publications and the Chatauqua organization. She was raised on Republican politics and Christianity, believing in the virtues of self-reliance and self-control, but, on the sly, as a girl, she read the racy crime- and sports-filled *National Police Gazette* (Tarbell, 1939: 13). She attended Allegheny College in Meadville at the same time that Sam McClure was at Knox. Tarbell wanted to be a biologist. Instead, she found herself helping to edit the national Methodist monthly *Chatauquan*. From this beginning in the 1880s, she grew into a reliable author of books and articles on famous men and women. She seasoned herself by spending years in Paris, supporting herself by writing pieces for magazines like *Scribner's* and then *McClure's*. She also became interested in reformist politics and deeply sympathetic to the interests of working people and small entrepreneurs.

She was an accomplished magazine writer and staffer at *McClure's* by the time she undertook her investigations of Standard Oil. Of course, the oil business had been a lifelong concern of her family, and her father had been a victim of the Standard's monopoly. She also knew Henry Demarest Lloyd and his treatment of the Standard in *Wealth Against Commonwealth*. Most of her material was not new. Much of it came from congressional investigations and hearings, and Lloyd personally guided her through some of this material. But she put her own stamp on it, with her own voice and lucid prose, and with augmenting material from interviews. (She found that she was in fact personally comfortable with men who figured as villains in her stories.) Her series was sensationally successful.

The History of Standard Oil is a tale of capitalist dysfunction. But the series is not anti-capitalist. Tarbell admired the business world at its best, and thought that the cure for bad business was good business. She shied away from socialism. She hoped her exposé would prompt outraged citizens to demand that their state and national governments adopt laws that would make it impossible for companies like Standard Oil to overpower the honest forces of the market. In this she succeeded. Her series is credited with sparking anti-trust actions against the Standard in many states and in federal courts, and speeding the breakup of the company.

Lincoln Steffens's articles on municipal corruption embodied a similar dream, but pitched farther to the left. Steffens was born in San Francisco in 1866, the son of a prosperous paint and oil merchant. After earning a degree from the University of California in 1889, he went to Europe to do postgraduate work in psychology at Leipzig and to season himself in Paris. He returned to the States in 1891 and went to work soon after at the *New York Post*, the newspaper that Alexander Hamilton had founded and William Cullen Bryant had edited through the middle of the century. It was then under the editorship of E. L. Godkin, one of the nation's premier reform politicians and the founding editor of the *Nation* magazine. While Steffens worked there, the paper campaigned against vice – prostitution, gambling, drinking. Through his friend Jacob Riis, who was then becoming famous photographing slum life, Steffens met Theodore Roosevelt, the future president and rough rider, who had been appointed New York's Police Commissioner. Steffens made his name reporting Roosevelt's sensational crimefighting career.

Both Steffens and Tarbell piggybacked their reporting on official investigations. This reflects a general change in the nature of governance. As industrialization allowed the emergence of larger and more expansive business interests, governments were called upon to regulate and supervise more areas of life. The same era that produced the railroads produced the Interstate Commerce Commission. Big business needs big government. And big business and big government together suggest a need for big media to supervise on behalf of all the little members of the public. Investigative reporters like Tarbell and Steffens rode the wave of paper that big government produced. Ordinary reporters shadowed government in much the same way, walking beats in the shadow of the police.

Journalists took the information generated by the new bureaucratic structures of industrial society and resolved it back into individual stories with dramatis personae – heroes and villains. Steffens's *Shame of the Cities* articles are the best example. In each, he profiles a city with a particular problem – organized vice in St Louis, for instance. This problem is truly social – generated by large forces acting through individuals. Most commonly, muckrakers called the ultimate culprit the "money power," the inevitable corruption that results from concentrations of wealth. But the solution was the individual citizen. In each of Steffens's profiles, an ordinary man, acting out of concern for the public welfare, tackles the problem by bringing it to the attention of fellow citizens, who then help the hero activate the machinery of the polity – the courts, the churches, public opinion. The end of the story for Steffens is not always happy. Sometimes the hero fails. But usually the hero has given the community a fighting chance. Article by article, muckraking was a hopeful journalism.

But cumulatively muckraking was a journalism of despair. Thomas Leonard has argued convincingly that ordinary citizens reading a steady diet of muckraking would take away a collective meaning, that corruption was everywhere and unavoidable (Leonard, 1986: ch. 7). As muckraking became a dominant genre of magazine and newspaper reporting, and as institution after institution was revealed to be riddled with corruption, readers would learn that disease rotted under every surface of the body politic. Some citizens, the highly involved ones, might be moved to take action. Others would simply dismiss all of public life as a dungheap. Leonard blames the muckrakers for the decline in political participation that occurred around the turn of the century (for another interpretation, see McGerr, 1986).

Certainly the journalism of the Industrial Revolution taught ordinary readers that they could not meaningfully take action in the great society. It taught them this because it was true. The economy had grown so large and abstract that, for the first time, non-specialists had begun to refer to it as "the economy" and not as "farming" or "manufacturing" or "the tariff." The society had grown so diverse and translocal that universities sent specialists into bordering neighborhoods to study populations as if they were exotic primitives. Government had grown so vast and privatized that the bulk of it was immune to politics – regulatory agencies, operating according to specialized discourses, and staffed with professionals protected by civil service rules from political interference. An ordinary citizen expected little to result from marching in a torchlight parade, attending a ward meeting, or voting – because the world said so, not because reporters implied it.

Industrial Journalism and Public Life

The journalism of exposé posited a new and different relationship between the news media, the citizen, and the political process. In this new relationship, the journalist (now so-called) inserted her or himself in between the flow of information and the ordinary citizen. Earlier reporters had sought to simply collect and transmit the flow of information, and newspapers had presented themselves as compendia of information for citizens to consult, the same way as they would a city directory. If a citizen wanted to be told what to do about this information, he (normatively) would turn to the editorial column, where he would be told to attend meetings, march in demonstrations, and vote for a particular party ticket. The editor's directives would be reinforced by the newspaper's correspondents, who would offer more personal observations of distant scenes. Reporters strove for accuracy, correspondents for insight, and editors for forcefulness, and all of them claimed to be fair, independent, and sometimes neutral, but no one pretended to be objective.

In the journalism of exposé, and especially in the American muckrakers, one finds the beginnings of a theory of how objective reporting would help democracy work. Objectivity came from the disciplined attempt to reconcile conflicting versions of real situations and events by not just gathering information but by actively evaluating it (Matheson, 2000). The great muckrakers followed in the trail of fact-finding commissions and supervising regulatory agencies, who in turn followed the practices of academics in research universities, scientists in laboratories, and managers in large banks and corporations. The expert observation of the real that journalism promised was supposed to allow ordinary citizens to make informed decisions as voters.

Journalism thus promised to take on that part of the work of citizenship that industrialization had made too complicated for ordinary people. Who among the plain folk could be expected to face up to the complexities of financial markets? How is an ordinary person supposed to come to judgment on the business practices of railroads and refineries, or on the likely repercussions of tariffs and currencies? The journalists would interpose themselves between the citizens and the governing process, posing in effect as supercitizens. Journalists would represent the public.

5

Institutionalization, the Professional Media and the Expert Public Sphere

In the first half of the twentieth century, "the press" became institutionalized in the west. By institutionalized, I mean that the press claimed a place alongside other institutions like the military, the legislature, banking, and organized religion as part of the apparatus that maintained the social order. One marker of the institutionalization of the press was the way in which it came to be discussed as a single, unified entity. Until the second half of the nineteenth century, in English-speaking countries, it was customary to refer to "the press" in the plural, using the noun as a shorthand form of the phrase "the gentlemen of the press." When the press was used in the singular, it referred to the printing press. So in eighteenth-century discussions, "freedom of the press" meant the freedom of gentlemen to use the printing press as a tool of expression, not the freedom of the press as an institution. By the beginning of the twentieth century, the press had come to be recognized as an institution that had achieved some autonomy from other institutions, and thus had taken up a place in the institutional order.

The configuration of the press in the institutional order differed widely, but several patterns are apparent. In some countries, the press system continued to map on to various estates. This was the case in the Netherlands, for instance, where media resources were parcelled out to the various social "pillars," or subcommunities, Protestant, Catholic, Socialist, and Liberal (Hallin and Mancini, 2004: 53). In others, particularly in the socialist countries, the press became an element of a party-state. In this chapter, I will continue to focus on a hegemonic western model, coming from the Anglo-American tradition. It emerged by mid-century as an evangelizing force in a world caught up by the globalization of capitalism and liberal political ideals embodied in the institutions of a post-World War II international order.

Across the various models of institutionalization, certain conditions prevailed. Mass penetration of media had been achieved in the most advanced countries by the 1920s. Accompanying this fact was a new language of talking about the media, including the use of the word "media," then its variant "mass media" or "media of mass communication."

Although some believe that the term "media" was coined by Marshall McLuhan in the 1960s, it actually has a much older history. John Peters notes that in the nineteenth century it was used to refer to agents of communication with the spirit world (Peters, 1999: 96–101). It was also used to refer to the biological media used to culture germs and to the physical media through which light passed. Architects and artists began to use the word to refer to the materials they used to make things. Then, around the beginning of the 1920s, the word began to be used by advertising agencies to refer to the things that carried ads. "Media" replaced "space" as a term of art in advertising because agencies began to place ads on radio programs as well as in newspapers and magazines. From there, the term came to be used by social scientists in the 1930s. Around the same time, the terms "mass media" and "mass communication" became used to refer collectively to newspapers, magazines, radio, and motion pictures.

Accompanying these terms was the notion of the "marketplace of ideas" (Peters, 2004). Notions of market competition had influenced news discourse since at least the commercialization of newspapers in the mid-nineteenth century, but the idea of a marketplace of ideas was something entirely different. In an age when the media marketplace allowed for widespread competition among newspapers and periodicals that had different points of view and offered competing versions of reality, no one bothered talking about a "marketplace of ideas," perhaps because they assumed that the media marketplace was the marketplace of ideas. The term itself came to be used at about the time that the faith in market competition disappeared both in the media and in the economy more generally. By the 1930s, with capitalist economies undergoing global depression amid widespread recognition of market failure, common sense seemed to dictate that the future belonged to industrial combinations and centralized planning rather than market competition. Fascism made sense, absent its murderous side, to people as diverse as Henry Ford and William Randolph Hearst, who retained both Benito Mussolini and Adolf Hitler as paid columnists for his media empire (Nasaw, 2000: 472–90). It was only in the context of institutional consolidation that thinkers began to imagine a virtual marketplace of ideas, a simulation of market competition provided by mass media of communication. The notion of the marketplace of ideas was compensation for the demise of the actual media marketplace.

Journalism developed a fraught relationship with the media industries. News was obviously a product of media combines, but journalists wanted to distinguish themselves from other media producers, like motion picture studios. That part of the media system seemed to be about producing spectacles that would distract audiences while extracting income from them. Journalism insisted that its mission was to enhance citizenship. Journalists identified with the image of the muckraker, then, even though most of the content of a daily newspaper or a serious news magazine had little to do with enterprise journalism. In fact, the very period in which the image of the heroic investigative journalist was erected also saw the creation of quasi-independent sections of newspapers devoted to sports, fashion, shopping, business, and entertainment (Barnhurst and Nerone, 2001: ch. 7). As the media industries developed and converged, journalism would find it continually more difficult to assert its independence from the less sanctified sectors of the media.

These developments in media sociology coincided with a three-decade period of war and turbulence in the European world. A fundamentally changed global order emerged at the end of this period. Gone were the empires of the old European powers. In their place was an expansionist liberal system, promoting markets and electoral democracies through both peaceful and belligerent means, wrestling with a socialist bloc that equally sought to transform the developing world. Both blocs exported journalisms and media practices and products.

Among the markers of this changing world order was a redrawn map of gender norms. Women had been campaigning for equality in the west since the mid-nineteenth century. After the turn of the century, remarkable successes were achieved, including suffrage in Britain and the US. At the same time, women found careers and voices in the media industries, and the gender line in journalism was redrawn.

Again I turn to the US narrative for a finer-grained look at these developments.

The Business of the Media in the Twentieth Century

William Randolph Hearst began his career in the media as a newspaper publisher. But his ambition spread in two directions. After he'd make a success of the *San Francisco Examiner* and the *New York Journal*, he began to turn his attention to politics and to other media. He got himself elected to the US Congress in 1902 and 1904, and in 1904 he narrowly failed being nominated for president by the Democrats. He continued to pursue politics in the coming decades, running for Mayor of New York City and Governor of New York State. Hearst's political career was a tale of inflated ego and disappointment.

Hearst was rather more successful in his second ambition, building a national media conglomerate. Here Hearst's strategy differed from Scripps' and Pulitzer's, the other great innovators in the newspaper industry at the turn of the century. Pulitzer built a chain consisting primarily of two newspapers, the *St Louis Post-Dispatch* and the *New York World*. He focused his company's energy on cultivating and refining these two news organizations, and increasingly after the embarrassing excesses of the coverage leading up to the Spanish–American War turned his attention to journalistic excellence (Juergens, 1966). Scripps, on the other hand, expanded his chain nationally by establishing newspaper after newspaper, all aimed at working-class readers, all cheap to buy and cheap to publish, sharing content and cutting costs wherever possible (Baldasty, 1999). In the process, the Scripps chain generated some non-newspaper units – a features syndicate, and later a wire service, United Press. But Scripps, like Pulitzer, remained firmly in the news industry.

Hearst developed his chain not just as a part of the news industry but increasingly as a player in the media industry. His newspapers, like the Scripps chain, sprouted a features syndicate and a wire service (the International News Service, or INS, formed in 1909). On top of his newspaper properties, he began accumulating magazines, establishing a magazine for automobile enthusiasts called *Motor* (1902), and acquiring *Cosmopolitan* (1904), *Good Housekeeping* (1911), and *Harper's Bazaar* (1912). And then he leapt into new media.

Motion pictures had already been established as a form of popular culture as early as 1905. By the early 1910s, some film companies had tried to sell movies as a news medium, but had failed to turn a profit at it. Hearst's INS included a news photo syndicate, run by a man named Eddie Hatrick. Hatrick bought a motion picture camera and began shooting important events; in 1913, he sold footage of

Woodrow Wilson's inauguration to Harry Warner (one of the founding Warner Brothers). Warner turned this footage around quickly, and had it showing in movie theaters the day after the inauguration (Nasaw, 2000: 234).

Hatrick had hit upon another profitable subsidiary market for the Hearst chain. Using the Hearst name as a brand, and promoting its motion picture capsules in Hearst's newspapers and other properties, the chain's newsreels soon became the prototype for visual news in the US. But the newsreel was just the entering wedge for the chain's involvement in motion pictures.

In 1914, the Hearst organization became involved in motion picture entertainment when it entered an arrangement with the French movie pioneer Pathé. The two media organizations cooperated in producing and promoting films. Hearst newspapers began by serializing Pathé movie plots, then got involved in co-producing serial movies, the most famous of which was the *Perils of Pauline*, an early example of synergy. The papers ran a Sunday feature previewing each episode, and, when the whole series was done, the Hearst chain published a novelization. Hearst himself was personally involved in all aspects of this venture, previewing scripts and making suggestions, and dropping in on sets during the actual shooting. By the middle of the decade, David Nasaw asserts, "the Hearst name was omnipresent in the nation's movie theaters" (Nasaw, 2000: 236–7).

Hearst also saw great potential in radio. By 1926, he was encouraging his newspapers to explore producing radio programs as a way of advertising what was in the newspapers. His west-coast newspapers were the first to respond; many of them bought radio stations, and by 1928 had formed the five stations they owned into a network, inaugurating the Hearst Radio Service (Nasaw, 2000: 390–1).

So, on the eve of the Great Depression, the Hearst chain had formed the prototype of the modern US media conglomerate. It owned properties in every medium – newspapers, magazines, motion pictures, broadcasting – and, in the infrastructures of these media, wire services, features syndicates, and distributorships. The chain continued to maintain the holdings in mining and real estate that had financed Hearst's first newspaper ventures. It did not shy away from directing all these resources at political ends.

If the Hearst chain was the prototype of the media conglomerate, Hearst himself embodied all that critics fear in the power and influence of the media mogul. His political trajectory seems to prove that capital interests exert an irresistible gravitational force on convictions. At the beginning of his career, Hearst batted from the left side of the plate, positioning himself as a voice for the working classes.

In those days, Upton Sinclair, the great radical journalist and novelist, compared him with Abraham Lincoln. Later, Hearst switched sides. When Sinclair captured the Democratic nomination for the California governorship in 1934, Hearst committed his resources to an unlikely media coalition that included Louis B. Mayer of MGM and Harry Chandler of the *LA Times* and worked to defeat Sinclair through a multimedia campaign that set a standard for later political scare ads.

Nineteenth-century US Americans had already been wary of the influence of news organizations. As newspapers formed into chains, and as chains diversified into other media, their anxieties sharpened. A media mogul like Hearst seemed to have unlimited influence answerable to no one. The world seemed to have grown much bigger, much more complex, and at the same time much closer; an ordinary citizen seemed to have become much more dependent on the media to explain the world, and much more vulnerable to media influence. The media included now not only traditional textual media but also pictures – engravings, photographs, and motion pictures – which could bypass the ordinary citizen's traditional defenses against persuasion. The Hearsts of this new media world wielded a menacing arsenal of weaponry against a public ill-prepared to withstand them.

The possibility of manipulating public opinion became obvious in the second decade of the new century. The World War I experience, in which a federal Committee on Public Information (CPI), headed by the experienced muckraking journalist and public relations figure George Creel, flooded the nation's media with pro-war propaganda, confirmed for many the power of the new media. By the 1920s, the power of the media had become a familiar problem for those thinking about democracy.

Public Opinion and the Problem of the Media

The new media environment challenged traditional notions of public opinion and its role in a democracy. The traditional model called for a public sphere in which individuals could deliberate on matters of common concern in a rational manner. Through the nineteenth century, the press became ever more central to providing such a public space. Observers and journalists alike saw that the press had come to assume more and more of the work of the public. All understood that political contests consisted of maneuvers by politicians and their allied newspapers to represent the public, and that ordinary citizens often would not be involved except as spectators or bystanders. As the media grew more powerful and more pervasive, the gap between people and the public yawned larger and larger, and the myth that the people were the public stretched ever thinner. The appearance of media conglomerates in the early twentieth century seemed to snap it.

By the 1920s, thinkers announced the death of the public. The most famous was Walter Lippmann, whose book *The Phantom Public* (1925) coined an enduring term. Lippmann had nailed down the terms of debate about the public in an earlier book titled *Public Opinion* (1921), in which he questioned whether ordinary citizens could ever have the capacity to be decision-makers in a modern industrial democracy. Because his argument in *Public Opinion* has crystallized so much common sense about media industries and democracy, it will bear examination in some detail.

Walter Lippmann might stand next to Walter Cronkite and Edward R. Murrow as a figure of enormous respect and credibility among twentieth-century US journalists. Beginning as an undergraduate student at Harvard, he interested himself in reporting. He worked as a "leg-man" for Lincoln Steffens, was a founding editor of the *New Republic*, and became the chief editorial writer for Pulitzer's *New York World*. His syndicated column was reprinted in hundreds of newspapers until his retirement in 1967 (Steel, 1980).

Lippmann was scarred by his experience in World War I. He had stepped down from the *New Republic* to work for Newton D. Baker, the Secretary of War. As a propagandist himself, Lippmann strongly disapproved of George Creel's efforts, and especially of government moves to censor socialist newspapers. Lippmann believed in the stated idealism of Woodrow Wilson's war administration, and participated in the drafting of the Fourteen Points, the platform that the Administration meant to provide a blueprint for a peaceful world order after the war. Lippmann also was part of Wilson's entourage at the Versailles negotiations that concluded the war, and was thus an eyewitness to the death of idealism as the peace process turned into a cynical orgy of deal-making. He returned to the US, to the private sector, and to the press, and in 1920 published a series of critical articles about the war and freedom of the press in the *Atlantic*, later reprinted in book form as *Liberty and the News* (1920). In these pieces, he undertook one of the first scientific content analyses of press coverage, concluding that news appearing in US newspapers about the 1917 Bolshevik Revolution in Russia had been hopelessly distorted by the press's own agenda.

Press bias was not, however, the real target for Lippmann's criticism of public opinion. He begins his 1921 book *Public Opinion* with the passage from Plato's *Republic* in which Socrates tells the myth of the cave. In this parable, Socrates asks his listeners to picture a society of people chained in place in a cave. On the wall of the cave in front of them, they see shadows of cut-out objects cast by a flickering fire. Because they have never seen anything else, they think that these shadows of cut-outs are the real things. But suppose, Socrates continues, one fellow manages to free himself from his chains and find his way out of the cave. At first, sudden exposure to the sunlight would blind him, but gradually he would learn to see in the daylight, and would come to realize that the real world was quite different from the appearances he had mistaken for real in the cave. All that he had taken for real had been just a shadow of a representation of something real. Eventually he would want to return to the cave and to try to free his fellows. But, on his return, he would find himself suddenly blinded – because his eyes had become accustomed to daylight, the dimness of the cave would leave him disoriented and clumsy. Then, when he told his story, his friends and neighbors would not believe him, would in fact think that he'd gone crazy. They'd try to talk him back into his chains, and hope that he would eventually return to his senses.

Plato meant this story to be a parable about the education of the philosopher. In the actual world, as in the cave, most people mistake the superficial appearances of things for their real substance and nature. The philosopher, however, learns to look deeper, to penetrate to the really real nature of things; but, in the process, ordinary people come to think of the philosopher as an idiot. The conflict between the many, who are trapped in a world of appearances, and the few who know how to dispel illusions was a central problem of democracy for Plato and would remain one in western philosophy.

Lippmann's *Public Opinion* is not a mere repetition of Plato's *Republic*. Rather, it revises the *Republic's* conclusions for a mediated world. Instead of using the metaphor of a cave, Lippmann refers to the "pseudoenvironment," his term for the collection of pictures in people's heads that they mistake for the real world. The pictures in our heads in some measure derive from the media, but the pseudoenvironment is more complicated than that. The pictures in our heads also answer to our personal and cognitive needs. Human beings want to think in terms of simple stories with sharply drawn characters, so they reduce complex realities to stereoptypes and heroes. It is simply human nature to distort the world in grasping it. The media intensify the distortion. First, the people who work in the media will have distorted understandings of the world, for all the same reasons that ordinary people do. Then, media operators will intentionally distort the world further to make it conform to what they think people are capable of or interested in understanding. At the end of the day, it would be a miracle if anyone who depended on the media for information could be well informed about anything. But in a democracy these very people are supposed to make judgments that will determine actions taken in the real world.

Lippmann argued that the problem of public opinion had become acute in the twentieth century. The cognitive shortcomings of humans had not previously presented a big problem for democracy. In the eighteenth century, when modern forms of representative government were created, ordinary people could, in fact, meaningfully understand their world, which still functioned on a human scale. Moreover, representative systems of government allowed people to delegate some of the work of grasping the world to more capable men [*sic*].

By the early twentieth century, Lippmann argued, all this had changed. The world had become much bigger, much closer, and far more complicated. The tasks of government had multiplied. And the media had also grown more complicated and more implicated. News media bombarded people with information deformed by the pressures of commerce and the need to turn complex affairs into compelling stories. Both ordinary people and their elected representatives relied upon this pseudoenvironment for knowledge about how to act in the real world. World War I had fully revealed the mischief and carnage that could result.

World War I taught (and should continue to teach) every thinking person the fragility of progress, reason, and civilization. People had actually believed that advances in science, industry, and technology would make poverty and war obsolete. Suddenly, in 1914, through a series of accidents, coincidences, and exigencies that historians still argue about, the most advanced nations of the world fell to slaughtering each other. Progress, reason, and civilization had given them the tools to slaughter in greater numbers with fewer restraints and less human contact. The killing done by new technologies like mustard gas and artillery bombardments was vastly more indiscriminate yet astonishingly less productive than older tools of war. Bodies piled up, but battle lines hardly moved. Meanwhile, propaganda bureaus set about convincing people of the righteousness of one side and the villainy of the other, even though the actual differences in terms of values, beliefs, and behaviors seem small in retrospect. Both sides included monarchies. Both sides were predominantly Christian. Both sides used weapons of mass destruction. Both lied about the other, and manipulated the media to do so.

World War I convinced Lippmann that the media intensified the problem of public opinion. His solution aimed not to fix the media system – that was not possible – but to create a layer of expert information and judgment to insulate decision-making from the pseudoenvironment. These "intelligence bureaus" would dispel the fog of bias and correct the distortions of stereotypes, making it difficult for popular misinformation and miscommunication to drive policy.

In retrospect, we may doubt Lippmann's faith in expertise. Surely any number of recent fiascos can be cited in evidence of the point that experts can be deluded too. But just as surely we have come to live in Lippmann's world. More and more of the governing process of modern societies has been removed from political processes and bureaucratized, working under the model of expert scientific management insulated from public opinion. The global system of central banks is exhibit A. Staffed by appointees nominally shielded from partisan interests, central banks make decisions on key matters of economic policy according to models supposedly derived from economic science in pursuit of goals supposedly agreed upon by everyone – sustainable growth, low inflation, available credit for capital investment and home ownership, and so forth. Critics may charge that central banks are in fact highly politicized, but such criticism has not dented their authority, even in the wake of global financial catastrophe.

We live in Lippmann's world in other ways as well. Even if you disagree with Lippmann's solution, and even if you disagree with Lippmann's condescending evaluation of the cognitive abilities of ordinary people – aren't we really smarter than that? – on another level you'd have to admit that he's seen clearly the alienated relationship between individual people and the world. The modern emphasis on individual freedom of choice reflects this. People have more resources available and more opportunities to form "pictures in their heads" that conform to their own interests and desires. But, at the same time, the content of people's heads has less and less to do with the execution of public policy and with the simulated public deliberation that legitimizes it. Put another way, the personal and the social have migrated farther apart.

The Subject of the Culture Industries: Individual Rights and Public Opinion

The culture industries foster and profit from a split between the personal and the social. The industrial logic of cultural production and distribution emphasizes identifying and targeting particular market segments with particular kinds of messages, texts, and images, providing an experience of choice amid abundance, in the same way that department stores, the great iconic locations of consumer desire in the age of the Industrial Revolution, allowed people to find their own way through a maze of abundance and come away with a feeling of wants sharpened and satisfied (Leach, 1993; Lears, 1994). In the process, individuals join up in communities of consumption. But these communities are thin: their inhabitants share only one thing in common (owning Saabs, say), whereas, in the traditional thick community of the polity or the town, inhabitants were thought to share everything in common – place, identity, faith, commerce, family, face. The thick community was supposed to be the location for self-government. The prototypical institution of such self-government was the town meeting, occurring in a situated space, transacted face to face, and operating against the background of a dense, negotiated life-world of common sense. As thick communities attenuated into thin ones, dense polities abstracted into the increasingly bureaucratized state – the Lippmannized state of expert control. The state manages the population, but not the persons within it.

Parallel to the rise of the bureaucratic state is the rise of a constitutional tradition of individual and civil liberties. This is another thing we have World War I to thank for. When the national government of the US decided to fortify the war effort with propaganda, it also decided to pass laws limiting the freedom of expression of dissenters. In 1918, it passed the first federal Sedition Act since the lapse of the Sedition Act of 1798, which had sparked the controversy over federal power that had helped elect Thomas Jefferson president in 1800. A Bureau of Investigation had been created within the Justice Department in 1908 under President Theodore Roosevelt, charged with fighting interstate crime like the "white slave trade" and monitoring radicals and anarchists. The brief course of US engagement in the Great War energized the Bureau, which guided federal prosecutions of anti-war and anti-draft activists. At the same time, the postal system hampered the circulation of radical and socialist newspapers and German-language publications. In addition, the government encouraged local groups to exert extra-legal pressure on dissenters. After the war, the same energy was turned on the left. Given new urgency by the 1917 Bolshevik Revolution, opponents of socialism, communism, and working-class activism passed Red laws, established Red Squads in police forces, and stoked a burst of anti-communist paranoia that resulted in the excesses known as the Red Scare of 1919 (Murray, 1955; Murphy, 1979). Attorney-General A. Mitchell Palmer led in the persecution of the left, a role that was soon passed on to J. Edgar Hoover at the FBI.

These abuses of federal authority prompted a response. A civil liberties coalition, consisting of both members of the old left and representatives of the center, the right, the legal profession, and the academy took organizational form as the American Civil Liberties Union, or ACLU. The position the ACLU articulated in the years after World War I drew on a new line of First Amendment jurisprudence, expressed forcefully in a series of Supreme Court opinions written by Oliver Wendell Holmes (especially his dissent in *Abrams* v *US* (1919) and his opinion on behalf of a unanimous court in *Schenk* v *US* (1919)). The guiding metaphor for this jurisprudence was the "marketplace of ideas," a phrase that now seems timeless but was in fact quite novel when Holmes deployed it in his Abrams dissent. The force of that metaphor is to insulate the realm of personal choice from the guiding hand of the government.

The constitutional recognition of personal freedom seems at first glance to run counter to the rise of a managerial state. In fact, the two are part of the same process. Both embody the split between the personal and the social, although in different directions. Lippmann wants to prevent the anarchy in people's heads from interfering with government; Holmes wants to prevent the government from interfering with the anarchy in people's heads.

The redrawing of the relationship between citizens and governments was embodied in the rise of public-opinion polling. In the politicized world of the nineteenth century, there were many ways of representing public opinion, and actual citizens enthusiastically participated in them. Torchlight parades, crowd actions, mass rallies, and all kinds of ritual displays of the people amplified and invited popular politics, leading to extraordinarily high levels of voting participation in elections. By the end of World War I, this age of "popular politics" was coming to an end (McGerr, 1986). In its place appeared more scientific methods of representing public opinion.

The pioneer in this field was George Gallup. Gallup's career, taking shape at the nexus of journalism, politics, and advertising, began with nineteenth-century techniques of representing public opinion – journalism and voting – then moved to refine new techniques for the twentieth century. He was born and raised in Iowa, where he attended the University of Iowa and edited the student newspaper, the *Daily Iowan*. When he graduated in 1923, he took a position as an instructor in the school's new journalism program. Meanwhile, he continued to pursue his education, finally earning a PhD in 1928 in "applied psychology." His doctoral thesis was entitled "A New Technique for Objective Methods for Measuring Reader Interest in Newspapers," the new technique being essentially in-depth interviews with readers.

From 1929 to 1931, he headed the Drake University School of Journalism in Des Moines, then left to teach at Northwestern University and conduct newspaper research in the Chicago area. In 1932, Gallup took over the leadership of the advertising agency Young & Rubicam's advertising research department in New York City. This led him further in the direction of the scientific analysis of public opinion, and in 1935 he set up the American Institute of Public Opinion at Princeton University.

Polling was a new science but an old idea in the late 1920s and early 1930s. Public-opinion polling is abstracted from voting (which is where the term "poll" comes from). And certainly Gallup thought of his polling as a form of voting – as a technique of using a representative sample of the population to simulate the likely voting behavior of the entire population. But it also deviates from voting in crucial ways. Voting is supposed to be rooted in the public deliberation of the body of citizens – it is meant to be an abstraction of the town meeting. Polling, however, seeks to identify the private preferences of individuals. It is rooted in market research. Gallup's own career moved first from teaching journalism to doing market research for newspapers to doing market research for advertisers, and only then to public opinion.

Polling epitomizes the twentieth-century relationship between the personal and the social. Personal preferences, which are assumed to exist independently of any social order, are seen as purely self-regarding; they are measured scientifically in order that providers (retailers, governments, politicians) may more accurately tailor available choices (Herbst, 1993, 1998). Together with the new profession of "public relations" (Ewen, 2008), this scientific knowledge allows managers to efficiently steer bureaucracies, whether in government or in business.

One particular realm of business that came to rely in special ways on this new science involved the culture industries. Market research was an important way for media to identify their audiences and show them to advertisers. Media industries became early sponsors of the emerging field of communications research. Radio broadcasters funded the studies that came out of Paul Lazarsfeld's research institutes in Princeton and at Columbia.

Critics of the media also sponsored research. One of the signal themes of Progressive reformers in the first third of the twentieth century was the corrosive influence of popular culture. When the motion picture industry emerged, vice commissions and censorship boards quickly labeled it a corrupter of the youth (Nasaw, 1993). In the 1920s, a private philanthropy called the Payne Fund sponsored a series of academic studies at the University of Chicago, the University of Iowa, the Ohio State University, and elsewhere that examined the influence of motion pictures (Jowett, Jarvie, and Fuller, 1996).

Fear of Media Influence and the Professionalization of Journalism

If the media had the power to influence public morals, public knowledge, and public opinion, then the survival of democracy required that such power be controlled or neutralized. In the past, in theory, the marketplace neutralized the power of the media. But because of industrialization, the most powerful media had outgrown market disciplines.

The press dealt with the problem of media influence in part by making itself the answer. The press positioned itself as a force of public reason in opposition to the entertainment media. The motion picture industry obviously would do anything to make money, including glamorizing crime and transgressive sexuality. In contrast, the press took on the responsibility of informing the public to reinforce morality and public order. Adopting this exalted position meant that the press had to repress its own dark side. The superego of the press would be public affairs reporting. It hoped that its performance in this high-value enterprise would obscure or excuse its id: crime reporting, celebrity gossip, advertising, and trivialities like sports and amusements, where the bulk of its income was earned.

This positioning implied a settlement to a long-running three-party struggle between owners and the public, on the one hand, and owners and their employees, on the other. The public agreed to leave the press unregulated, in return for which the owners agreed to moderate their pursuit of self-interest through a norm of public service; embracing this norm allowed reporters to upgrade their status through professionalism, while squeezing more autonomy and income from owners. This settlement was embodied in the appearance of schools and departments of journalism in universities and of codes of ethics in news organizations.

Some version of this drama occurred in most developed countries in the years between 1890 and 1940. In some places, newsworkers were more active in seeking autonomy through unions; in others, governments enforced norms through censorship or other means of regulation. But, in the bulk of the developed world, the rise of the perceived power of the media and the rise of concentrations of industrial control in the news business produced a professionalization project as a defensive response.

The professionalization project coincided with the achievement of true mass circulation in the most developed countries. By the end of this period, news media had achieved total or nearly total penetration of the population. Britain led the world in number of newspapers per person; Raymond Williams estimated – using three readers per copy as a multiplier – that the daily press in Britain reached 75 percent of the population in 1930, and that the Sunday press reached 125 percent in 1920 (Williams, 1965: 233). In the US, when sociologists Robert and Helen Lynd performed their famous intensive study of a typical town that they called "Middletown" in the mid-1920s, they failed to find a household that did not take a daily newspaper (Lynd and Lynd, 1929).

But professionalizing journalism was fraught with contradictions. In 1904, Joseph Pulitzer published an article in the *North American Review* calling for the establishment of a college of journalism at Columbia University. Pulitzer understood the obstacles to his project. First, there was him. He was an outsider, an immigrant of Jewish descent who spoke with an accent, a populist who marketed newspapers to common folk, and so not a natural fit for the still very waspish university, which had in fact rejected his proposal to establish a school of journalism in 1892. Then there was his newspaper. The *World* had acquired a reputation for sensationalism and vulgarity in the recent period of yellow journalism leading up to the Spanish–American War. But Pulitzer was convinced that a school of journalism was a necessity. His article in the *North American Review*, the most prestigious of the nation's intellectual organs, pressed the case.

What one notices when reading this article today is the hollowness at its center. Pulitzer's main premise, that journalism badly needed uplifting, and that higher education for journalism could do it, seems on its face unobjectionable. But the obviousness of the argument ends when Pulitzer turns to the content of the education. Here the parallel between journalism and other "professions" breaks down.

In the years of the Industrial Revolution, middle-class occupations generally had adopted the forms of professions (Bledstein, 1976). What is a profession? The easy way to define professions is to say that they are middle-class occupations, like medicine and law. Although historically accurate, this definition doesn't really help us understand what the term has come to mean. Professions distinguish themselves from other occupations in obvious ways, of course: they are more prestigious and more lucrative, usually, than other occupations, and they are also harder to enter. To become a professional usually requires training and certification.

The requirement for training, especially higher education, gives a profession autonomy. A profession is able to control entry to its own field. To enter medicine, an aspiring doctor must pass a series of examinations that are administered by the state but of course written by doctors: in other words, the state authorizes the medical profession to control its own field. Likewise, the state licenses lawyers through bar exams written by lawyers. Lawyers decide who gets to be a lawyer, and doctors decide who gets to be a doctor; the state then grants the profession a monopoly on its field. Non-lawyers and non-doctors are forbidden to practice. So, for instance, pharmacists, who may know a great deal about medications but are not licensed physicians, in many countries are not allowed to prescribe drugs. Monopolizing a field is a necessary but perhaps not a sufficient condition of professionalization.

In addition to having collective autonomy, individual professionals also typically have independence. Professionals answer to no higher authority in their practice. Ideally, they have no bosses. They contain within themselves, in their hands and heads, the tools of their practice, and do not require an employer to enable them to work on or for their clients. This ideal becomes more remote all the time, as doctors and lawyers work for larger and more commercially and industrially organized firms, but nevertheless the claim of occupational independence is central to both the prestige and the income of professionals.

Independence and autonomy both mean power, and power requires responsibility, or the next best thing, a code of ethics. A professional works in situations where the client is in a dependent and submissive position: think of a gynecological exam. The professional works with a client's most intimate affairs, and clients submit themselves to the mastery of the professional. The power in this relationship needs to be justified by a guarantee that it is exercised on behalf of the public. The medical profession's autonomy and the doctor's independence serve the public health, then; the legal profession serves the justice system. All professions write codes of ethics to govern their members and to assure the public that their power will be exercised responsibly.

Independence and autonomy both come from science. Doctors have licensing requirements because medical practice is based on medical science. Science is difficult to learn; the medical profession distinguishes it from the practical knowledge of midwives and pharmacists, which can be acquired through apprenticeship or emulation or picked up here and there. Science is theoretical and arcane and you need to go to college to learn it. Without science, the autonomy and independence of the professions would be arbitrary.

You could argue that it always *is* arbitrary, of course. Take medicine. Medical schools and licensing arrangements and codes of ethics and all the other professional apparatus had appeared and solidified by the mid-nineteenth century, although "heterodox" medical practices persisted. But medical science of that era, it later became apparent, was no damned good. If you were seriously ill, you were better off going to a faith healer. Orthodox medicine still poorly understood germs and hygiene, and orthodox doctors were still likely to prescribe mercury-based medicines or "heroic" treatments, like starving and lengthy bedrest. If you had dysentery, a disease that produces uncontrollable diarrhea, an orthodox physician would have recommended avoiding liquids. This would dry up the diarrhea, curing a symptom. Alas, dysentery kills by dehydration. The point is that medicine invented its science after it achieved the social status of a profession. Some would argue that this is true of all the professions. Knowledge doesn't confer power; power creates knowledge (Foucault, 1980).

Whatever the case, to be a believable profession, an occupation needs to make a believable claim to some kind of science, and that was what Pulitzer needed to do in arguing for higher education in journalism. And that was a problem. A few months earlier, Horace White, whose bona fides as a journalist matched Pulitzer's, had argued in the *North American Review* that higher education in journalism was irrelevant (White, 1904). College education was a good thing, of course, and White valued his own, but it was a good thing because it was *not* about being a journalist. Journalism one could learn by doing, and that's the way it ought to be. White recognized that the quality of journalism left much to be desired, and criticized the recent epidemic of yellow journalism. But the problem of yellow journalism was a problem of demand and not supply. The market rewarded yellow journalism. Until the public stopped patronizing sensationalism, it wouldn't go away, and training journalists wouldn't help.

White was certainly correct in noting that journalism never has had and probably never will have a science attached to it. Instead, it has techniques and know-how and craft and a lot of miscellaneous intelligence. Some of this is teachable. A journalism professor can teach a student how to craft a lede or a nut graf, and how to interview a school-board member, how to look up census data, and so forth. But this kind of knowledge doesn't really require higher education. At the beginning of the twentieth century, and also at the beginning of the twenty-first, many in journalism thought that the craft was better learned on the job, through a kind of apprenticeship.

Pulitzer rejected that notion, and insisted that journalists should study in college. "Before the century closes schools of journalism will be generally accepted as a feature of specialized higher education, like schools of law or of medicine" (Pulitzer, 1904: 642). Both law and medicine used to be learned through apprenticeship, or what Pulitzer called "the 'shop' idea'" (p. 647). In journalism, as in law, apprenticeship is ineffective and expensive: "One of the learned critics remarks that Greeley took young Raymond in hand and hammered him into a great editor. True. But was it not an expensive process, as well as an unusual one – the most distinguished newspaper-maker of his time turning himself into a College of Journalism for the benefit of a single pupil?" If you take apprenticeship out of the newsroom and turn it into college education, a single instructor could "turn out, not one Raymond, but fifty" (p. 647).

But what will journalists study? Well, everything, Pulitzer said. The second half of this very long article is a catalog of all the things a journalism student must master. This catalog includes all of the things a journalism educator would recognize today – style, the law, ethics, literature, history, sociology, economics, statistics, modern language – and many that would be considered extraneous, exotic, or pretentious, such as physical science, arbitration, truth and accuracy, the enemies of the republic, the power of ideas. So inclusive a curriculum is a sure sign that Pulitzer had no clear notion of a science for journalism. Ironically, when he comes to the end of the piece, he almost admits as much. When he reaches the center of the curriculum, the actual teaching of the "principles of journalism," he proposes running a laboratory newspaper – in essence, an apprenticeship system inside the university. And when he discusses "news" per se, he abandons any hope of systematic instruction, noting that news "is perennially changing – more varied than any kaleidoscope, bringing every day some new surprise, some new sensation – always unexpected" (p. 678). Not something you can teach. But Pulitzer is interested less in news here than he is in civics.

The kind of encyclopedic knowledge Pulitzer envisions will be necessary for a journalist to fulfill one's civic mission.

> A journalist is the lookout on the bridge of the ship of state. He notes the passing sail, the little things of interest that dot the horizon in fine weather. He reports the drifting castaway whom the ship can save. He peers through fog and storm to give warning of dangers ahead. He is not thinking of his wages, or of the profits of his owners. He is there to watch over the safety and the welfare of the people who trust him. (p. 656)

In Pulitzer's model of the profession of journalism, there is a strict line between the journalist, who is a public servant, and the proprietor, who is a private individual seeking profit. A wall of separation divides the sacred from the profane in the newspaper. Greeley and many others had preceded Pulitzer in the notion that the editorial side of the newspaper needed to be autonomous from the business side. But the nineteenth century had thought of the editorial side as being essentially political. Pulitzer's generation had begun to think of it in terms of a professional practice also autonomous from politics.

Pulitzer wrote his justification for journalism education shortly after Columbia University had accepted a million-dollar endowment from him. But the university did not open its School of Journalism until after Pulitzer's death in 1911. This reluctance reflected a cultural wariness on the part of Columbia and institutions like it. The better-established private schools, and especially the Ivy League, disliked "industrial" education. Where US journalism instruction flourished was in the land-grant universities of the south, midwest, and west, schools like the Universities of Wisconsin, Illinois, Missouri, Alabama, and Washington. Missouri claims to be the oldest of the colleges of journalism, having been established in 1908 – after Pulitzer endowed Columbia, but before Columbia's Graduate School of Journalism began instruction. Its founding father, Walter Williams, was also a tireless promoter of journalism education, helping to lay the groundwork for the organizations that would authorize and accredit programs, and internationalizing standards by traveling throughout the world, promoting the professionalization of journalism (Farrar, 1998). Williams also penned one of the more enduring formulas of professionalizing journalism, the "Journalist's Creed."

The Journalist's Creed is much like Pulitzer's argument. It is full of the language of uplift, and, although some of its language is dated, its sentiments are unobjectionable. But that is because they are so vague as to be virtually meaningless. Any journalist can justify virtually any course of action by appealing to some clause in this creed. At the same time, the creed doesn't define what is professional and teachable about journalism. One might say, in its appeal to gentlemanly virtue, it is profoundly anti-professional. I quote it in full:

> I believe in the profession of journalism.
>
> I believe that the public journal is a public trust; that all connected with it are, to the full measure of their responsibility, trustees for the public; that acceptance of a lesser service than the public service is betrayal of this trust.
>
> I believe that clear thinking and clear statement, accuracy and fairness are fundamental to good journalism.

> I believe that a journalist should write only what he holds in his heart to be true.
>
> I believe that suppression of the news, for any consideration other than the welfare of society, is indefensible.
>
> I believe that no one should write as a journalist what he would not say as a gentleman; that bribery by one's own pocketbook is as much to be avoided as bribery by the pocketbook of another; that individual responsibility may not be escaped by pleading another's instructions or another's dividends.
>
> I believe that advertising, news and editorial columns should alike serve the best interests of readers; that a single standard of helpful truth and cleanness should prevail for all; that the supreme test of good journalism is the measure of its public service.
>
> I believe that the journalism which succeeds best – and best deserves success – fears God and honors Man; is stoutly independent, unmoved by pride of opinion or greed of power, constructive, tolerant but never careless, self-controlled, patient, always respectful of its readers but always unafraid, is quickly indignant at injustice; is unswayed by the appeal of privilege or the clamor of the mob; seeks to give every man a chance and, as far as law and honest wage and recognition of human brotherhood can make it so, an equal chance; is profoundly patriotic while sincerely promoting international good will and cementing world-comradeship; is a journalism of humanity, of and for today's world.

But the incoherence of these calls for journalism education did not forestall the professionalization project. Journalism education spread not because journalists needed college degrees but because it served the social and political interests of the press. At the University of Illinois at Urbana-Champaign, where I taught for 30 years, a leading force behind the establishment of journalism education was the Illinois Press Association, the statewide club of newspaper publishers. They wanted a program at the flagship state university as a matter of prestige. Ultimately, they worked a bill through the state legislature mandating the creation of a College of Journalism.

Journalism education came only slowly to have an effect on journalism as an occupation. College-educated journalists remained a small minority until after World War II, and, of the college-educated, only a fraction had degrees in journalism. Not until the Vietnam era would most new journalism hires have journalism degrees. Journalism thus lacked the science to be a profession, and journalism education lagged behind other professional programs at universities in the US and elsewhere.

Other elements retarded the professionalization of journalism, especially the nature of journalism itself, signaled in the US by the First Amendment tradition. Constitutionally, the US forbids the licensing of journalists. The First Amendment clearly prevents the erection of legal barriers to entry to the field as "abridging freedom of the press." In this tradition, journalism by its nature should be hostile to the kinds of privileged knowledge that professionalism requires. Like doctors, good journalists should know all sorts of things that are not common knowledge, but unlike doctors they should try to translate their intelligence into common knowledge. To the extent that journalists hoard knowledge, they serve themselves and not the public. Journalists claim an exemption for protecting and cultivating sources, but even in those cases, to the extent that a journalist conceals the identity and motivations of a source, there is a risk of serving the source at the expense of the public. Professionalization can produce "source-capture."

The forces pushing professionalization outweighed both the intellectual incoherence of the project and the First Amendment tradition. The networks of relationships that constituted journalism as a media practice changed as the press industrialized and then institutionalized.

Institutionalization and the Demand for Professionalization

Industrialization, with its economies of scale, produced situations of "natural monopoly" in the news business. At the end of the nineteenth century, the telegraph had produced one kind of monopoly in the form of wire-service news. By the 1920s, in the US and in other developed countries, local daily newspaper markets had also become natural monopolies. At the same time, chain ownership had begun to produce artificial monopolies. So economic conditions provided "barriers to entry" that had a similar effect to what licensing requirements achieved for the learned professions.

People recognized the power of news. This is why newspaper proprietors like Pulitzer felt the need to propose uplifting the practice of journalism. They confronted critics like Upton Sinclair, who saw the press everywhere as corrupt (Sinclair, 1920; Lawson, 1993; McChesney and Scott, 2004). The public demanded transparency and responsibility.

Newswork, its divisions of labor, and their meaning continued to evolve. News organizations had distinguished between "correspondents" who had a voice and opinions and wrote authorly accounts, on the one hand, and "reporters" on the other, whose work was more stenographic, recording what was said at meetings and speeches and what was written in police blotters and hotel registries. This distinction was recognized widely in commentary and was inscribed in the organizational structure of newspapers. At the turn of the century, reporters worked under the "city editor," while correspondents wired their material to the "telegraph editor," who replaced what had earlier been called the "scissors-and-paste editor," the editor who clipped items from exchange newspapers (Bleyer, 1913: 2–6; Nerone and Barnhurst, 2003).

In the industrialized newspaper, the work of reporters was increasingly routinized. Reporters were paid by the line, for instance; a hostile copy-editor could starve a reporter simply by cutting copy (Smythe, 1980; Solomon, 1995). Reporters fought a continual battle with their superiors to raise their income and prestige. Part of what they desired was the recovery of the voice of the correspondent.

So newspaper owners were fighting two simultaneous battles. In one, an angry and suspicious public demanded more accountability from media that seemed to be pursuing special interests. This public knew that newspapers were often fronts for mining and railroad interests (like Jay Gould's *New York World* and the elder Hearst's *San Francisco Examiner*) or political operators. Rhode Island's Republican Senator Nelson Aldrich secretly owned the *Providence Journal* and Indiana's Republican Senator and later Vice President Charles Fairbanks secretly controlled both the *Indianapolis News* and the *Indianapolis Journal* at the beginning of the century (Lawson, 1993: 20). In response to these concerns, the reformist Democratic Congress elected in 1912 passed the Newspaper Publicity Act, requiring newspapers to disclose their ownership and imposing other measures designed to ensure transparency.

The other battle pitted reporters against their bosses. Owners had already been forced to accept unions among their production workers – typographers, pressmen, drivers, and others. They hoped to limit the labor activism of their newsroom workers, though.

Professionalization was a sort of negotiated settlement to both these battles. Media owners yielded some autonomy to reporters in return for protection from public movements for regulation. Reporters gave up their campaign to gain voices – opinions, distinctive authorial styles – in return for some autonomy. The public gave up their desire for media regulation in return for a guarantee of objective and authoritative information. This negotiated settlement played out over a long period of time and was perhaps never consciously expressed. The basic terms of the settlement were clear by World War I, and the decades between the world wars produced changes in the news industry that filled out what was meant by this compromise.

One notable set of changes was organizational. In the US, professions all have national organizations, like the American Medical Association (established in 1847) or the American Bar Association (established in 1878). In the news business, the key parallel organizations were the American Newspaper Publishers Association (ANPA, founded in 1887; it merged with several other organizations in 1992 to become the Newspaper Association of America, or NAA), the Society of Professional Journalists (SPJ), founded as Sigma Delta Chi fraternity in 1909, the American Society of Newspaper Editors (ASNE, first proposed in 1912 but not established until 1922), and the Associated Press Managing Editors (APME, established in 1933).

The ASNE, the most important of these for the professionalization project, understood itself as specifically a professional organization (Pratte, 1995). The prime mover in its founding was Casper S. Yost, editorial director of the *St Louis Globe Democrat*, who later recalled being pushed into action by an article critical of journalism in the *Atlantic Monthly:*

> The article attacked the newspaper profession very viciously and, I thought, unjustly. I thought of writing an editorial for my own newspaper in answer to it, and then it occurred to me that very few people ever read *The Atlantic Monthly* anyhow, and if I said anything, it would give much larger circulation to what this gentleman had said and wouldn't do any good. (ASNE, 2013)

Yost wanted to rescue the reputation of the newspaper industry. To do that, he needed to form a community of newspaper leaders, a way for people like him, who used their judgment to decide what went into newspapers, to form common standards and to influence the less scrupulous among them. "I didn't know a half-a-dozen editors in the United States at that time. I couldn't name a dozen of them. We were all living a sort of monastic seclusion in our individual offices, and I thought it would be a good thing if we could get together" (ASNE, 2013). Professional organizations always have a social component, of course. The ASNE was like any other organization in connecting the formation of a community with both the establishment of standards and the uplift of the field. It stated this set of purposes succinctly in the preamble to the Constitution it adopted in 1922:

> To promote acquaintance among members, to develop a stronger and professional esprit de corps, to maintain the dignity and rights of the profession, to consider and perhaps establish ethical standards of professional conduct, to interchange ideas for the advancement of

> professional ideals and for the more effective application of professional labors, and to work collectively for the solution of common problems. (ASNE, 2013)

The ASNE also adopted a code of ethics, the Canons of Journalism, in 1923. This code built on the many different codes of ethics adopted by individual newspapers since the turn of the century. As with the Journalist's Creed, it mingles values from many different news formations, and at root every plank is agreeable and unobjectionable. Many practitioners ridiculed the piety of this document and others like it. Stanley Walker, a stalwart New York City journalist whose book *City Editor* is a prototype of the newspaperman's memoir, puts it this way:

> In all this groping for a coherent philosophy there is much that is ridiculous; mostly such attempts to codify journalistic practices seem like the musings of a shyster lawyer, with a trace of the old college spirit still left in him, who in his day off tells himself that after all there are such things as ethics, and that henceforth life must be a little cleaner. Not a bad thing, this eternal seeking for sanctification. There is, it may be, some hope for any reprobate who is capable of turning his head on his pillow and asking: "Why do I have to be so rotten?" But the next day comes the avalanche of reality. (1934: 176)

Walker's skepticism toward ethics, and his dismissal of the "old college spirit," have been a common theme among the working press of the last century.

Along with the professional organizations and college degree programs, professionalization in journalism produced a set of publications. This again is typical of professional occupations: the American Medical Association began publishing its *Journal of the American Medical Association* in 1883. Various publications related to the news business had appeared around the same time. The most famous of these late nineteenth-century publications was *The Journalist* (established 1884), published in New York and achieving national circulation. It was absorbed in 1907 by *Editor and Publisher*, which had been founded just after the turn of the century. *Editor and Publisher* had become by the 1910s the chief organ of the newspaper business, filling two slots simultaneously – working as a trade publication, and also as a professional publication, with stories and essays about how journalism was practiced. (Journalism reviews as a genre came much later – *Columbia Journalism Review* in 1962, *St Louis Journalism Review* in 1970; *Washington Journalism Review* in 1977.)

The way business and professional concerns mixed in these organizations and publications is emblematic of journalism's half-hearted embrace of professionalism. Journalists could not claim freedom from the business side of the newspaper, no matter how earnestly they proclaimed the principle. In fact, the industrialization of the press had done too much to decrease the independence and autonomy of journalists. Even a columnist like Walter Lippmann had less independence, in practical terms, than a partisan editor like Thurlow Weed. Journalists continued to work for media owners who were legally entitled to fire and hire them at will. As a result, journalists would lack the capacity to do what was expected of them. Lippmann himself pointed this out in *Public Opinion*.

But Lippmann also pointed out that more and more was expected of journalism. As the world became more complicated and citizens in democracies were expected to know a great deal more about it, journalism seemed to be the indispensable public educator.

The Invention of Objectivity

Partly in response to this increased public reliance, and partly in response to their own ambitions, journalists developed their own notion of objectivity as a professional ideology in the 1920s and 1930s. They fashioned objectivity out of a melange of notions from common sense, the natural sciences, and psychology. They did this in opposition to and in dialog with developments in the news industry. Professionalizing journalists developed the ethos of objectivity to distinguish themselves from the tabloids, the advertisers, and the public relations professionals. They also drew on expectations from the new world of radio news.

Journalists rarely used the term "objectivity" before the 1920s. The earliest article that a search of the *New York Times* database for "journalism AND objectivity" turned up was published in 1924 (Strunsky, 1924). This is not to say that something like the concept wasn't already developing in the culture of journalism. Reporters were repeatedly admonished to faithfully record "facts" and to be "accurate," and newsworkers of all ranks knew what "neutrality" meant. These are all common-sense components of objectivity. Michael Schudson has argued compellingly, though, that these leave out a crucial element of the mature ideology that distinguishes it from an earlier "naive empiricism": an acknowledgment of the subjectivity of journalists (1978: ch. 4).

Naive empiricism became much less believable after World War I. Propaganda campaigns, the rise of public relations and advertising, and the new sense that public information was inherently unreliable (Lippmann's talk of a pseudoenvironment, for instance) convinced thoughtful people, some of whom were journalists, that the facts never speak for themselves. Instead, facts always required an explanation or a context.

Objectivity as used by journalists applies more to context than facts. It refers to the ways that journalistic accounts arrange facts, not for the accuracy of the facts themselves. It is a kind of discipline of storytelling. The opposite of objectivity, for journalists, isn't subjectivity, as it might be for philosophers, or non-replicability, as it would be for physical scientists, but bias. Journalists fail to be objective when they do not police their values to keep them from distorting their stories.

This disposition of journalists toward what would later be called objectivity seems to actually be part of a new job description for journalists, a merging of the correspondent and the reporter. The objective journalist would do some of the work of correspondents, reporting from afar, providing perspective and explanations and a sense of what it's like to be there. But the objective journalist would not have the same kind of voice – quirky, textured, opinionated. That voice would be reserved for columnists and commentators.

This shift in voice also involved a regendering of newswork. By this I mean both a repositioning of women in news organizations and a revision of what it meant for journalism to be manly. Manliness has been and remains one of the things that journalists recognize as important to "hard" news, and masculine–feminine binaries shoot through the norms and categories that comprise the hierarchy of news forms. Print, for instance, is masculine, while broadcast is feminine. Within broadcasting, war is masculine, while consumer affairs reporting is feminine. Weather is feminine; sports masculine. These designations come out of a nineteenth-century set of values that has changed more slowly in journalism than in other fields.

The irony is that journalism as it professionalized was more open to women than other professions, such as medicine or law. Women, like other outsiders, came into it through enclaved media. The great muckrakers Ida Tarbell and Ida B. Wells-Barnett both worked first in religious publishing. Literary publishing also opened doors for some, though the emergence of lines between serious literature, popular sensational fiction, and polite fiction hardened gender lines there. Others worked in the reform press, especially periodicals dedicated to temperance and woman suffrage (Solomon and Watson, 1991; Tusan, 2005).

Within news organizations, particular occupations opened up for women. As newspapers commercialized and appealed to new consumer publics, they naturally sought out women to edit society pages, where luxury items could be advertised, and pages designed for homemakers, where grocers advertised. And certain kinds of high-profile reporting positions also opened up, to the point where the "sob sister," the female reporter working human-interest angles, became a stereotype.

As technology transformed the news workplace, new divisions of labor opened up jobs for women. Typesetting remained an almost all-male preserve, with strong unions erecting barriers to entry, but copy-editing and the many tasks that involved working a typewriter were there for women. The typewriter is an invention that deserves more attention than I can give it here. But it does exemplify a more general point. Office technologies tend to be masculine when they are introduced; the first office employees who used typewriters were men. But as office technologies become more user-friendly, they lose their masculine mystique and become feminine. Wired communications show the same pattern as the typewriter. In the first generation, telegraph operators were mostly men, but as telegraph yielded to telephone, the occupation feminized. At the beginning of the twenty-first century, digital technologies followed a similar arc, with women emerging as a powerful presence in social media.

There is a gender dimension to the emergence of objectivity, then, but it is not simple or obvious. In general terms, the highest-value news beats emphasized objectivity the most, and journalists on these beats policed themselves by drawing bright lines between their work and the low-value beats – the cultural, society, religion, and human-interest ghettoes where women were most likely to be employed. Soft news was feminine, and hard news masculine. Women did work hard news – more often than one might expect. But when a woman took on such a beat, she was expected to pump testosterone.

Journalism redefined its job description before the word "objective" was applied to it. The early muckraking reporters (described in chapter 4) were objective in the modern sense of the word. They marshaled facts into narratives that explained the way things happened, and did so in a fashion that promised that the reporter's personal biases had not entered into the account. The stories they wrote, though, often advocated a particular position or movement.

Does advocacy contradict objectivity? No. That's a crucial difference between objectivity and neutrality or naive empiricism. An objective journalist is active, seeking out information, shaping it into stories, and putting the stories into play. A neutral reporter is passive, balancing opposing points of view in a mechanical fashion. A naive empiricist is passive also, not speaking but letting the facts speak for themselves. But an objective journalist is limited as an advocate. First, one's advocacy must always be able to make the claim that it's compelled by the facts. Second, and this is related to the first limit, advocacy must fall within the realm of consensus.

Present-day people, even if they are avid newspaper readers, have trouble telling what was news matter and what was editorial matter in older newspapers. It's not that there wasn't a distinction. It's just that the distinction between news and opinion at any point in time is not a distinction between news and opinion. It's a distinction between items on which everyone is supposed to agree and items on which disagreement is expected. News items are items with consensus opinion, in other words. Consensus opinion continually changes, however. In the mainstream press before World War I, for instance, consensus opinion in Europe and North America embraced white racial superiority. A present-day reader confronted with articles about imperial expansion or about lynching in newspapers from those days would call them opinionated; in their own day, they were considered neutral and factual. You can be sure that much of what we find "objective" today will be considered opinion by future generations.

Objectivity, with its careful balancing of the active and subjective with the effacement of the identity of the journalist, was central to the development of professionalism. In many ways, it came to stand in the place of "science." But it is not a matter of science, unlike objectivity in chemistry or other physical sciences. It remains a matter of craft. It is a form of craft that allows journalists and readers to distinguish between different kinds of journalism. Gaye Tuchman (1972) argues that it is a "strategic ritual" that consists of certain practices designed to signal professionalism – balancing points of view against each other, for instance, and attributing to sources any expression of opinion. Balancing and sourcing can be used in any number of ways, of course. A manipulative journalist can package anything in such a way as to make it look like an objective report – "There is a range of opinion on whether cigarettes cause cancer," for example, or "Experts dispute the existence of global warming." It's easy to make a pretense of being "fair and balanced." But the sense of shared endeavor that professions require makes it difficult for a journalist who wants respect to challenge common sense in this fashion. Not science, then, but consensus forces journalists to restrain themselves from abusing their techniques.

Journalism, like any "ism," defines itself in terms of what it is not. Journalism in effect divides the universe of news practices into journalism and not-journalism. The 1920s produced all sorts of innovative news styles that professionalizers could cast as "other": tabloid journalism, for instance. The tabloid form, pioneered in Europe and especially Britain, where it pursued a trajectory established by the Sunday press, filled half-sheets with shorter items, heavy illustration, and sensational content to market aggressively to new, downscale urban readers. The US pioneer in this field, the *New York Daily News*, was established by Joseph Patterson, the left-leaning cousin of *Chicago Tribune* co-owner Robert McCormick. But most tabloids tended to be shrilly socially conservative. Hearst's newspapers frequently adopted the tabloid format. Tabloid journalism then, as now, was known to bend the truth for the sake of making stories stand out. Notorious in this regard was the *New York Graphic*, begun by fitness guru Bernarr Macfadden, which invented the "composograph," a photoshop-like composite of photographs claiming to faithfully represent scenes like the surgery of screen idol Rudolf Valentino.

Photojournalism itself emerged as a new and vigorous field in the 1920s. New and more portable cameras, with shorter exposure times, were introduced. Techniques of halftone reproduction, which made it easier to print photographs along with text, and techniques of sending photographs by wire made it ordinary for newspapers to include pictures everywhere. And news media specifically devoted to photojournalism began to appear. The most enduring entrepreneur in photojournalism was Henry Luce, the son of missionaries to China, educated at Yale and Oxford, who worked for a year on the *Chicago Daily News*, itself an innovator in news pictures, and then went on to found *Time* magazine in 1923 and *Life* in 1936.

Professional journalism defined itself against pictures and tabloids. Tabloids represented primitive and debased news for readers who didn't know any better. Photographs were more complicated. They appeared to be entirely neutral and factual, and as such seemed objective. But they were not, in two complementary ways. First, they were traces of reality, not reports of reality. A photograph is more like the raw material of a news report than an actual report. Second, they were inevitably emotional. They invited the reader to imagine an immediate experience of the thing pictured and did not allow the detachment and distance that objectivity demands.

What a professional journalist needed to do was "interpret." "Interpretative journalism" became a common term almost as soon as "objectivity" entered the reporter's lexicon. It was already in common usage when it became the title of a leading journalism textbook (McDougall, 1938). The turn to interpretation in reporting owed a lot to pictures. It seems that, as pictures took over more of the labor of telling readers the who, what, and where of the news, journalists could devote themselves more to the why and how (Barnhurst and Nerone, 2001: ch. 5). Interpretation, the work of explaining the world to readers rather than merely tickling or scaring them with it, implied that journalists had the kind of authority that other professionals, like doctors and lawyers, claimed.

One other new element of the news environment that interacted with professionalization was broadcasting. The impact here was momentous and complicated. With the birth of broadcasting in the 1920s, especially in the US, newspapers tried to prevent radio from becoming a news medium. In the early 1930s, newspapers conspired to prevent the wire services from selling news to the radio networks. This "press-radio war," as it's been called, raged from 1933 to 1935 (McChesney, 1991), But eventually the parties negotiated a modus vivendi in which radio news reached a division of labor with the printed word. Radio would carry the live events and headlines, along with commentary, that would impel listeners to go out and buy the newspapers to read fuller accounts and explanations. In this fashion, radio promoted the kind of interpretive print reporting that supported objectivity and professionalism.

But there were other dimensions to radio's impact on objectivity. One was the neutrality required of radio. Both government regulation and business concerns mandated neutrality. In most countries, a national broadcasting authority was created, usually with monopoly power, and along with it a commitment to responsibility and fair representation of the various legitimate social interests. The US was exceptional in its failure to embrace a public-service sector in broadcasting, but even there a federal regulatory agency licensed broadcasters under a mandate to serve the "public interest, convenience, and necessity," so that broadcasters were continually encouraged (threatened, more likely) to avoid anything that might seem like partisanship. And because US broadcasters drew their sole income from advertising, they shied away from any content that would alienate advertisers or any market segment that advertisers might like to target. The combination of government and business pressure explains why radio stations, which competed in markets in a way that newspapers in their partisan era used to, did not adopt partisan affiliations.

The very nature of radio listening added another dimension to objectivity. Radio, like the photograph, promised a kind of immediacy. But radio's immediacy required an announcer's work. Early radio announcers tried to let listeners feel that they were actually experiencing the events that were being described, a media encounter that Susan Douglas calls "dimensional listening" (Douglas, 1999: 33). In concentrating in silence on the words coming from the radio, listeners work to construct in their minds an image in depth of the scene of live action – for example, the World Cup final. This is like photography, but through the medium of words.

The broadcasting of live events thus involved an objective performance on the part of the radio correspondent. But radio carries voices. It was not possible for radio announcers to efface their presence in the same way that print journalists could. The announcer's voice established a signature, a face, a personality. Listeners would attest that the unique staccato tone of noted commentator H. V. Kaltenborn, the complex bursts of voice coming from gossip correspondent Walter Winchell, and the soothing familiarity of World War II correspondent Edward R. Murrow gave their broadcasts a deep feeling of intimacy. Broadcast announcers were personalities. So, even more than in print, objective broadcasting required a balancing of subjectivity.

The style of journalism that came to be called objective was not the only solution to the problem of professionalization. As some western countries developed objective styles, a larger part of the world moved in different directions. In the socialist countries, the press was often reorganized as a state institution; in fascist countries, journalism became a propaganda tool in a system of command capitalism. In such systems, the achievement of a monopoly on practice by journalists was more complete; arguably, then, journalism became more professionalized in those systems. But it would be a mistake to take party-controlled or propaganda systems as the primary alternative to objectivity. In fact, several alternative styles developed.

One particular style of journalism that set itself apart from objectivity in the US and western Europe was called "reportage." Reportage traces its lineage to diverse styles, such as the French feuilleton and its English equivalent, the sketch, made popular by writers like Charles Dickens. John Hartsock (2011) sees its most formative practitioners as linked through a Russian genre of *ocherk*, or essay, and then practicing in the global radical journalism that followed the establishment of the Soviet Union. The most influential of these writers included familiar names like Maxim Gorky and the US American John Reed, but also figures who are now more obscure, especially the Czech Marxist Egon Erwin Kisch. Writers in this tradition self-consciously deployed Marxist theory to animate factual accounts; in doing so, they sought to counter the covert capitalist ideology of western professional reporting.

The tradition of reportage was tremendously influential in the years between the world wars in and outside the emerging Soviet Bloc. In Europe, practitioners flourished in all the major countries. It was especially important in France, where it informed the pedagogical style of elite newspapers like *Le Monde* (Benson, 2013). In the US, writers on the left, both in communist publications and in the larger movement called the "cultural front" (Denning, 1998), wrote reportage that documented the hardships of workers and the unfairness of capitalist social relations. Seemingly presented in a neutral, factual manner, reportage of this sort aimed in fact to push emotional buttons (Stott, 1973). As part of a literature of agitation, it appealed to political movements throughout the developing world also, and had a particular impact in China, where a form of literary reportage appeared at the end of the nineteenth century. It first was called by a specific name, *baogao wenxue*, in an article describing the work of Egon Erwin Kisch in 1930. Kisch himself visited China in 1932 and published a book of reportage about his experiences, *Secret China*, which was translated into Chinese. Adopted as a style by the press of the Chinese Communist Party, literary reportage has had an important place in the news system ever since (Chen, 2011).

World War II and the Media

The professionalization of the press was intensified by the World War II experience. As in World War I, all the involved governments actively worked to direct the media. In the fascist powers, control included censorship and direct production of news and entertainment by ministers like Josef Goebbels in Germany. In the USSR, media control rested with the party-state. In Britain, the broadcast authority, the BBC, functioned as a semi-official propaganda bureau, while the press presented a more complicated problem.

The British press had matured by the 1930s into an industrially concentrated combination of national dailies, national Sunday papers, and provincial dailies and weeklies. Roughly half of the circulation of the British press overall was under the control of a handful of companies, most of them controlled by press barons who tended to be conservative politically. Before the war, some of them had flirted with fascism, and some had supported Prime Minister Neville Chamberlain's line of appeasement, but none were officially anti-war in 1939. The exception was the communist press, led by the *Daily Worker*.

At the outset of the war, a set of regulations was passed giving the Home Secretary the authority to regulate the media under the rubric of maintaining morale. One of these, Regulation 2D, allowed him to ban any paper that published material "calculated to foment opposition" to the war (Curran and Seaton, 2009: 56). The *Daily Worker* was shut down under this provision, though it was later allowed to resume publication after its editorial line changed to reflect the USSR's entry into the war on the side of the Allies. More complicated were cases of publications that supported the war but criticized the Churchill government's prosecution of it. One newspaper that particularly irked Churchill was the tabloid *Daily Mirror*. The *Mirror* had been conservative in tone before the war, but several factors encouraged it to migrate leftward during the war, as James Curran has pointed out. One was a shortage of newsprint. Newsprint supplies had always influenced the news industry, and usually in the direction of concentrated ownership. Shortages tended to favor market leaders, after all, and when new technologies began to alleviate shortages, this ironically produced a new economy of scale that also favored market leaders. But the war produced shortages that in turn entailed government rationing. This meant a reduced number of pages for all newspapers, which also meant a reduction in the space available for advertising. That in turn meant a decline in advertising revenue relative to circulation. So it became more important to serve readers than to serve advertisers. And because tabloid readers tended to be downscale, that meant becoming more friendly editorially to the Labour Party (Curran and Seaton, 2009: 58–62). The dynamic of the war effort itself also tended to promote collective interests and a social welfare agenda. So the *Mirror* came to look like a political enemy to Churchill. But when he tried to act against it, his Cabinet resisted, and then the Commons resisted, appealing to a broad interest in maintaining freedom of the press. Much of the tension eased when the war effort took a positive turn for the Allies in 1942–3, and Britain did not exercise the kind of press control that the mainstream press would have found hostile.

In the US, an Office of War Information (OWI) was formed in June 1942, six months after US entry into the war. It censored reports related to the war, but also produced and encouraged news, images, and information. It was led by Elmer Davis, a veteran of the *New York Times* as well as a radio commentator. Because of an overwhelming consensus on the necessity of the war effort, journalists enjoyed almost unlimited access to troops and battle zones. The military and the OWI were only somewhat concerned that war correspondents might violate secrecy or propriety; in fact, World War II correspondents seem in retrospect to have been as integrated into the war effort as nineteenth-century partisan editors were into their party's organization. Symbolic of this integration were figures like Ernie Pyle, a roving reporter for the Scripps-Howard owned *Washington Daily News*, who began reporting on the war in 1940, during the aerial phase of the war known as the Battle of Britain. After US entry, he traveled with the infantry in Europe and then in the Pacific, sharing their hardships and relaying their point of view in a syndicated column that appeared in 400 newspapers. Pyle was the archetype of the World War II correspondent. He identified with the troops, referring to them as "we," and calling himself their "mouthpiece." He became a public symbol of the appropriate relationship of news media to the war effort; after his death in battle in the Pacific, his war reporting became the subject of a movie, *GI Joe*.

But the media did see a danger in this arrangement. Ironically, both the news industry and the film industry had been at odds with federal policies in the years preceding the war. The leading press lords, like Hearst and Col. Robert McCormick of the *Chicago Tribune*, were anything but objective in their rejection of Roosevelt's New Deal. The news industry and the film industry, which had always been hostile to labor organizing among its artists, craftspersons, and talent, vigorously opposed the pro-labor initiatives begun under the National Recovery Act and continued by the National Labor Relations Act, one side effect of which was the breakout growth of the Newspaper Guild (Leab, 1970).

The war presented media owners with conflicting interests. On the one hand, demonstrating their patriotism and public-spiritedness would help them win the confidence of a public that had questioned their hatred of the New Deal and had worried about their undue influence in the halls of power. On the other hand, the cooperative arrangement with the OWI, if it worked too well, might look like it should be made permanent. If fascism proved anything about the media, it was that government management of the media system could be very effective. Media owners preferred that business return to normal immediately after the war.

The end of World War II provided an opportunity for the victors to rebuild much of the world's media systems. In the vanquished countries of Japan and Germany, Allied occupiers designed media systems that included strong market-based sectors coupled with significant public-service elements including national broadcasting. In both cases, the pre-war media were carefully purged of fascist influences. In liberated countries, such as South Korea, which had been under Japanese colonial authority for decades, a similar process occurred (Cha, 1994). The media systems that the Allied powers imposed after the war reflected an emerging settlement of the competing interests in their domestic media systems. This settlement was fully articulated in Britain's Royal Commission on the Press, and in the so-called Hutchins Commission Report in the US (Commission on Freedom of the Press, 1947), as well as in the liberal language of the emerging UN regime, especially the Universal Declaration of Human Rights. These enshrined a set of relationships defined by the master terms "mass communication," "objectivity," and "the marketplace of ideas," and produced what Dan Hallin has called the "high modernism" of journalism (Hallin, 1992).

Postwar Media and Responsibility

Henry Luce had become deeply concerned about the post-war media order shortly after the war had begun. By World War II, his news magazines had come to be an empire, and he had added ventures in the newer media too, including the *March of Time* syndicated radio newscasts and film newsreels. Luce thought it was a matter of urgency for the future of the US media that deep thought should be devoted to how the press, and with it the notion of freedom of the press, had changed in the twentieth century. Luce tapped Robert Hutchins to lead this effort. Hutchins was simply the most famous educator in the US – the president of the University of Chicago as well as chairman of the Book of the Month club. Hutchins assembled a blue-ribbon panel of deep thinkers, including Archibald MacLeish, a poet and writer who had served in the Office of War Information; Zechariah Chafee, Harvard Law professor and arguably the nation's foremost thinker on the First Amendment; Arthur Schlesinger, Sr, one of the nation's leading historians; and Reinhold Niebuhr, the most prominent Protestant theologian. The commission began its work while the war was still in progress. It interviewed important figures in the media, government, and the academy, including many of the most powerful media owners and many members of the working press.

Its work climaxed in 1947 with the publication of *A Free and Responsible Press*. In that succinct report, the commission argued that grand changes in the structure of the media and the nature of society had conferred upon journalism the responsibility for explaining the world, representing the society, and clarifying or formulating values for an increasingly challenged citizenry. Much of the report reads like a direct translation of criticisms of the media business from

Upton Sinclair and Will Irwin on (Pickard, 2010; Pickard, 2014). Media businesses had become so powerful that they no longer looked like the "press" in the First Amendment. Freedom of the press, the commission found, had been invented for the numerous little newspapers that competed in the early Republic's marketplace. Modern newspaper chains resembled Standard Oil and US Steel more than *Porcupine's Gazette*. Modern agencies of mass communication constituted radically different networks of relationships than the printerly newspapers for which the theory of freedom of the press had been constructed. The eighteenth century could pretend that freedom for the press was the people's freedom, but the twentieth century really could not. In fact, and to a certain extent in law, freedom of the press had come to be the property of the press rather than of the people.

The Hutchins Commission therefore suggested a new rationale for freedom of the press. If the press now referred to the agencies of mass communication, then freedom of the press should be understood as something the people entrust to the press to exercise on their behalf. Ultimately, it was the people who owned freedom of the press, but they loaned it to the press. Moreover, people had freedom of expression not because it was their natural right but because it was their moral right. They had a moral right to freedom of expression because it was their duty as citizens to speak out on behalf of truth and justice. The justification of this moral freedom was utilitarian. The society needed the people to exercise their moral right to free expression for the society to remain fair and progressive. The justification for freedom of the press was also utilitarian. The press allowed an active citizenry to be knowledgeable and to participate in public deliberations. Only inasmuch as the press served these purposes did it deserve its freedom.

The commission did not recommend changing First Amendment law. The legal rights of the media would remain the same as ever, and, because corporations were considered to be fictional persons under the law, these rights would be understood as identical to the rights of any individual citizen. But the commission drew attention to the sociological and philosophical absurdity of this legal status. This made media owners nervous. They denounced the commission's report as the first step on a slippery slope to government control and unlimited censorship (Hughes, 1950).

Working journalists, however, found much to agree with in the commission's work. The requirements the Commission announced for the press corresponded rather well to the journalist's sense of what a professional should strive for. The commission bestowed a tremendous leadership role on journalism, expecting it to not only explain the world to citizens but to orient citizens morally toward that world, to articulate for them the "ideals and values of the society." Although the commission accorded journalists an elevated role, it suggested that journalists had not yet lived up to that elevation. Journalists resented this criticism. They thought that they had done a pretty good job already of meeting the requirements.

The Hutchins Commission's work is both at the heart of twentieth-century journalism and completely irrelevant to it. The commission expressed the ideals of a professional press better than perhaps anyone else. It also comprehended the realities of the modern media system quite well. Why then call it irrelevant? Well, because it refused to bring its realism and its idealism fully to bear on each other. It announced responsibilities for the press, and, as ideals, these became incorporated into journalism ethics. But journalists don't run the media. Media owners do. And, increasingly, media owners are publicly held corporations legally obligated to maximize shareholder return on investment. They couldn't exercise journalistic responsibility if they wanted to, unless they could justify it economically. Journalists were then and are now constrained by this economic structure. But professionalism generally, and the Hutchins Commission particularly, pretend that journalists are autonomous and independent, and that they therefore have the capacity to do the work required. They didn't and they don't, but, in the years immediately following World War II, it was easier to believe that they did.

At almost the same time as the Hutchins Commission published its report, a British Royal Commission on the Press produced a similar document. In the British case, a similar reckoning with wartime media policy was involved, though the inquiry began later than in the US and had been prompted more specifically by party politics. At the end of the war, a Labour Party government had come into power. During a protracted economic recovery it maintained many wartime practices such as rationing of consumer goods, but found itself facing continual criticism from the press, most of which remained solidly conservative. Labour activists thought the press unreasonably hostile, while newspapers feared what they saw as government ambitions to control the flow of information and to stifle criticism. Continuing controversy led to the appointment of a Royal Commission in 1947 (Williams, 2010: 178–80).

Like the Hutchins Commission, the Royal Commission noted strong trends toward industrial concentration. But it rejected the notion that the press was monopolized, and turned away from structural remedies for problems of representation in the press. The commission suggested that "free enterprise" would allow the press system to present all the appropriate information and points of view and to represent all the principal class, social, and ideological groups, so that democratic deliberation could properly function (Curran and Seaton, 2009: 348).

Instead, the Royal Commission established a national Press Council that would in theory work as a conscience for the news industry. The Press Council offered citizens a mechanism to lodge complaints and seek redress, and supposedly would encourage more responsible and professional behavior on the part of the press. It is a point of contention whether it made a difference. British news culture, with a more active oversight role and more restrictive range of legal protections, remained significantly more raucous than its US counterpart.

The High Modern Moment

Factors combined to make the press seem professional and responsible in the years following World War II. The institutionalization of the press on both sides of the world divided by the Cold War provided the kind of monopoly on the journalistic field that made claims to professional status seem reasonable and appropriate. This was particularly clear in the former Soviet Union and its satellites, where party-controlled state offices monitored the media system, and required licensing for practicing journalists. In institutional terms, Soviet journalism was closer to the kind of profession that medicine represents than any place in the west. In Italy, it became a requirement that one pass an examination to join the official union of journalists, but political conditions were such that practicing journalists tended nevertheless to be plainly partisan, a situation that would persist. Elsewhere in the west, licensing was rare.

But the institutional structure of the news system in most western countries supported professionalization. In most countries, a core of national newspapers coupled with a national broadcasting authority dominated the news system. The journalists who staffed these prestige media generally formed an ideologically coherent group that had learned during the war to assimilate to an equally ideologically coherent political class. Political contests proceeded within agreed-upon frameworks, and professional journalism took on the role of ensuring it all made sense to serious people. Journalism had the capacity to ensure the world made sense because of its institutional power. It had become, in the words of Timothy Cook, part of the governing process (Cook, 1998).

Television journalism became the most stylized corner of the profession. National broadcasts featured somber newsreaders who drew authority from the obvious realism of the accompanying filmed display of current events. Although at first confined to headlines and brief reports, national television newscasts expanded in the 1960s to present apparently thoughtful accounts of the day's events. In the US, the television coverage of the Kennedy assassination, which preempted regular programming and featured live tracking of the unfolding aftermath, became the central moment in the profession's memory of itself (Zelizer, 1992). At the same time, prompted by licensing expectations, local television stations turned their news departments and their signature evening broadcasts into their primary producer of original content. Although daily newspapers continued to set the agenda for national news systems as a whole, ordinary citizens began in the 1970s to report that they relied more on television for news (Gans, 1979).

By the 1960s, journalism had entered a stage that Dan Hallin has called "high modernism" (Hallin, 1992). The press, characterized by a relatively monopolistic set of industrially organized companies, had become an institution, charged with a public responsibility and armed with an ideology and canons of ethics, and capable of creating and preserving cultural hegemony.

By the mid-1960s, the press on both sides of the Atlantic could point with pride to achievements as an institution of independent moral criticism that seemed to justify its professional status. In Britain, a team of investigative reporters at the *Sunday Times* had shocked the nation with its revelations of birth defects related to the drug thalidomide. This series, like W. T. Stead's famous *Maiden Tribute* series in 1885, or Ida Tarbell's investigations of Standard Oil at the turn of the century, established a genre, in which corporate malfeasance was concealed by a complicitous government, and courageous but helpless citizens struggled in vain until fearless journalists, protected by a powerful media enterprise, drew public attention to the problem. In a world of big business and big government, the people need big media to get justice. Led by pioneering editor Harold Evans, the "Insight" team at the *Sunday Times* became the most famous crew of investigative reporters in the English-speaking world, and produced a number of equally spectacular revelations, including exposing the notorious spy Kim Philby (Evans, 2009).

In the US, the most impressive journalistic accomplishment was arguably coverage of the Civil Rights movement (Alexander, 2007). But the relationship of mainstream news organizations to the movement also underscores some of the ironies of the high modern moment.

First, and most obviously, the moral voice of the press as an institution took its sweet time making itself heard. For a century after the Civil War, the industrializing press and then the professionalizing press collaborated in repressing the "race problem." With the exception of a few northern liberal newspapers and far fewer southern eccentrics, the white press gladly accepted the narrative of racial inferiority and innate criminality that justified second-class status. The black press, on the contrary, was outspoken, especially as newspapers like the *Chicago Defender* acquired a national presence and considerable commercial power in the 1910s and 1920s. These papers never acquired recognition in the mainstream public, but they did produce a generation of able reporters who were available to be recruited by mainstream news organizations when their racial calculations changed in the 1950s (Roberts and Klibanoff, 2006).

The national political calculus of race changed in the 1950s because of global and domestic shifts. Globally, World War II had unleashed a wave of decolonization; the most dramatic peaceful example was the liberation of India under the leadership of Gandhi; the most dramatic violent example was the long war for national liberation in Vietnam. The leftward shift in US politics in the 1960s can be seen as at least in part a response to this global tide of decolonization. The Civil Rights movement in fact saw itself as part of this wave of change. Martin Luther King, Jr, famously read Gandhi, and activists looked to the newly independent nations of Africa for inspiration. The US government, positioned geopolitically as a sponsor of democracy, offered some material and much rhetorical support to decolonization, even while fighting against it in Vietnam and elsewhere. This put the Federal government in an uncomfortable spot. Racial apartheid in the US violated both US rhetoric and global moral sense. On the other hand, southern votes remained crucial to gaining power in Washington.

The Civil Rights movement achieved its signal successes in the 1960s because the Democratic Party changed its national posture. In the 1960s, John Kennedy had won the presidency with a large turnout of African American voters, even while the party's southern wing still included diehard segregationists. For a brief time, it was possible for the national party to oppose segregation while the southern wing embraced it. This strange pas de deux could not endure, however, and in the aftermath of the legislative landmarks of the 1960s the southern states turned to an increasingly white Republican Party.

In the brief moment of racial detente in the Democratic Party, national news organizations were able to position themselves as unproblematic champions of desegregation. It helped that there was a radical black power movement on the left of the Civil Rights movement, of course; having extremists on the left made it possible to depict the resisters in the south as extremists on the right. But it would be churlish to deny that the press as an institution came to play an important enabling role in promoting racial equality in the 1960s.

The classic journalism of the high modern moment, like the London *Sunday Times* series on thalidomide or US coverage of the Civil Rights movement, shows the redemptive possibilities of an institutionalized objective press. But it also underscores how many things have to fall into place for the good guys to win. When the structures of the high modern moment came under strain in the final decades of the twentieth century, many worried that an agency of great moral authority would weaken. Without the press, public life would have no referee. On the upside, though, good things might come of having more players and fewer rules.

6

The Late Modern Press, the Digital Media, and the Network Public

The high modern moment of journalism always depended on a series of bottlenecks for its infrastructure. In the western countries, these consisted of monopolies – the natural monopolies of wire services and local daily newspapers, and the state monopolies on broadcasting. In the communist countries, state and party monopolies performed the same function. In both west and east, the ethos of professionalism concealed deep ideological tensions between the tendency for professional knowledge to be privileged and journalists' commitment to publication. The infrastructure provided spaces to control information flows, which in turn seemed to require professional behavior from journalists, and journalism responded by creating university training and codes of ethics. But no one was able to answer the fundamental question of the intellectual basis of all this. Professionalism in medicine has been legitimated by the development of medical science, but there is no journalism science.

Moreover, it was never the journalists who controlled the bottlenecks. In the west, journalists answered to the people who owned news organizations; in the east, they answered to state and party bureaucracies. Even in the public-service sector of the social democracies, the autonomy of journalists was circumscribed by forms of politically influenced supervision, and managers remained aware of their reliance on continued funding. So the professionalization project proved a curse for journalists. It conferred responsibility but not power. Professional journalism has always lacked the capacity to perform the functions that the high modern moment expected. This lack of capacity has been evident even in the moments that professional journalism has cherished as its greatest accomplishments.

In the final decades of the twentieth century the bottlenecks began to erode. The social democracies rejected state-owned monopolies in favor of market forces, often foreign-owned. In market systems, cable and satellite TV, talk radio, and free weeklies and dailies challenged the supremacy of monopoly media. The collapse of the Soviet Bloc after 1989 and the rise of market-based systems in eastern Europe, followed by the development of the Internet in the 1990s, accelerated these changes. At the same time, surging economies in East Asia produced hybrid authoritarian market systems.

The end of the twentieth century thus produced a global crisis in journalism. In the United States, this began with a crisis in credibility that preceded the erosion of media markets. The news media became aware of a disconnect with their publics in the reaction to Reagan administration news control during the Grenada invasion in 1983. Media organizations responded by initiating projects to monitor public opinion on the press and to educate people on the importance of an adversary press in democratic systems. Another response came in the form of the public journalism movement. But the intensification of media conglomeration and vertical and horizontal integration reinforced public suspicion of the mainstream media, and the encroachment of digital competitors weakened the business models of news organizations.

The age of professional mass media seemed to be in eclipse not because of public opinion or press behavior, but because of the long arc of mobile privatization (Williams, 1974). Technologies reinforced social practices (including marketing behavior) that disaggregated mass audiences into audience fragments. The resulting network public provides new challenges for the system of public intelligence.

The End of the Age of Mass Communication

Structural changes in the years since 1960 have altered the relationship between individuals and the media. Walter Lippmann's major insight, discussed in the last chapter, has to do with the increasing gap between the worlds inside people's heads and the big world outside. Lippmann drew attention to this gap in 1922. In the years that followed, the gap was institutionalized in the form of a professionalizing press and culture industries marketing mass-produced fictions to a mass audience. By the 1950s, all sorts of observers complained of a "mass society." To radicals and conservatives alike, the forms of cultural regimentation and alienation created by mass media threatened democracy; responsible leadership from news professionals was essential as a kind of compensation.

Since the 1960s, the fear of mass culture has waned. It's not just that generations have now grown up on TV, but that TV too has changed. Where before tight groups of national broadcasters controlled most programming, competing national and international channels available by broadcast or through cable and satellite arose, as well as a seemingly limitless range of digital content. Similarly, film production has exploded into new formats. Not that industrial control has disappeared. A few global companies still command a huge share of the total media universe. But they provide individual members of the public with remarkably more choices than the last generation imagined possible. This combination of tight economic control at bottlenecks with a vast array of personal choices is characteristic of the late modern moment of the media.

Perhaps the clearest example of how the late modern culture industries operate is the recorded music industry. Music has always been a way for societies to express their repressed tensions and discontents, and in the twentieth century popular music had offered a platform for marginal or non-mainstream performers. African Americans especially have dominated popular music in certain periods – think of the global influence of jazz and blues. At the beginning of the twenty-first century, the list of best-selling artists worldwide featured a disproportionate number of rap and hip hop performers. Music has also been a way of expressing frustration with cultural norms. The career of rock music exemplifies this.

Rock emerged at a particular conjuncture of US social, cultural, and media history. In the 1950s, a large youth population with some disposable income and a restlessness with conventional morality encountered the medium of radio, which had recently been emerging from the dominance of network programming. Before World War II, network radio had featured sitcoms, soaps, news shows, and game shows that were vehicles for national product advertising. After World War II, television displaced radio from this role. Then, instead of seeking mass audiences for national product advertising, radio came to seek segmented audiences, like youth, and to feature cheaper programming, like recorded music. So the medium for rock appeared at the same time as its audience. Meanwhile, recording technology remained at a stage where individual entrepreneurs could readily enter. This permitted a flow of new sounds.

Within a fairly short time, concentration appeared at the center of the rock music industry. A few large labels, all now part of international media conglomerates, came to control the vast majority of music revenues. But this core of vertically integrated companies has never been able to capture and plan the next hit sound. The appeal of rock has a lot to do with rebellion and innovation. The element that makes a hit song or performer is inscrutable, charismatic: it can't be formulated.

As a result, rock, like many other culture industries, requires a large frontier of independent producers at the edge of the dominant core. The periphery – local garage bands, inner-city dance clubs, or, in Louis Armstrong's day, the sounds of New Orleans whorehouses – produces music that unpredictably captures the ears of large audiences. The major labels have been successful at signing artists who are emerging from this frontier, and they invest a great deal of money in identifying and recruiting new talent. They never have and never will be able to produce it raw. The same situation arises with film. New talent emerges unpredictably, in independent movies, in Hong Kong, on Mexican telenovelas, in Bollywood or Nollywood. The major distributors maneuver to capture talent with charisma.

This balance of core and periphery works quite well economically. The major firms displace risk on to the independents. The independents, meanwhile, are motivated not just by profit but also by something else – artistic vision, integrity, a sense of what's cool, politics. To the majors, these concerns of their recruited talent are inconsequential.

This means there is a disconnect between the cultural meanings of the product and its economic impact. Sixties' rock bands like the Grateful Dead or the Jefferson Airplane believed that they were creating music with meanings that would help alter the social order. The revenues from this music flowed to those most invested in the social order, who showed little concern for the content of the music they profited from – though they preferred love songs.

Mass audiences have waned, and the disconnect between cultural meanings and economic impact has grown stronger. The marketing logic of the culture industries has become more sophisticated, and media companies are now much better at targeting narrower audiences. The more abundant media environment has made it possible for people to locate and purchase the music, TV shows, and films they find most appealing. But the share of the market that goes to the largest transnational conglomerates has continued to grow.

The firms created by industrialization in its classic phase were monopolies, like Standard Oil and US Steel: huge, lumbering beasts with massive torsos and tiny heads. They were dinosaurs. In communications, the dinosaurs were Western Union, Reuters, AT&T, the BBC, *Time Magazine*. There is much in the late modern moment to indicate that the age of the dinosaurs may be ending. Mass-circulation magazines started to falter by 1980, yielding to magazines that targeted narrower consumer interests (Abrahamson, 1996). Radio changed earlier, especially on the FM dial. (Rothenbuhler and McCourt, 2002). Television has migrated steadily away from the mass audience, till now only extraordinary events like the World Cup Final capture as high a percentage of viewers as regular programming did in the late 1950s. The new media are supposed to be rapid, darting, shifty critters – the age of dinosaurs has ended, and the era of the mouse has begun.

The mouse is the symbol of Disney and a metonymic term for the computer. Disney is a remarkable example of the emergence of the new media conglomerate. It began as a specialized film company – not a major, but one that targeted a niche audience with high-quality animation. From there it spread to other areas of the entertainment industry, most famously theme parks. It also began to aggressively market products associated with its movies – clothing, toys, books. It was one of the great movers in the 1980s, beginning to produce more and different kinds of movies through subsidiaries. It also moved into cable television. Perhaps its most remarkable new revenue stream came from videos. Before the introduction of home video, Disney's film catalog made money only at release or through television. After home video, old movies like *Sleeping Beauty* or *Pinocchio* became steady sellers. By the beginning of the twenty-first century, the company had also merged with ABC, and had come to control some of the most lucrative cable networks, including ESPN. So the mouse in this case is the highly diversified media giant.

But the mouse also symbolizes the conduit through which much of the public now encounters the new diversified media. Especially for younger audiences, time online surpasses time spent in front of the television, and TV content is increasingly accessed on mobile devices. The computerization of the media has occurred at every level, of course, not just in transmission but also in production.

Digital media promise a new kind of media public sphere with enhanced diversity and new interactivity. You can answer back in ways you couldn't to your dinosaur media. Whether public life will be transformed remains to be seen.

But it is already obvious that digital media have allowed for a great increase in commercialization. The web is a very rich marketing environment, allowing retailers to profile and target particular consumers, and allowing consumers to quickly shop and compare prices. So the web presents the same aspect as the late modern media generally – very wide choice for consumers, yet increasing concentration at a number of bottlenecks. Dominant firms, like Microsoft, Google, Apple, Verizon, Comcast, and Cisco, all enjoy something like a monopoly at a crucial bottleneck in the transmission system, and in some cases are leveraging that monopoly into content-provision. Proliferating choice at the bottom is wedded with concentration at the top.

The changing media environment challenges and stimulates public communication. On the one hand, the media environment no longer gives nations a unified set of texts and information. In the US, in the age of the dinosaur media, you could talk with strangers about last night's TV news with a fair degree of confidence that they would either know what you were talking about or not think it strange that you should expect them to. This is no longer the case. Fewer people now watch the President's State of the Union address. In any random group of young people, it is harder and harder to find movies that everyone has seen. Even though media use has grown, the store of common knowledge has shrunk.

At the same time, the late modern moment seems to invite more voices into the realm of public discourse. The chatter from cable TV, talk radio, and social media has infiltrated the post from which the high modern media "gatekeep" the arena of public discussion. When the Hutchins Commission defined the responsibilities of the media, it assumed that their size and level of organization allowed them to be responsible and effective gatekeepers – that they could shut out the fascists and racists, for instance, and enforce decorum. But the news media in particular lost their grip on the flow of public discussion in the years following Vietnam. This has involved another reconfiguration of the media's relation to the public sphere.

The News Media and the Shifting Public Sphere

The institutionalized press, the high modern manifestation of the news media, implied a particular model of the public sphere. In any modern public sphere, there is a bifurcation between an active and a passive public sphere. The active public sphere is the realm where empowered persons engage in interactive deliberation and discussion. A legislature, for instance, is a locus of the active public sphere, as is a presidential press conference. The passive public sphere is the realm where ordinary people observe the active public sphere as it is represented to an anonymous and indefinite public. Ordinary people enter into the active public sphere only rarely and peripherally. There is a chance that a letter you write to your local newspaper or to your congressional representatives will attract attention. But typically you will not have a voice in the active public sphere. Your letter will be tallied, your opinion will be surveyed, and your vote will be counted as a number, not as a voice. You will not have the opportunity to persuade. Instead, your voice will be delegated to a representative, and you will (passively) observe your representatives in action. If you are a member of the American Association of Retired Persons (AARP), for instance, or of the National Rifle Association (NRA), or of the United Automobile Workers (UAW), you can expect that organization to speak on your behalf in the active public sphere. In any modern public sphere, there has been such a delegation, or a mechanism of representation, or a bifurcation. In the high modern period, this meant that voices that mattered were relatively few, privileged, and coherent (Verba et al., 1995).

In any modern public sphere, the media play a role in the bifurcation. The media are part of the mechanism of representation. They represent the passive public to the active public, and the active public to the passive public. So, for instance, partisan editors in the nineteenth century represented their readers both in the pages of their newspapers and in the deliberations of their party committees and caucuses. At the same time, they represented the party leaders for the reading public. They did this as partisan advocates, with clear preferences and voices and, to their local readers, faces. Their representation was explicit. Prior to the partisan press, a different kind of press, one claiming to serve rational liberty through an ideology of impartiality and impersonality, represented the active public through pseudonymous "contributions." In that public sphere, the mechanisms of representation were more opaque. Editors claiming to be above party allegiances kept the identities of their writers secret, trying to give the impression that they were simply ordinary citizens writing as "Publius" or "A Farmer" or "Cato," even if they were actually James Madison or John Adams.

The high modern moment, the moment of professionalization and the institutionalized press, combined explicit and opaque representation. The journalist, now often visible on TV, was clearly an agent, but she was not supposed to be an explicit participant, like the partisan editor. Nor was she supposed to be an ordinary citizen. She was a kind of supercitizen, much smarter and more discerning than you. In objective journalism, she was also a non-person, one who suppressed her own interests as a citizen, to the extent that some refused to vote. She thereby earned access to the deliberations of the active public sphere. She could question the president on your behalf. Her learned impersonality authorized her to represent you to the president and the president to you.

The function of representing the public has evolved in a similar fashion wherever there has been an industrialized news system. The US has been atypical in many ways – other nations' media are mostly less commercialized and less pious about objectivity and First-Amendment-style independence from government – but the place of journalists in the process of representing the public has been similar. One could argue that US journalists are more alienated than, say, Italian journalists, who work for media with more explicit political allegiances, but this is beside the point. In both systems, journalists are professionals involved as experts in the process of representing the public.

The high modern moment claimed that this mode of representation was better, more democratic, than other modes, like partisanism. It promised the people that it would ideally serve the combined interests of both the active and the passive public spheres. In the active public sphere, the professional journalist would be a probing, disinterested seeker of truth and exposer of falsehood and corruption. The professional journalist would be above the game of power and able to referee it. At the same time, in the passive public sphere, ordinary citizens could be assured that the representations they observed were authoritative and reliable. The professional journalist would filter out the distortions and propaganda of the powerful and allow ordinary people to see what was truly going on, behind the idealized images that the powerful sought to erect. They would be our bullshit detectors.

The high modern moment has waned. As newer media have elbowed their way into the active public sphere, professional journalists have seen their always ad hoc monopoly on news practice dwindle. With it have slid many of the standards of professional conduct. Meanwhile, interactive media have promised ordinary citizens that they may have access to the public sphere without having to rely on journalists, that they can represent themselves. New forms of the public sphere have been created online. Many of them straddle the modern divide between active and passive publics. Some would hail this as a postmodern moment. I prefer to call it late modern, noting the endurance of modern forms of distributing power.

From the vantage point of the late modern, we can look back to the high modern and try to judge whether it really did live up to its claims. Did the ideology of objectivity and the pull of professionalization allow journalists to better represent the public? Did it describe the working of the public sphere? Or did it function as a useful ideal, giving journalists something to strive for, something they could not, perhaps, attain, but could approach, and in the striving make the world a better place? Or did it simply mystify the way power was distributed by making people think that they were represented, when in fact they were only spectators? If we judge the ideology of the high modern moment to be a description of practice or an ideal for practice, then it has been useful and we should try to preserve it. If we judge it a mystification, then we should hope it passes quickly and something better replaces it.

The best tests of high modern journalism are the moments that the professionalizers take the most pride in.

Vietnam and Watergate

In the collective memory of journalists, the 1970s was the strong time of the profession. In the first part of the decade, the news media humbled a presidency in Watergate and ended a war in Vietnam. These twin accomplishments seemed to prove that journalism had become what the professionalizers had promised – an independent agency of criticism, an adversary of entrenched power. On closer examination, neither of these triumphs seems all that convincing. Let's begin with Act I, Vietnam.

US involvement in Vietnam began accidentally and ended tragically. The end of World War II began a wave of decolonization throughout Asia and Africa; Indochina had been a French colony, and local nationalists waged a successful war of liberation that culminated in a stunning defeat for the French in 1952. After agreeing to a cease-fire and then a plebiscite, the French withdrew from the scene and the US moved in. The US feared that the nationalist movement would deliver the region to the Soviet Union, and therefore opposed the plebiscite, instead supporting a conservative regime in the south of the country, and in effect triggering a 20-year-long civil war, in which the north drew support from communist regimes and the south from the US, Australia, and other western powers.

Direct involvement in fighting in Vietnam began during the Kennedy administration and accelerated dramatically during the Johnson administration. Claiming Cold War necessities, both Kennedy and Johnson skirted constitutional restrictions on using the military, a policy that Richard Nixon continued. By 1965, 184,300 US troops were in Vietnam. The number would increase to over half a million in 1968, and the network news carried weekly tallies of US, South Vietnamese, and Vietcong casualties. By the end of the war, 56,000 US soldiers and between 2 and 3 million Vietnamese combatants and civilians had been killed, the north prevailed, and everyone agreed that US policy had been disastrous for all concerned, though people disagreed as to why.

In the US, hawks argued that the war effort had failed because it had been half-hearted. Had the US prosecuted the war with full vigor, the south would have prevailed and would have become a viable independent country. But the military had had its hands tied by the politicians, who in turn had been cowed by the media. To hawks, the reporters had lost the war. This was preventable, they argued – if reporters had been kept in check, and information restricted, the US press would not have become a propaganda instrument of the enemy. Instead, naive US reporters told a frustrated public that the war was unwinnable, and that US forces and their South Vietnamese proxies were committing hideous atrocities in a losing effort. Faced with a flood of embarrassing images, with a TV war that brought the carnage into everyone's living room, and with a returning tide of disenchanted veterans and body bags, the electorate turned against the war and the Congress followed.

To doves, the war was evil in its conception and prosecution, and the press had done heroic work in ending it. The South Vietnamese puppet regime oppressed its own people, who hated it and would have overthrown it had not a US army of occupation propped it up. In fact, far from being a war on behalf of the people, the US was waging a war against the people. In his memoirs, Colin Powell, who would become famous as the victor in the Persian Gulf War and as Secretary of State, recalls US policy by invoking Ho Chi Minh, the leader of the north, who said "the people were like the sea in which his guerillas swam." Powell continued: "We tried to solve the problem by making the whole sea uninhabitable," by torching villages and crops, and sometimes by killing civilians (Powell, 1995: 87). The bloodiness of this policy was brought home in reports about a massacre at My Lai. In the anti-war view, heroic journalists like Seymour Hersh, who won the Pulitzer for his reporting on My Lai, and David Halberstam, whose dispatches poked holes in official accounts of military success, supported by fearless editors in New York and Washington, humbled and crippled the war effort, while television, again bringing the carnage into living rooms, elevated public disgust. The media served notice that US chieftains wouldn't get away with their abuses, and thus saved democracy.

To both hawks and doves, the media played a crucial role. Both sides have lived long and have nourished their memories; emotions over Vietnam still run strong. In 1998, CNN aired a news report, *Valley of Death*, on the use of chemical weapons by US forces in Operation Tailwind. The counterattack by veterans' groups and apologists for the military was so fierce that CNN apologized and punished the producers, who then sued for compensation and settled for large sums, reportedly around a million dollars apiece. One of the bizarre features of the controversy was the continuing ire against Jane Fonda, who had been one of the most famous anti-war activists, visiting North Vietnam during the War and earning the nickname Hanoi Jane. When *Valley of Death* was televised, Fonda was married to CNN owner Ted Turner; hawks saw her nefarious hand in the whole episode.

Both hawks and doves magnify the role of the press in the war, but there is surprisingly little historical evidence that the media helped end the war. One telling fact is that the army's own official investigator concluded that press coverage had little if anything to do with turning public opinion against the war. He argued that it was the body bags, not the *New York Times* or CBS, that turned people against the war (Hammond, 1998).

In fact, the press and especially television strongly supported the war effort until quite late in the game. Most accounts see 1968 as a turning point. In that year the US and South Vietnamese forces were stunned and humiliated by a northern offensive timed to coincide with Tet holidays. The penetration of Vietcong forces deep into urban areas in the south seemed to demonstrate the complete failure of a policy aimed at pacification. Walter Cronkite, the stalwart and highly trusted anchor of the CBS evening news, visited Vietnam and announced that the US was "mired in a stalemate." That moment figures in one of the right's more durable accounts – that the media misreported Tet as a US failure rather than a victory, and so caused a collapse of public support for the war (Braestrup et al., 1977; see also Herman and Chomsky's refutation: 1988: appendix 3). But this account doesn't ring true.

Cronkite's assessment is remembered as a thunderous rejection of the Pentagon's aims. Rereading it today, one can't help but notice how balanced it was. Even while casting doubt on the projections of "optimists," Cronkite allows that they might turn out right this time. Even more remarkable is his blanket endorsement of the nobility of the US war effort. It would be rare for the mainstream media to question the morality or motivations of the people who framed war goals and policies.

Media attitudes were well to the right of public opinion in both their optimism and their acceptance of the morality of the war. Long before the Tet offensive, the US public had turned against the war, and along with them a large chunk of the political leadership, including much of Congress and several leading presidential candidates. In this case, the media reluctantly followed public opinion, after balking at pursuing the claims of the heroic journalists on the ground, the Hershes and Halberstams. Reporting on the My Lai massacre, which occurred in the wake of the Tet offensive, shows the extent to which the really bad news of the war was kept out of the mainstream news media. Rumors of the massacre had spread through the military and among reporters in Vietnam in the months after it occurred. A report of it reached army Major Colin Powell's desk several months later – he was new to the theater of war then – and, after a cursory investigation, he concluded that there was nothing to it. As long as the rumors remained vague, the army was able to deny the massacre. Several months later, Vietnam veteran Ron Ridenhour began writing letters to Pentagon officials, members of Congress, and the White House, asking for an investigation into My Lai. By May 1969, the army had begun its investigation. The army's Inspector General in Vietnam looked into it for seven weeks and then recommended the investigation be shut down, but by then a separate investigation in the Pentagon had begun, which would lead to the prosecution of William Calley. Seymour Hersh had also begun pursuing the story, but his climactic article on the massacre would not appear until mid-November. Hersh himself was working as a freelancer at the time, not as a journalist on staff of a major news organization. So, even in this most dramatic case of critical Vietnam reporting, the story broke almost by accident, after an army cover-up failed, a heroic whistleblower had managed to alert investigators in several branches of the military, and a dynamic independent reporter had produced an account that could not be ignored.

But the press as a profession and as an institution has a real investment in the notion that the media ended the war in Vietnam. It has marked a key moment of validation for the professional mission of the press. In journalism's collective memory, the government set up a system of spreading official lies; the public was helpless in the face of it, and would have been consistently deluded and misinformed; but reporters, who were willing and able to face official disapproval and physical danger, got on the ground and got the facts. And this proves that, without the press to be their eyes and ears, the people will be helpless, and self-government cannot work.

For most of the war, the press as an institution had modified but not abandoned its World War II position as a friend of the enlisted man and a patriotic rallier of public opinion. Only a few journalists challenged official accounts before non-journalists had cast doubt on them. How different would the moral of this story be if we were to conclude that the press had in fact been a conduit for government misinformation?

In Vietnam, as in other moments in the history of journalism, there is a lack of fit between the tales of heroic journalists and the performance of the press as an institution. Undeniably, the energy, commitment, skill, and courage of specific war correspondents merit admiration. They represent the best in high modern journalism. But the performance of the institution of journalism was more determined by the set of relationships that structured its work in the governing process, and in this set of relationships, journalism as an institution has been dependent upon official sources and impotent when those sources are united. Only when things go seriously awry does journalism as an institution assert itself as an agency of independent moral criticism.

The Watergate story is inextricably bound up in Vietnam. It begins with the Pentagon Papers case. The Pentagon Papers were a secret history of US involvement in Vietnam commissioned by one of the architects of US policy, Robert McNamara, who was Secretary of Defense under Kennedy and Johnson. They were leaked to the press, and the *New York Times* and *Washington Post* began to publish lengthy excerpts. The Nixon administration went to court to put a stop to their publication, asking for a prior restraint for national security reasons. The documents were full of embarrassing details, but hardly contained the kind of information that would compromise US intelligence or endanger US troops. Moreover, all of the embarrassing misdeeds had been committed by Democratic presidents. Why did the always opportunistic Nixon want to prevent their publication? Probably because of a combination of factors – a deep suspicion of the press, an abiding interest in maintaining presidential privilege, a commitment to winning the political battles surrounding Vietnam, and a sense of being embattled by liberal forces. In any case, the Nixon administration's effort failed. The Supreme Court upheld the right of news organizations to publish the material without prior restraint (Rudenstine, 1998).

After this battle, the White House became obsessively sensitive to leaked information. Nixon's staff assembled a team of operatives, dubbed the "plumbers," who would go after leaks. Eventually this team was caught burglarizing the headquarters of the Democratic National Committee in the Watergate building in Washington during the presidential election campaign of 1972. The White House attempted to cover up its links to the crime, and eventually was found out, producing a cascade of embarrassing revelations about abuses of power that undercut Nixon's congressional support, fueled an impeachment drive, and forced him to resign.

In the common sense of journalists, two heroic reporters, Bob Woodward and Carl Bernstein, unraveled this whole fabric of abuses and concealments. In journalism's collective memory, Watergate is the defining moment (Schudson, 1992). And there are good instrumental reasons why this is so. In the conventional account of Watergate, just as in the conventional account of Vietnam, the people would have been helpless without the press. In the melodramatic account that Woodward and Bernstein authored, and in the even more melodramatic movie version of *All the President's Men*, the reporters are credited with saving democracy itself.

Surely this account is overblown. Edward Jay Epstein (1975) has argued that very few of the key revelations came from Woodward and Bernstein, or indeed any of the other reporters working on Watergate. Most came from the FBI or from congressional investigators, or from some other source within the Federal government: from the very institution that figures in the conventional account as a monolith of corruption. Most of the legendary information in Woodward and Bernstein's reporting concerned a kind of sideshow. When, many years later, the confidential source for much of this information became known, his identity as a high-ranking FBI official confirmed Epstein's surmise.

Nevertheless, it is true that, by the mid-1970s, popular attitudes toward the press had reached a remarkable level of respect. Journalism was closer than it had ever been to acquiring the aura of professional public service, and idealistic young men and women were drawn in larger numbers to the nation's journalism schools. It was because journalism had become recognized as an institution that politicians like Richard Nixon could gain advantage by claiming that they were victims of systematic bias (Ladd, 2012: 76–9) – even after 80 percent of the nation's newspapers had endorsed Nixon for President in 1968. In fact, recognition as a profession and an institution carried with it the causes of journalism's subsequent crisis.

In the early 1980s, it became clear that public support for critical journalism was rather soft. The wake-up call for the mainstream media was the US invasion of Grenada. The invasion of Grenada was the sort of maneuver that an aggressive adversarial press should have punished an administration for. Its justification was thin, its execution was clumsy, and its timing was more than suspect, following just two days after a suicide bomber's devastation of a marines barracks in Beirut, in which the Defense Department reported 241 deaths of US service personnel. During the invasion, reporters were kept uninformed and away from the action, presumably because of a need for military secrecy. In fact, media in neighboring Caribbean countries were able to report on ship movements, and journalists suspected that the operation was secret only from the American people.

But when journalists began to complain about secrecy and the manipulation of public opinion, they quickly sensed that the public seemed to side with the Reagan administration against the press. To members of the news media, this constituted a crisis of credibility, and hence a crisis for democracy. If the people did not trust the news media to be impartial and authoritative sources of information and commentary, then they would be defenseless before government and big business. Already anxious over declining daily newspaper circulations and a general sense of malaise in the news business, news executives began urgently asking how they could regain the public's confidence (MacNeil, 1985; Nimkoff, 2008).

Since the 1980s, the news media have become overly conscious about the gap between their own high seriousness and the public's perceived disrespect. News executives claimed that they didn't want to do pack journalism (Crouse, 1973), they didn't want to have "feeding frenzies" (Sabato, 1991), and they sure didn't want to do gavel-to-gavel coverage of the O. J. Simpson trial and Bill Clinton's impeachment hearings, but that a debased audience, jaded after years of overstimulation, demanded more and more titillation. The ratings, they say, prove it. Who watches PBS?

The attempt to cultivate a healthier relationship with the public took many forms. Programs like the Gannett (later Freedom Forum) Foundation or the Pew Charitable Trust's Center for the People and the Press intensively studied the problem. Gannett's First Amendment Center undertook an educational program, and has since performed annual surveys to test the public's grasp of the conventional version of First Amendment theory. Over the past three decades, one of the many findings that hasn't changed is that only about one in four identify freedom of the press as one of the rights guaranteed by the First Amendment. Three in five name freedom of speech, however. One suspects that, for many, freedom of expression *is* freedom of speech, whereas freedom of the press seems like a set of privileges for an industry.

Well-intentioned journalists and scholars in the 1990s developed the notion of public or civic journalism as a way of trying to recuperate public engagement in news and governance. They proposed to cultivate a larger public by finding ways to let it be active in the news, to set an agenda for news coverage, and to form itself into a self-aware community (Merritt, 1998; Rosen, 1999). On a theoretical level, the leaders of the public journalism movement had all read or read about Habermas's analysis of the public sphere; they had also been stunned by the argument behind Robert Putnam's seminal studies of declining "social capital" in US communities (Putnam, 1995). They were persuaded by Putnam's data that ordinary people simply had fewer human connections in their own localities, and they reasoned that news organizations, and especially daily newspapers, were among the few institutions outside of government that had both a capacity for and an interest in reaching all the groups in a town or city. Among the techniques favored by the public journalism movement were public forums, facilitated by journalists, in which community members could engage in direct dialog with elected officials and opinion leaders, setting the agenda for politics rather than passively responding. Public journalism also liked to survey communities.

The public journalism movement encountered fierce resistance from many professional journalists, especially at elite news organizations. They saw it as redirecting resources away from enterprise reporting and toward outreach activities that were the proper province of the marketing department. They also saw it as an attack on the characteristic detachment of the professional journalist. Public journalism, to them, was cheerleading; professional journalism was muckraking.

The public journalism movement waned after the turn of the century. Mostly this can be attributed to a migration of media reformism to the rapidly developing realm of Internet media, particularly the blogosphere. Public journalism seemed so twentieth century. It can also be attributed to a reordering of priorities after 9/11.

Neither the corporate media First Amendment offensive nor the public journalism movement made any measurable impact on popular attitudes toward the media. The First Amendment Center's annual surveys showed dramatic movement between 2001 and 2002, but this was almost entirely a short-term result of the reaction to 9/11. Moreover, it was ambivalent. The public was temporarily more approving of the main elements of the First Amendment, but it was less tolerant of non-western religions, and deeply skeptical of the rest of the Bill of Rights. Robert Putnam's surveys also showed a temporary increase in positive civic attitudes and behaviors among young people, who became more interested in trying to build a vibrant political community; but this too receded toward cynicism. Mainstream news media identified the disaffection of young people as a key to their prospects. They knew that readerships and viewerships had begun declining well before the wake-up call of the Grenada invasion, and were fully aware that they hadn't done much to cultivate the next generation of audiences. Newspapers in particular tried to recapture younger readers through schools, through special pages in the paper, and through spin-offs. In the first few years of the twenty-first century, for instance, the Chicago daily newspapers produced daily editions for young readers – the *Tribune*'s *Red Eye* and the *Sun-Times' Red Streak*. Sold at a lower price or given away free, they featured short, brisk news items with a heavy accent on night-life and lifestyle. In theory, they would cultivate an audience for the grown-up paper. More honestly, they were intended to capture advertising dollars from the city's thriving alternative press, especially the free weekly *Chicago Reader*.

None of these attempts proved successful. Young readers simply decline to be interested in conventional daily newspapers, network evening news, or all-news cable channels, which all serve an aging population – the average age of a Fox News viewer is now above 65 – and are stupid and boring to boot. The newer media have worked only when they express alienation toward the mainstream news media. The *Red Streak* folded, and the *Red Eye* survives as a free daily without producing new news audiences. But Jon Stewart's *The Daily Show*, a parody of a network news show on the cable channel Comedy Central, and other "fake news" projects have done quite well (Baym, 2009). News parodies have a long history on television, running back through *Saturday Night Live* to the genre-establishing British show *That Was the Week That Was*, which starred David Frost and nurtured writers and comics like famed children's writer Roald Dahl and Graham Chapman and John Cleese of Monty Python; its launch in November 1962, shows that parodies of television news are almost as old as television news itself. The success of fake news where "real news" has failed indicates that the nature of the problem has something to do with the seriousness and responsibility with which journalism as an institution views its function in the system of democratic governance. The real journalists have bought into Lippmann's analysis, but the ordinary people they mean to steward have not.

Meanwhile, however, the morbid fascination of the press with public approval seems to have left it uncomfortable with the role of adversary, watchdog, and advocate that the professional model assigned it. Many complained that, after Grenada, the press took a servile line toward the Reagan administration (Hertsgaard, 1988). Such criticism may be politically motivated, and certainly subsequent administrations got a fair share of sharp scrutiny from the press, but even in the case of the events leading to President Clinton's 1998 impeachment trial, it is remarkable how little "enterprise" reporting was involved. Even more so than in the Watergate scandal, the key revelations were made by partisans or congressional or judicial investigations. The journalists seemed to relay this material with little gatekeeping or original investigation. Their reliance on other news producers only increased after 9/11.

By the 1980s, then, and certainly by the 1990s, the professional press had come to seem a vulnerable institution. The people didn't trust it. The powers that be were able to manipulate it. Journalism no longer seemed the institution of public intelligence that it wanted to be. President George W. Bush could characterize it in a 2004 remark as just another "special interest" (Auletta, 2004).

The sense of malaise in journalism was exaggerated, however, because of the way its past had been mythologized. Popular distrust of the media was hardly new. The public had consistently voiced doubts about news media precisely because the public was so dependent on them. Nor was this doubt unique to the news media. In fact, the public doubted the news media's intentions and motivations in exactly the same register as it doubted the motives and intentions of all other powerful businesses. The real crisis was a crisis of identity for the news media. Throughout the high modernism of journalism, the media had conceived of themselves as responsible professionals, identifying with their superego and forgetting the material side of their operations. The public never lost sight of the id.

The Movement for a New World Information and Communication Order

The decline of post-World War II high modern journalism coincided with a recalibration of western hegemony in global communications. The infrastructure of global communication – the underseas cable system, the wire services built on top of it, and then the satellite system after 1958 – were controlled by developed countries, especially in western Europe and North America. At the end of World War II, the birth of the United Nations produced a series of meetings and documents, like the organization's Charter, that were meant to establish a new age of international law. Perhaps the most famous document was the Universal Declaration of Human Rights (Glendon, 2002). In the west, these founding documents were understood as endorsements of conventional modern notions of constitutional rights, including freedom of expression and freedom of the press. To the committees that drafted them, and to non-western signatories, including countries in the Soviet sphere of influence, they were carefully vague, couched in language that would accommodate many philosophies. In practice, in the first two decades after World War II, these documents seemed to endorse the existing western-dominated system of global communications. Western treatments acclaimed the world's embrace of the "free flow of information" and the "right to know."

But the same documents could also be read to authorize other, more challenging norms. In the 1960s and 1970s, as the Cold War intensified and the group calling itself the Non-Aligned Movement rose in salience, the rights to free expression in the Universal Declaration became the site of a messy debate over interpretation. To the rising chorus of critics of the existing international communication order, they called for a "right to communicate" that could only be achieved if circumstances were reordered; instead of simply a "free flow" of information, which in practice amounted to the ability of western industrialized countries to dominate, the critics called for a "free and equal" or "free and balanced" flow. Instead of one-way flows from north to south and west to east, the critics proposed two-way flows, contraflows, and rights of reply. Nodding to arguments about "cultural imperialism" (Schiller, 1976), critics suggested that communication rights were not simply the property of individual persons as consumers, but that communities and cultures also had communication rights as sovereign entities.

These criticisms found their international forum in the United Nations Educational, Scientific, and Cultural Organization (UNESCO). In geopolitical force, they seemed to parallel and harmonize with the movement for a New World Economic Order, which had found its forum in the International Labor Organization (ILO). UNESCO traditionally works by consensus, and engages primarily in uncontroversial initiatives – who doesn't like education? So this politically charged set of questions presented novel problems for it. The organization responded by creating a committee.

The International Commission for the Study of Communication Problems was established at the suggestion of the US delegation in 1977. At that moment, US foreign policy under President Jimmy Carter was unusually open to multilateral initiatives. That moment didn't last very long. The committee was chaired by the Irish Sean MacBride, and included a good cross-section of nations, regions, and professions. The two most famous figures in the west were Gabriel García Márquez and Marshall McLuhan (for whom a substitute was found, as he became ill). In 1980, after a series of meetings reminiscent of the Hutchins Commission, the commission issued its report,

Many Voices, One World. The report summarized the criticisms sympathetically, and, while including rejoinders to them, concluded that the world communication order was indeed beset with problems. It offered a long list of suggested remedies, all presented in the subjunctive – "may," "might," "should" – not the imperative: "must."

By 1980, the landscape had changed. Conservative governments were taking power in the US and UK, and aimed to relocate the practice of international governance from multilateral settings like the UN and its subsidiary organizations to less risky forums where bilateral arrangements allowed for a plainer implementation of national interests. These governments found unexpected allies on communication issues in their most powerful news organizations, which leaders like Thatcher and Reagan had long demonized as liberal and adversarial. These news organizations Viewed With Alarm the movement for a New World Information and Communication Order (NWICO), which they saw as cover for authoritarian governments seeking to restrict press freedom. Certainly some bad actors played along with NWICO, but it would be extremely difficult to name any international movement that didn't offer something to bad actors.

The strategy of the UK and US was to end the conversation by threatening a boycott of UNESCO. This was a serious threat – the two nations accounted for a disproportionate share of UNESCO's budget – and they did in fact make good on it. UK and US withdrawal had the expected effect, chilling discussion of the issues raised by the MacBride Commission report, and depriving the NWICO movement of its most effective forum.

The debate did not die out. It did, however, move from political arenas to the arena of global commerce. Issues involving international media became not cultural issues but issues of intellectual property and trade, and were addressed in settings like the Global Agreement of Trade and Tariffs (GATT) and the World Trade Organization (WTO). For those institutions, the working of the media as cultural or political forces disappeared into negotiations on "non-tariff trade restrictions" and rights over data like personal biological and genetic information. Because those settings interpret every issue in terms of property rights, the same principles that govern gene-modified soybeans are also thought to be applicable to *Le Monde.* This is not a ridiculous notion, but it does tend to make serious consideration of public intelligence difficult, in the same way that understanding labor relations as bilateral negotiations between individual workers and employers makes consideration of class and social justice difficult.

The media sector, however, changed dramatically in the years following the "neoliberal" turn of the 1980s (Harvey, 2005). Partly this was the result of the neoliberal push against large state enterprises and the stiffening of national borders that they tended to produce. State broadcast authorities became more commercial and lost their monopolies, as national and international commercial broadcasters and cable and satellite companies captured large shares of markets. National telecommunications companies were privatized and sold to international investors or swallowed whole by transnational corporations. Advertising agencies with global reach inserted themselves into media industries throughout the world. This process accelerated with the fall of the Berlin Wall in 1989 and the collapse of the Soviet Union in 1991; at the same time, mainland China's party-controlled media system embraced commercialization with new fervor.

Media in Rising Asia

The "cultural imperialism" critique remains compelling in the age of neoliberal globalization, but it is also important to acknowledge that media history from the early modern period on also involved complicated negotiations, even in countries under direct colonial rule. The most interesting histories in this regard are those of the world's two largest countries, India and China. Both came under European trading hegemony in an earlier age of globalization, and in both the initial commercial concessions turned into forms of political and military subjugation. In both, reformist intellectuals adopted the newspaper form as a way of promoting national revivals that combined traditional and modern values and ideas. Finally, in both, media have undergone a commercialized explosion in the last generation.

In both India and China, the first newspapers were published by and for westerners. India's first newspaper was the *Bengal Gazette*, established in 1780 by James Augustus Hicky (Kohli-Khandekar, 2006: 23). It was suppressed for publishing unseemly gossip. The first newspaper published in an Indian language was the *Bengali Sambad Kaumudi*, established by Raja Rammohun Roy in 1820; he had earlier (1816) started an English-language weekly called the *Bengal Gazette*. Between 1820 and 1947, more than 120 publications appeared in various Indian languages. Some were missionary publications run by Europeans proselytizing Indians; others were run by Indians fighting colonial rule. They were all advocacy organs, then, rather than commercial ventures. The most important impulse for

Indian-owned publications was the independence movement. The most important of these was *The Times of India*, founded in 1838 in Bombay. Other still thriving newspapers in both English (*The Hindu*) and other languages (*Mumbai Samachar*, *Malayala Manorama*) came out of the independence movement (ibid.: 26–7).

The rise of an Indian media system was partly an unexpected by-product of British colonization. Administration required the creation of a network of communication that could supsersede what Athique calls "the 'native' public sphere," which operated through "the manual circulation of handwritten messages, despatch of oral emissaries and the function of commercial intermediaries between different parts of the subcontinent." The "native public sphere" was attenuated by long distances, and had to deal with too many languages and jurisdictions to be suitable for the kind of uniform political space that British administration required (Athique, 2012: 14–15). Bayly identifies a different sort of public sphere in northern India that he calls the Indian "ecumene," composed of "Hindustani-writing literati, Indo-Islamic notables, and officers of state (which included many Hindus)," and which he suggests was able to "mount a critical surveillance of government and society" (Bayly, 2009: 52).

British rule required the creation of a new space of communication, but once the British had built the infrastructure of such a space, Indians came to be familiar with its practices and assumed control over these tools of empire. Among the tools of empire was the language itself. Indian businessmen who sought to engage in commerce and a growing class of Indian bureaucrats who sought to work in the expanding British bureaucracy acquired English literacy, which "inexorably gave rise to a pan-Indian public sphere that transcended the numerous localized public spheres that had previously characterized Indian public life" (ibid.: 16).

This public sphere was itself divided into English language and vernacular (Orsini, 2002). The English-language press was sponsored by businessmen and reformers who were generally recognized as a native liberal elite by the British administration. The vernacular press was far more popular, engaging more directly with local and regional traditional discourses, reaching a broader middle class, and tapping into a pool of resentment and antagonism less visible in the English-language press. Athique points to a meeting of the English-language and vernacular public spheres, with the mediation of Indian traditional discourses resulting. Britain made an attempt to control non-English-language publication through the 1878 Vernacular Press Act, but this failed, and the attempt itself gave a further impetus to vernacular publishing.

By the time of independence, the newspaper press in India was dominated by ideologically oriented papers owned by wealthy families and located in large cities. India's first premier, Jawaharlal Nehru, who had himself been a journalist, promoted policies to guarantee that the English-language press would be owned by Indians; he subsidized the press so that it could be part of the infrastructure of multiparty parliamentary democracy (Thussu, 2006: 129). In 1953, the Indian Press Commission – apparently inspired by the British Royal Commission – identified the power of metropolitan papers as a problem, and proposed pricing rules that would level the playing field for local and rural titles. Despite various policies meant to promote local publishing, and despite the tremendous diversity of Indian society, a relatively small number of highly successful dailies continue to draw a disproportionate amount of revenue and exercise a corresponding amount of influence. This is more true of the English-language press than of the rapidly expanding vernacular press (Jeffrey, 2000).

Because the Indian press remained strongly partisan after independence, it has often been blamed as a cause of political instability, and attempts have been made to regulate it. In June of 1975, the government of Indira Gandhi declared a State of Emergency, and began an extended period of harassing the press – shutting off the power to the street where most of the publications were located, for instance. Legislation passed during the Emergency made it very difficult to publish criticism of the government. This attempt to repress the opposition backfired, resulting in a flourishing underground press, mostly magazines, and an intensification of partisan divisions. After the Emergency, control relaxed both for print and broadcast media. Television, both terrestrial and satellite, expanded rapidly, overtaking print as the most popular medium, and adding an alternate dimension to public space. Television has been the most important domain for the new popularization of Hindu classics like the *Ramayan*, which was broadcast in 78 episodes in 1987; mythologicals had been a popular genre in Bollywood film, but their breakthrough success on television has been linked to the rise of a new identity politics (Rajagopal, 2001). Though Gandhi's Congress Party has been in and out of power, a pattern of political division cross-pollinating with class and religious communal tensions, and irrigated by partisan media in multiple languages, has made public life in India particularly dramatic.

At the same time, Indian media have become much more commercial since 1977. Both of the major coalitional parties have embraced neoliberal economic reform, which, among other things, has meant lifting import restrictions on printing equipment, relaxing restrictions on foreign investment, and opening the media to the internationalized advertising industry. India had been unusual in the world for having very low percentages of advertising income in its newspapers. Using 1951 data, the Press Commission found that advertising accounted for 40 percent of revenue. But after 1977, English-language newspapers moved closer to global norms for advertising revenue, and new titles like Mumbai's *Mid-Day* became extraordinarily successful by using new technology and marketing techniques.

The figure that epitomizes the newly commercialized Indian press is Samir Jain, who took over his father's firm (BCCL, parent company of the *Times of India*) and turned it into India's biggest media company. Much of the turnaround came from ruthless cutting of unprofitable titles and savvy adoption of marketing techniques used for consumer goods. In the process, the *Times of India* became the world's largest-circulation English-language newspaper (Kohli-Khandekar, 2006: 33–4). BCCL has diversified rapidly in recent years; its holdings include radio networks, television channels, a movie production house, the leading automobile magazine in India, an advertising agency, and numerous Internet properties, including a very successful matrimonial website. As a model of a communications conglomerate, it has also become a global company, investing in British radio, distributing its movies and television channels worldwide, and following the immense Indian diaspora with its Internet properties. It remains small in comparison with global giants like NewsCorp and Time-Warner, but its core properties continue to grow.

China's media arc diverges from India's in two key ways. First, China achieved a unified political space centuries before the encounter with Europe, which deranged rather than created it. Second, in the post-World War II moment, China's political history placed it outside the capitalist world order. In other regards, however, the two countries' histories are similar.

The first newspapers in China were published for the European residents of Treaty ports; the first newspapers in Chinese other than official government gazettes for the bureaucracy were missionary newspapers. So, despite its early history of intensive literacy, its invention of printing well before Gutenberg, and its extensive and largely meritocratic bureaucracy, China encountered the modern printed newspaper form as a European import.

The first wave of Chinese-language newspapers printed by and for Chinese people were reformist newspapers of the late Qing period, agitating prior to the 1898 constitutional reform. C. C. Lee characterizes these newspapers as "Confucian liberal" (Lee, 2006: 107–8). After Empress Dowager Cixi crushed the movement, the leading journalist, Liang Qichao, fled to Japan and published a newspaper there (Chen, 2011: 149–50). In this reformist period, the Chinese newspaper was a transnational form. The westernness of the form lent cultural force to the content, which featured political agitation by Chinese reformist intellectuals (Judge, 1996; Mittler, 2004). Liang's *Shibao* was of crucial importance in the 1911 Republican Revolution, and with the collapse of the Qing dynasty, the very weakness of the central state allowed newspapers to flourish and experiment with new forms as in a kind of laboratory (MacKinnon, 1997; Mishra, 2012).

China experienced yet another European humiliation when the Treaty of Versailles continued the practice of assigning spheres of influence in Chinese territory, turning the German concessions over to Japan. In response, a movement begun by students but drawing large popular support and the backing of prominent intellectuals emerged. Called the May 4th Movement, it led to a nationalist consolidation of power under the Guomindang (KMT). But it also led to the founding of the Chinese Communist Party (CCP). As the KMT consolidated power, it quickly began restricting press freedom and producing a party-state press. Meanwhile, the CCP created a contrary press system. Both operated as propaganda systems, citing norms enshrined in a Confucian tradition of the educational role of the written word.

The next two decades of turbulence saw a variety of styles of journalism. In the 1930s and 1940s, the war following Japan's invasion of Manchuria prompted a large output of literary reportage, documenting the barbarity of the war and the corruption of the KMT government. This journalism was influenced by international trends, as we saw in a previous chapter. Meanwhile, the CCP articulated the role of the press in the Yenan rectification campaign of 1942, invoking the formula "from the masses, to the masses." The CCP press was meant to be both an intellectual vanguard of the revolution, a voice of ordinary people, and an instrument of "self-criticism." After the 1949 revolution, the CCP directed the press to concentrate on pro-state propaganda; from then until the 1970s, the press remained a relatively predictable component of the party-state.

After the Cultural Revolution (1966–76), the role of the press became a topic of discussion again. After 1978, there was a revival of critical reportage, authorized in part by a seminal quasi-official essay, "Practice is the Only Criterion for Testing the Truth," which appeared in the *Guangming Daily* on May 11, 1978. A surprising and robust public debate followed on "the standard of truth," with opinions circling around a center of gravity marked out by Deng Xiaoping's famous dictum: "White or black, if it catches mice it is a good cat" (Wang, 2004: 2). Deng's pragmatism allowed for experiments with market reforms, which brought in their wake more commercial media forms.

The key areas for experimentation were in the southeast, especially in Guangzhou, separated by a narrow body of water from Hong Kong. This was a natural area for a special economic zone, in which freer trade was allowed, encouraging the rise of export-oriented manufacturing and drawing a huge migration in from the countryside. It was also an area in which people had relatively easy if not always legal access to Hong Kong cultural production. In the 1970s, the streets of Guangdong were flooded with illegally published tabloids mimicking Hong Kong newspapers; the state tolerated these for a time because they seemed to pose no threat, while offering a kind of inoculation against more potent imported media. But the state was also interested in capturing this new media market. So party-owned newspapers began publishing weekly "literary" supplements.

The most famous of the new tabloid supplements was published by *Nanfang (Southern) Daily*. *Southern Weekend*, as it was called, began as a primarily literary supplement with a very small staff, outsourcing most of its production to its parent daily. Gradually in the late 1970s and 1980s, it grew in both size and originality. It became hugely popular, producing revenue out of all proportion to its size relative to its parent organization; it added staff, and expanded its news-reporting operations; and it published a series of investigative reports that, depending on the observer, followed western professional journalistic principles, or enhanced the party-state's avowed media strategy of self-criticism. It also achieved national recognition, and created a network of outlets that reprinted its reporting (Zhao and Xing, 2012). *Southern Weekend* became a premier national news organization, and continues to be so today, though some argue it has lost its edge in the process.

This account seems to lay out a smooth and inevitable process of liberalization, but that has hardly been the case. There were major crackdowns in 1978, 1983–4 (the "Campaign against Spiritual Pollution"), 1987 (the "Campaign against Bourgeois Liberalization"), and 1989 (post-Tiananmen Square, or the "June Fourth Incident") (Cheek, 1990: 419). A broader view of media that would take in the expanding television, satellite, and Internet sectors would show the same crablike course. The pattern seems consciously experimental.

The party-state retained ownership control of media, and continued to oversee practice through its propaganda office and the State Administration of Radio, Film, and Television (SARFT) and the State Internet Information Office (SIIO). The state allows innovation, but walks it back when it senses danger of instability or opposition. In this way, the state has managed to combine the increasing material comforts of market competition with continuing political monopoly, in a form called "market authoritarianism." To western liberals, this accommodation seems thoroughly ad hoc and impermanent: economic freedom will inevitably demand political rights. But one might easily refute this by pointing to recent western history, where economic privatization has supported depoliticization, both in media and in social life more generally.

Meanwhile, in China as in India, media have become global. The Chinese diaspora is as immense as the Indian diaspora, and media have followed populations around the world. The clearest expression of the sheer size of the overseas Chinese population is the stunning success of Alibaba, the Internet marketing company, whose revenues in 2014 were 50 percent higher than its leading western rival, Amazon. But it is still a world of nation-states and the national borders, along with language and cultural barriers, restrict the flow of Chinese media even more so than Indian media. And it is still a world of capital, with the largest concentrations in the G-8 and OECD countries, in spite of India's and especially China's growth in the era of neoliberal globalization.

The rise of the Asian giants, India and China, as well as Japan and Korea, who make up in commercial dynamism what they lack in population, have provided regional contraflows to the still mainly western world information order. But, with the exception of diasporic markets, these have not penetrated western national publics. US cable news systems are an interesting case in point. In the years since 9/11, a variety of news channels with foreign sponsorship sought US viewerships. China Central Television (CCTV) managed to place its English-language service on US satellite and cable systems, for instance, and seems to consider this presence a priority. The content of CCTV-9 is relentlessly respectable, uplifting, and unwatchable. Russia's similar service, RT (for Russia Today), is more argumentative, and sees itself as offering an alternative to US cable news, but also has a very small audience. France 24, which has the look and feel of BBC's news service, lags far behind the BBC itself, which has the most experience with US audiences of any international news service.

The most interesting case is Al Jazeera, the international news service owned by the government of Qatar. On the one hand, Al

Jazeera has a far greater impact on both the global and US national news environment than any of the other international channels. On the other hand, its impact in the US comes almost entirely from being talked about rather than being watched. Al Jazeera was launched in 1996, filling a vacuum in Arabic-language news left by the closure of the BBC's Arabic-language service. It aspired to a significant degree of independence from the state, and contrasted itself to the main national broadcast authorities in the Arab world. It built a huge audience in the Middle East, and acquired global fame in the years following 9/11, but also was derided as the voice of Osama bin Laden and denounced as anti-Semitic. US and other western news organizations recognized its enterprise as a journalistic organization during the wars in Afghanistan and Iraq, and frequently used its reports. In 2003, Al Jazeera began an English-language website, and built it into Al Jazeera English, a 24-hour news channel, in 2005. It then tried and failed to achieve a presence on US cable systems. Resistance came from political groups, who seized on its reputation for anti-Semitism, but also from cable systems themselves, who claimed that there was no significant audience. But Al Jazeera has very deep pockets, and has been able to circumvent this problem by buying the news channel Current-TV and converting it into Al Jazeera America, acquiring a place on major cable systems. It is not clear at this writing whether its audience will expand, though I find it to be by far the most watchable of the international news channels and superior in the quality of its journalism to Fox News, CNN, and MSNBC, its main US-based competitors. Of course, all of these also have relatively small audiences. Old, too.

Regardless of its lack of a primary audience in the US, Al Jazeera has had tremendous influence. There are two major reasons for this. One is its huge audience elsewhere, which means that it is a factor to be reckoned with by governments in the world, which target it for both positive and negative treatment. Leaders and movements wishing to influence the broad public in the Arab world seek out its journalists, but so do censors and military police, who seem to find it more acceptable to jail Al Jazeera's journalists than those of the BBC or *New York Times*. The second reason for its influence is its credibility among other journalists, who recognize and respect both its unique access in certain areas and its generally high standards.

The Limits of Late Modern Journalism

At the beginning of the twenty-first century, the situation of journalism in the developed west and in the world more generally has moved beyond the conditions that made professionalization seem obvious and necessary. One can argue – I would – that there remains a need for journalists in their role as advocates of the public, watchdogs against corruption, and adversaries of the powerful. But the by-now traditional stance of objectivity does not obviously make that role practicable. Meanwhile, many other forms of journalism practice seem emergent.

It is not clear whether there will be a de-institutionalization of journalism, but it is clear that journalism as an institution has not been operating according to its best self-image for some time. This was made painfully obvious to the US and UK publics in the events leading to the 2003 Iraq War. In both Britain and the US, leading news organizations offered skewed reporting, evidently the result of too much reliance on official sources. After much soul-searching, both the *Washington Post* and *The New York Times* apologized to their readers. *The Times* apology admitted that key articles

> depended at least in part on information from a circle of Iraqi informants, defectors and exiles bent on "regime change" in Iraq, people whose credibility has come under increasing public debate in recent weeks. Complicating matters for journalists, the accounts of these exiles were often eagerly confirmed by United States officials convinced of the need to intervene in Iraq. (*New York Times*, 26 May 2004)

That *The Times* acknowledged distortions from source-dependency shows unusual awareness of the density of its ties to officialdom. But that's one reason why intelligent people read *The Times* in the first place, to get the official story.

No intelligent citizen in the UK or US had any excuse for believing the official story about Iraq's weapons-of-mass-destruction programs in 2003, however. There was no end of disconfirming information available from credible sources, including arms inspectors from both countries and of course the United Nations team. So it is remarkable that the people who followed the news most closely, and were the best equipped to figure out the truth, were also more likely than people who didn't follow the news at all to believe the official story. It says something about the way that public opinion was formed in the developed west.

The ideology of professional journalism holds that an investigator can produce truth, her news organization will publish it, and an intelligent supervising public will recognize it and act on it. We all know that happens sometimes. In that way, a journalist can be a champion of democracy. But it is important to distinguish between individual journalists and journalism as an institution. Journalists continue to win awards for behaving in ways that set them apart from what journalism as an institution routinely does.

Even when individual journalists produce important news, their news organizations often fail to publish it effectively, and have been remarkably wobbly in defending their reporters in recent years. In 1998, something happened in my hometown, Cincinnati, that strikes me as a parable about the limits of journalism in our times.

The *Cincinnati Enquirer*, unlike the infamous *National Enquirer*, has not been known for rocking the boat. And so it came as a surprise to long-time readers when the *Enquirer* published a special section in its Sunday newspaper on May 3, 1998, which consisted of more than a dozen articles criticizing one of Cincinnati's most prominent local businesses. Chiquita Brands was the descendant of the former United Fruit, one of the more notorious of the US transnationals. The burden of the reports, whose main reporter was Mike Gallagher, was that the new Chiquita was not all that different from the old United Fruit. The articles, the result of a year-long investigation that took reporters to Europe and Central America, offered convincing evidence of corporate violations of standards and laws regarding finance and ownership, labor relations, working conditions, and political influence. This was classic muckraking. The managing editor, Laurence Beaupre, and the reporters all believed that they were living up to the highest standards of their profession, doing the kind of work that wins Pulitzer prizes.

The reporters had gathered a lot of information from many sources, but the most damning evidence came in the form of voicemail messages retrieved from the corporation's internal system. Gallagher, the lead reporter, had a source inside Chiquita who had given him the code to tap into the voicemail system. He had put it to canny use. He would call Chiquita's public relations and legal officers, and ask them pointed questions; they would promise to get back to him with the answers; then he would eavesdrop on the voicemail traffic that followed as the answers were formulated. The result was tremendously embarrassing, as you can imagine.

The voicemail proved to be the reporters' undoing. Chiquita's lawyers alleged that the voicemail messages had been stolen. If that were true, Gallagher would be guilty of breaking the law. Gallagher and Beaupre disagreed, believing that, because their source had given them access, they had a right to this information. But the *Enquirer*'s parent corporation, Gannett, sensed a legal disaster looming. The head offices immediately took charge of the affair and quickly brokered an agreement with Chiquita, running an apology, and paying upwards of $10 million, stunningly before a suit had even been filed. Gallagher was fired by the *Enquirer* and became the subject of an investigation by a special prosecutor – an odd maneuver, necessary because the elected prosecutor in Hamilton County, along with almost all of the leading elected officials there of either party, had accepted campaign contributions from Carl Lindner, a principal owner of Chiquita's parent corporation. (In a related trial, three judges were obliged to withdraw before one was found who hadn't accepted Lindner contributions.) Gallagher subsequently pleaded guilty to two charges and cooperated with authorities investigating a "conspiracy" of current and former Chiquita employees in the theft of the voicemail messages. As part of this deal, he gave up his source, a cardinal sin for a professional reporter.

The Chiquita case was much noted by the nation's media critics and conscience keepers. Oddly, the major media took no notice of the investigative reports themselves. The other newspapers in the Gannett chain, including the flagship *USA Today*, at the time seeking to heighten its reputation as a serious newspaper, did not carry or mention these stories. The Chiquita exposé, it seems, was not a national story. But the apology and repudiation was. The nation's media did cover the *Enquirer*'s endgame, and commentators treated it as an ethical embarrassment, another example of a journalist flaunting ethical guidelines in the interest of winning glory and recognition. Beaupre and Gallagher particularly were accused of conducting a high testosterone Pulitzer-seeking crusade. Journalists and media critics did a lot of soul-searching about their declining ethical standards and their abysmal public image, and readily clumped the Chiquita episode with a few other recent embarrassments – cases where columnists had fabricated interviews or characters, and the notorious Valley of Death or Tailwind report on CNN, which presented controversial allegations of nerve gas use by the US military in Vietnam. (In that case, CNN retracted the material, settled lawsuits out of court for large sums of money, and fired the producers of the report; but the producers fought back, and eventually won big settlements themselves from CNN.) Lost in this orgy of self-reprimand was the stuff of the controversy. Although the *Enquirer* repudiated the series and apologized for it, the paper never admitted that anything printed was untrue. And even subtracting the stolen voicemail messages, any candid reader would have to admit that the series presented a mountain of evidence of corporate wrongdoing.

The corporate structure of the media clearly produced a chilling effect. The mere threat of legal action made Gannett take the case away from the *Enquirer* and impose a gag order on the paper's personnel. Unlike the editor and reporter, who arguably acted according to overriding journalistic interests, the chain was concerned only with the financial danger. It did not support any further investigation into the truth of the reports – something that journalistic integrity should require. In fact, Gannett actively discouraged such reporting, a posture that makes excellent business sense, considering that its newspapers are almost all monopolies situated in medium or small markets and which therefore have nothing to gain from pulling the noses of the local corporate goliaths.

The professional ideology of journalists, which is supposed to make them the implacable adversaries of the powerful, also seems to leave them curiously impotent in the face of corporate power. Professional ethics became the enemy of journalistic independence. Because reporters thought of the *Enquirer* case as the story of a reporter's ethical lapses, all of the substantive concerns faded into the background. This runs counter to common sense, which has it that when journalists are concerned with professional standards they will produce media matter that will be a richer resource for democratic polity. But that equation assumes that journalists have more autonomy and independence than they actually do. Journalists are not like other professionals in this regard.

The media owners who hire and fire journalists concern themselves with maximizing profit. This is not a matter of personal evilness or a conspiracy of dark forces. It is a matter of law. Publicly held companies are required to seek to maximize shareholders' return on investment. More and more of the news media are owned by publicly held companies. As the press industrialized over a century ago, the public expressed fear of media moguls who would use their power to advance their personal interests. The grandest example here was William Randolph Hearst. The media companies in the late modern period are not like Hearst. They are not run by individuals who impose a vision or a set of personal interests on their media – with notable exceptions like Rupert Murdoch and Silvio Berlusconi. Rather, they are run by managers with an interest in the bottom line and often an indifference to the traditions of professional journalism.

Working reporters have long deplored this situation. The complaint that the MBAs run the newsroom, and that the people who run news organizations no longer believe in the "elements of journalism," resonates well with the actual working experiences of reporters for whom budget and personnel cuts have become routine (Kovach and Rosenstiel, 2007; Underwood, 1995). Ironically, though, the complaint comes at a time when people are exposed to an ever larger amount of news matter. Local television news departments have increased the amount of time they fill even while economizing on staff; all-news radio and cable channels are manifold; and Internet media are flourishing too. Can you die of thirst in the middle of the ocean? Obviously, yes.

The corporate structure of the media has altered the quality of news while it has increased its quantity. The change in quality might be hard to specify, but two characteristics seem quite obvious. First, the line of demarcation between news and other media content has diminished. Second, the news media no longer offer a map of the world through the news that makes sense of the day's affairs to a mainstream audience. Both relate directly to the increase in consumer choice in the media.

The high modern moment of journalism allowed for a firm distinction between news and entertainment. This had not always been so, of course. Much of the most compelling news of the century before the institutionalization of the press was packaged as fiction, such as *Uncle Tom's Cabin*, *The Wizard of Oz*, and *The Jungle*. Reporters strived for an authorly voice in those years, and many went on to become important novelists, like Theodore Dreiser, Mark Twain, and Ernest Hemingway. Newspapers often serialized novels. People watched newsreels in movie theaters. The distinction between news and entertainment was firmest in the period when journalistic professionalism was strongest. The sanctity of news (vs the profane entertainment) justified the professionalization of journalism, which in turn depended on de facto monopolies in the media business. When those monopolies began to shift, the line between news and entertainment shifted with them (Williams and Delli Carpini, 2011).

Television personality Jerry Springer's career is a case in point. In the 1970s, he attracted attention as Cincinnati's most progressive young politician, and served several terms as Mayor (interrupted by a scandal over a call-girl ring). In the 1980s, he converted his political celebrity into a television news career, first by providing "Commentaries" and then by anchoring the evening news on Cincinnati's NBC affiliate. In the 1990s, he moved to Chicago and began a talk show on syndicated television. *The Jerry Springer Show* quickly earned a reputation as least common denominator entertainment, exploiting whatever social pathologies its guests could offer for the amusement of an audience that included a surprising number of bored college students. If Jon Stewart's *The Daily Show* was the comic face of news-as-entertainment, *The Jerry Springer Show* was its tragic face. At the end of each episode, positioning himself as a Greek chorus commenting on the mayhem he's just orchestrated, Springer gave a summarizing thought, pretending to redeem the entertainment as public education. Everyone – the guests, the audience, and certainly Springer himself – knew better. In 1997, Springer tried to cross the threshold back into mainstream television journalism by arranging to do commentaries on Chicago's NBC affiliate's local evening news. This attempt aroused unexpectedly strong opposition from journalists – unexpected to Springer. In 2003, he flirted with the idea of running for the US Senate. Certainly his credentials competed with high elected officials like Minnesota Governor Jesse "The Body" Ventura and California Governor Arnold Schwarzenegger, whose careers in exploitation film might have been considered disqualifying in other times and places. Springer explored then declined, finding his chances of success slim. Perhaps there are still some lines that can't be crossed.

The success of *The Jerry Springer Show* underscored a rising amount of noise in the public communication system. Shows like that had become possible because of the large number of independent broadcast stations with airtime to fill in the afternoons. The creation of new channels had allowed for a great proliferation of all sorts of stuff, especially on television but also in every other medium.

Abundance and the Age of Digital Media

Abundance strained the sense-making organs of the body politic. Walter Lippmann had hoped for intelligence bureaus to make sense out of the world for decision-makers and ordinary citizens. The Hutchins Commission had instructed the news media to perform this function. But in the late modern period, the news media could no longer do that for a growing percentage of the population. Even the prestige daily newspapers conceded ground to the growing dissonance of the news. And with the end of the Cold War, the prevailing frame for making sense of the world lapsed too. You can argue that shows like Springer's work because they try to find an emotional common sense behind the apparent social chaos (Lunt and Stenner, 2005), and so work to create the kinds of solidarity that theorists of the public sphere claim is a necessary precondition for democratic deliberation. That argument would be more convincing if the proliferation of such shows didn't coincide with plummeting respect for public institutions throughout the developed world.

This shift is most noticeable on the Web. Most of the hard news on the Web still comes from legacy news organizations, whether broadcast (the BBC, NPR, Fox) or print (*The New York Times*, the *Guardian*). At first it consisted mostly of "shovelware," stuff uploaded directly from the newspaper or broadcast; now, the

Internet presence has eclipsed the old media publication in many news organizations, perhaps most dramatically for the *Guardian*. Even as staid an outfit as *The New York Times* has married its print and online efforts in a reorganized newsroom and bent its journalists to incorporate digital news values like immediacy, interactivity, and participation. Because of the continued updating that web technology allows and web readers expect, it is common for audiences to follow a big story as it is being worked up: as Nikki Usher points out, "the process of journalism was laid bare, mistakes and all" (Usher, 2014: 12).

The organization of news on the Web is strikingly different. Compare news on the Internet to the high modern front page of a newspaper. The front page offered a succinct map of the world. It arranged a few stories in terms of hierarchy, with the most important coming at the top, above the fold, and traditionally on the right-hand side. It further divided its inner pages into discrete sections, each of which dealt with a supposedly coherent chunk of the world – sports, for instance. Little of this organization remains on the Web. There news sites pile far more stories into their home pages, and then they frame those within dizzy columns of hyperlinks to other sections and other media.

Much of this material is "disintermediated." News sites routinely portal readers to sources of raw information or to institutions that produce their own authoritative accounts of sports, weather, crime news, and so forth. This is wonderful for highly involved readers, who can now go directly to, say, the official text of the majority opinion in a case decided by the Supreme Court of the United States, or who can construct their own statistical profile of baseball players on FanGraphs. In the not too distant past, people had to rely on the judgment of the news organization, and all people, no matter what their level of interest, had to tolerate being exposed to the same international news and the same grocery store ads. In the digital age, instead of creating a map, a news site provides an index, something without hierarchy or necessary order, which different people will navigate however they choose.

This is a throwback to older news media formats, especially printerly papers, which clipped items from many sources and presented them often in scrambled order, counting on the reader's own sophistication to form a coherent picture from them. It is ideally suited to the highly informed, highly mobilized reader, on the one hand, and the thrillseeker on the other.

The disaggregation of web news has allowed other throwback forms to emerge, like the blog. Bloggers compose a series of entries, with hyperlinks, giving their take on matters of many sorts and in the process provide access to items appearing elsewhere on the Web, on mainstream media sites, on other blogs, or in public information sources. Bloggers work much like nineteenth-century partisan editors. The most politically motivated of them, many of whom are working journalists, produce daily editions that can be read just like a personal newspaper made up of clippings. Bloggers engage in dialogs in the same way that editors did. And bloggers hope to drive a larger public agenda. Sometimes they succeed in capturing the attention of mainstream journalism, and influence headlines in daily newspapers. Like talk-radio hosts, they became a force to be reckoned with. Within a short time of their initial flowering in the public imagination, media executives began expecting every working journalist to blog. Within a few years, blogging yielded to microblogging and social networks like Twitter.

Add these augmentations to the increased availability of non-local and international news sources, and you have a news environment in which an ever-increasing amount of information is publicly available to ordinary people. We should hope that publics are getting more intelligent as a result. So why does it feel like we're living through a golden age of stupid?

The Lost Promise of the Digital

Anyone who has been observing the effects of the digital revolution on public life has by now outlived many versions of predicted media utopias. In the 1980s digerati celebrated the egalitarianism and practicality of Usenet groups; in the 1990s they hailed the populism and plenitude of the World Wide Web; in the first decades of the twenty-first century we've already exhausted the enthusiasm for the rational-critical phase of the blogosphere and the enthusiasm for citizen journalism and user-generated content. Each of these media utopias promised a redistribution and democratization of voice. Ordinary people would become more active in the public sphere as access to information and the means of publication escaped the control of media organizations. Only a few years ago Manuel Castells greeted "mass self-publication" as a new regime of communication power (Castells, 2009).

Although these dreams are unfulfilled, digital technologies have transformed the media and political landscape in developed countries. They have done so by allowing changes in the networks of relationships that form organizations. Matthew Hindman argues that the Internet has changed politics on the back end, not the front end. Political expression remains very scripted, increasingly partisan, and dominated by a few voices – so the Internet hasn't revolutionized the public sphere. But fundraising and political organizing have been transformed. Digital tools allow campaigns to crowdsource funding; they let campaigns guide supporters into networking with each other; they facilitate the recruiting of activists and surveillance of ordinary voters (Hindman, 2008). Even though any particular news cycle can be hijacked by a random meme from Twitter, the net effect of digital technology has been to allow more effective and thorough management of electoral politics.

For legacy news organizations, changes on the back end have been equally impressive. New efficiencies in acquiring news and producing it for distribution have upset old routines and divisions of labor: every journalist is now her own photographer, and sometimes typesetter and proofreader as well. The same efficiencies that allow Amazon to displace brick-and-mortar stores allow media organizations to eviscerate their production workers, especially the unionized pressworkers and drivers, and to decimate newsroom staffs, while maintaining quantity and accelerating the speed of the flow of content. This is what managers wanted, even if their satisfaction is cloaked by their cries of despair at the erosion of audiences and ad markets. This shift in the network of relationships, though not readily apparent in the front end of legacy media, has nevertheless been epochal.

Take advertising. Twentieth-century newspapers owned the only set of really big pipes for distributing key genres of advertising – department store display ads, classified ads, grocery store coupons, and so forth. Digital technology has made that sort of mass advertising very inefficient, however. Why should an advertiser pay to reach consumers who aren't specifically interested in what she wants to sell? Digital technology allows the narrowcasting of ads to more specific consumers, and allows ads to float free from specific placements, following their target consumers as they wander the Web. This new efficiency has enraged old media managers. Mel Karmazin, then CEO of Viacom and later CEO of Sirius Satellite Radio, when introduced to Google's ad system by Sergei Brin and Larry Page, protested, "You're fucking with the magic!" (Auletta, 2009: 5).

If Google takes away on the back end, it gives back on the front end. Google and other search engines have introduced a new bottleneck to the flow of content; their algorithms work to focus attention on a fairly small number of content producers, chief among them legacy news organizations like the *New York Times* and the BBC, and on the local level the old monopoly daily newspapers and broadcast news organizations. That these news organizations don't know how to "monetize" these visitors is hardly Google's fault. Likewise, social media applications like Twitter and Facebook direct friends and followers to traditional media.

These new front-end relationships inflect the way media content reaches people. A Facebook user, for instance, is highly likely to run across a steady diet of news items in her newsfeed. But this diet will be stewarded by her friends, in the first instance, and by Facebook's algorithm in the second. So one's news diet will quietly voice and reinforce the common sense of a community, much as the public journalism movement had hoped a daily newspaper could. But there is a big difference. A daily newspaper's community was locally situated and supposedly universal – it was the same for each member. But everyone's Facebook community is unique to her.

For the public of network media (which I'll call the "network" public, which means something slightly different from Yochai Benkler's (2006) "networked" public), life, both private and public, is increasingly "mediatized," and the distinction between them becomes attenuated. They continue to encounter the media organizations that have traditionally produced and distributed content, but they tend to do so through another mediated contact – through a search engine or a social media application. At the horizon, the entire media system might seem to collapse into a single networked entity called "media," no longer a plural noun but a singular. At that horizon it might no longer be possible to distinguish media from public life.

The network public might experience the threshold between oneself and media as porous. One might imagine oneself producing while using, for instance. And this is certainly true, at least inasmuch as users continually produce data about themselves that can in turn be sold as a commodity to advertisers.

But hegemony continues to operate in the network public. Bottlenecks shift and erode, but they don't disappear. In addition to search, there are bottlenecks in retail, hardware, operating systems, social networks, and other applications that afford many kinds of power.

In the network public, everyone gets one's individual sovereignty but ordinary people have no power. Everyone gets to choose one's mediated reality. Everyone can migrate to the public sphericule (Gitlin, 2002) that promises maximum comfort. But this doesn't allow one to participate meaningfully in forming the public agenda, contributing to public discussion, and steering public affairs. Perhaps this explains why, even as choice expands, people in developed countries have come more and more to despise their public institutions.

Conclusion: Coming to Judgment on Public Intelligence

The beginning of the twenty-first century promised to reconstruct the sets of relationships that constitute the news media. The commencement of an apparently never-ending "war on terror" intensified the neoliberal turn in all forms of governance just as the impact of new media technologies eroded the economic basis of the system of professional news. As in previous moments of the long communication revolution, utopian and dystopian narratives competed to capture the import of these changes. Where some saw enhanced flow of information and opinion and the return of an active citizenry, others saw the increasing incoherence of public discussion.

Critics maintain that these are signs of a collapse of high modern journalism, caused in part by the weakening of its business model. In the liberal version of this argument, weakening news organizations employ fewer and fewer journalists, who produce less and less important information, which allows the powerful to become increasingly corrupt (Starr, 2009).

Another version of this argument would see the key absence as not information, which remains abundant, but the sense-making capacity of a high-modern media system that could represent an intelligent public. I've discussed this point in the introduction and here and there in the book. In this point of view, the role of the press in the public sphere has not been as information-provider but as part of the mechanism by which public opinion is represented. As that mechanism has changed in the late modern west, the representation of public opinion has grown more problematic, and the belief in an intelligent supervising public has been weakened to the point where it has ceased to function as a regulative fiction.

In what remains of this book, I will try to think through whether there is any merit to this argument by looking at some tests of capacity of the late modern system of public intelligence. If the slavery question was a good test of the capacity of the US partisan press, and the Civil Rights movement and the war in Vietnam were good tests of the mid-twentieth-century professional press, then I think issues of class, climate change, and war and empire are good tests of the capacity of the late modern system. Although I think the system is currently failing those tests, I remain optimistic.

Tests of Capacity

The professional press always had a difficult time dealing with class, more so in the US than in other countries. This is because the professional press tended to think of the people as independent citizens rather than as social groups, except in the case of inferior or oppressed groups. In addition to this ideological tendency, the news industry as a business sector had and continues to have less interest in working-class audiences, which it has shed in pursuit of upscale markets. This upscaling of news markets increased as ownership became more corporate. The temporality of the quarterly report led news executives to pursue increasingly well-off audiences, and discouraged investment in reporting working-class news, in covering working-class neighborhoods, and in cultivating the next generation of working-class readers and viewers. In the US, newspapers once had reporters covering the "labor beat"; by the 1970s, outside of Detroit, New York, and a few other metropoles, labor news had become entirely the province of business reporters, and was framed almost entirely in terms of the interests of investors (Martin, 2008). Only in rare cases of spectacular strikes did labor news invade the general news pages (Kumar, 2008).

News organizations did not abandon non-elite audiences altogether. Instead, they constructed soft news ghettoes to isolate readerships as market segments that could be sold to specific advertisers. Some working-class readers were recruited for the "Women's" pages, the sports pages, and the pages that featured crime news. But these same readers would then be easily siphoned off from general news organizations by media specializing in their concerns – cable and satellite television channels, then websites. One segment in particular that general news organizations never seemed to find a way to capture was youth. Perhaps this is because professional journalists are constitutionally disinclined to make their reporting fun in any way.

General news organizations seem to have stopped producing new audiences some time around 1970 in the US. The average age of subscribers of daily newspapers or viewers of network evening news or cable news hovers at around 60 in the US.

The working class did not abandon news. News abandoned them. Journalists abandoned them in a hunt for prestige. News executives abandoned them in pursuit of advertising revenue. Investors abandoned them out of a failure to read the future beyond the horizon of the next quarterly report. And then the tipping point came, and they all blamed the Internet.

A key moment in this tragic history concerns journalists' rising misrecognition of their own situation as workers. Newsworkers began to call themselves "journalists" around the same time that they separated themselves as workers from the other workers in news organizations: the pressmen and typographers and drivers and deliverers and ad salespersons and so forth. Many of those other news occupations formed powerful unions and identified themselves with the labor movement generally. In many countries journalists did form such unions. On the whole, though, western journalists sought the distinctions enjoyed by professionals like doctors and lawyers. Even in Italy, where journalists created a powerful labor union, entry into that union relied upon passing an examination, much like the licensing exam for physicians.

This is a misrecognition because journalists have never anywhere enjoyed the kind of independence and autonomy that doctors and lawyers do. In a few countries, there are statutes that ensure editorial independence – the Netherlands, for example (Bergman, 2012). But even there, it would be absurd to say that journalists actually run media companies. By telling themselves that they are professionals like doctors and lawyers, journalists leave themselves less capable of resisting the forces that render them dependent. They are, for instance, less capable of challenging manipulation by empowered sources. And they are often incapacitated by a felt need to be balanced.

As a result, I would argue that news media make it difficult for working-class audiences to recognize themselves, and to intelligently pursue their concerns in the public sphere. This is one possible explanation for the salience among working-class voters in Europe and North America of anti-immigration politics. In the face of declining material prospects caused by a shrinking social safety net and corporate austerity justified by international competition, working-class voters misrecognize immigrants as the cause of their problems.

The challenge of global warming might be the clearest parallel now to the challenge of slavery in the nineteenth century. Both cases demand fundamental changes in the global economic structure. Both evoke basic moral questions. Both articulate clumsily to political systems. Both annoy ordinary people, who would prefer that the problem not be brought up. But both also produce compelling events and narratives that are taken up by activists and should make for good journalism.

Has the system of professional journalism done better with global warming than the partisan press did with slavery? I focus on the US experience, which is atypical, both because of the size and entrenchment of the interests involved, and also because its news system lacks the vigorous public sector that exists in other developed countries. But the US case remains important, both because of the prominence of the US as a producer of greenhouse gases, but also because the vulnerabilities of US journalism exist in other countries, as well as in the international news system, to some degree, and, I would argue, an increasing degree.

If we measure the effectiveness of the US news media by change in public opinion on climate change, we would conclude that the system has failed. Even as a powerful consensus has been built among climate scientists, and recognized by authoritative global institutions (like the Nobel Committee), while common-sense evidence has mounted, skepticism has been growing among the US public (Leiserowitz et al., 2013). Climate skepticism has increased because of, not in spite of news coverage. Aspects of professional journalism practice have worked to make skepticism viable in the public sphere. I will name two habits here; certainly there are others. The first is an addiction to balance. Journalists come to judgment on whether an idea or actor or event belongs in the sphere of deviance, consensus, or legitimate controversy. In the US, any matter on which the major parties disagree falls into the sphere of legitimate controversy by default. In the sphere of legitimate controversy, acceptable journalism must present balancing points of view. So it happened that, perhaps in response to corporate-interest lobbying, or perhaps in response to their own sense of how the world operates, the national leaders of the Republican Party decided at a certain point to embrace climate denialism. At that point, the emerging consensus among climate scientists became irrelevant to the form of climate-change stories, which were required to include a skeptical voice, which in turn authorized any reader or viewer to say, "well, that's a matter of opinion." This habit clearly helped produce the current situation, in which an emerging public consensus on climate change has receded, and opinion has divided on party grounds. Of course, the availability of non-professional bloggers to add to the noise level has made skepticism more acceptable.

The second feature of professional journalism involved here is an emphasis on events, conflict, and scandal. At first glance, the event-orientation would seem to produce movement in the right direction. When surprisingly powerful storms or surprisingly hot summers occur, and journalists look for news-size explanations, climate change is available and often used, which should reinforce public acceptance of the scientific consensus. But even in this dynamic there is a downside. If there is a cold winter, the same logic invites public scoffing at climate change. When there is a run of time without a weather disaster, public attitudes revert to more comfortable positions. And it becomes more difficult to draw the attention of both journalists and the public to the slow, boring, incremental creep of change.

Attention to scandal is more evidently a problem. Take the coverage of the so-called "Climategate" emails. Hackers copied thousands of emails from the computers of climate scientists at the University of East Anglia and published them on the Internet, claiming they showed that the scientists were engaging in a conspiracy to cook data. The "scandal" erupted shortly before the Copenhagen summit on climate change and quickly became a leading component of the news coverage. Even though subsequent investigations dismissed the charges of conspiracy, the support given to climate-change skepticism has been enduring, as is readily seen in the coining of the term "climategate." It is difficult to see how news organizations in the system of professional journalism would have resisted this story, even though knowledgeable reporters certainly saw it as misleading.

It is a feature of the system of professional journalism that reporters routinely falsify their own values and beliefs. This is evident in the fact that surveys of professional journalists usually reveal them to be center-left in values, while news coverage is usually slanted center-right. At times this systematic distortion is dramatically evident. The most compelling recent example is the run-up to the Iraq War, which I touched on in the last chapter.

This example is an index of the larger test of capacity that the system of professional journalism appears to be failing, the subject of war and empire. It seems that the contemporary news environment might be developing an increased capacity for dealing with that set of questions.

Two recent episodes bear on this point. The first, the publication by WikiLeaks in conjunction with professional news organizations like the *Guardian* and the *New York Times* of leaked cables from the US State Department, shows that the digital age first makes it harder to keep secrets and then makes it possible to disseminate them in the right circumstances. In this case, the right circumstances include an intermediary like WikiLeaks, which is truly outside of any national jurisdiction and savvy enough to recruit very capable journalists (Beckett and Ball, 2012).

The second, still unfolding story involves the publication, again by the *Guardian*, with assistance from the *Washington Post*, of revelations of surveillance by the US National Security Agency in partnership with private organizations and other national governments. The documents from which these revelations have been gleaned were copied by an NSA contractor, Edward Snowden – again indicating the precariousness of secret information in the digital age. And again the international nature of the coalition producing the revelations has been key. The initial publications occurred while Snowden was hiding out in Hong Kong – he later moved on to Moscow – and working with the UK-based *Guardian* through the blogger Glenn Greenwald, a US lawyer who emphasizes civil liberties and lives in Brazil.

But both the State Department cables and the Snowden revelations also show the limits of the digital age. The State Department cables peeled back a layer of confidentiality for US diplomats, showing them operating as a kind of shadow-journalism system for their own privileged public of foreign-policy professionals. Coincidentally, however you might feel about US policy in this or that place, the cables show the professionals to be rather good at their jobs – intelligent, clear-spoken, well-informed, discreet, and, on the whole, ethical. The State Department and the US government generally fought against publication and continue to prosecute the chief leaker, Chelsea (née Bradley) Manning, because of the embarrassing lack of fit between public postures and these more frank confidential assessments, arguing that good government requires a certain level of secrecy and a limited amount of disingenuousness. Let's grant them that argument, to be generous.

It remains troubling that the US government has apparently been able to recruit the private sector to help protect its confidentiality. At the height of the controversy, Amazon, which had been hosting the WikiLeaks website on its servers, withdrew its services, and Visa, MasterCard, and PayPal refused to process payments for WikiLeaks. In the more recent Snowden revelations, the NSA has been shown to mine data at a previously unknown level, but those data are mostly retained and archived by private organizations – telecoms, search engines, social media companies, and software manufacturers. These US-based companies have objected publicly to the way the NSA has obliged them to yield data for surveillance, and are quite worried about what the public knowledge of these activities will do to their global customer base. On the other hand, the same companies have maneuvered very effectively to retain and data-mine their own records of usage and transactions. Many of them make their money by targeting advertising to specific users, after all. What is scarier: the ocean of data that the Googles and Facebooks of the world hold, or the fact that the NSA occasionally inserts a straw and takes a sip?

But news organizations are very bad at holding private concentrations of power to account. It is rather easier for them to monitor governments. Partly this is because governments are supposed to be monitored; partly it is because the people who run governments often disagree with each other about significant matters, opening up a space for scrutiny. But it is also a function of professional ideology, which can authorize muckraking the state as objective citizen advocacy, but finds something uncomfortably biased about targeting private companies. And it is a function of the legal and public relations resources that private organizations can bring to bear: governments generally can't afford really good lawyers. This is one of the lessons of the Chiquita Brands episode, discussed in chapter 6.

So the combination of traditional professional values, corporate news media ownership, digital technology, and globalization has not yet produced the kinds of public intelligence that the present age seems to require. This doesn't mean that it won't. Previous moments of change in the news media had at first produced novel forms of news culture that alarmed observers and critics; within a decade or two, these had produced new disciplines of news – new journalisms – that enforced ground rules for making sense in public life. One can expect the creation of a new form of journalism to replace or sit alongside the old.

Shot through with Chips of Messianic Time

I believe that I can give this particular history a happy ending partly because I think it hasn't ended yet, but also because I think that one can see intimations of what a happy ending would look like at various points in the past. Walter Benjamin, in his *Theses on the Philosophy of History*, criticized what he called "historicism," the approach to history that sees it piling up, inexorably, an endless chain of overdetermined accidents, producing a narrative of tragic meaninglessness. Instead he appealed for what he called "historical materialism," which he said can find intimations of an eventual happy ending by sifting through a past "shot through with chips of messianic time."

Media history is often written in a historicist mode. In that kind of narrative, each new media technology carries with it the promise of pure communication, which should in turn produce stronger community, healthier public life, and more vibrant democratic governance. In every age of modern history, some innovation has produced the kind of fantasy that Thomas Jefferson and his contemporaries expressed about the newspaper. But these fantasies always crash against brutal reality, and every media technology gets captured by entrenched forces – authoritarian governments, exploitative corporations, violent extremists.

But media history is also a good location for panning for chips of messianic time. In media history there is in every period an energetic group of dynamic actors who believe in the possibilities of democratic communication. Although they turn out in the short run to be losers, and the Hearsts and Murdochs of the world get to headline the story, in fact it's the also-rans who are the ones later generations want to hang out with. Every generation will rediscover Tom Paine and Ida B. Wells-Barnett; not so much Duff Green.

The past allows us to tell an infinite number of true stories about it; it's up to us to decide when to begin and end them. Most of them end, at least implicitly, with us standing right here. But that is a sleight of hand, because it implies that we know where we are standing. And in fact we won't, not until we look back 50 years from now. But even acknowledging the fluidity of the present, I think we can identify some real vectors. One is an increasing emphasis on instrumental rationality. Industrial production, then professional organization, and certainly corporate decision-making continually invoke a kind of reasoning in which actions are to be selected on the basis of a careful balancing of costs and benefits. A second vector is individuation. The public, throughout the course of media history, has become increasingly composed of individuals, who, although distinguished perhaps by race, gender, class, sexual preference, religious belief, and other factors, have identical rights and will similarly pursue their individual interests.

The intersection of those two vectors is what Raymond Williams (1974) has called mobile privatization. In the course of the long career of the modern, society has been constantly revolutionized in order to make individuals more private and more mobile. The great technologies of the twentieth-century consumer society are cases in point. The refrigerator puts the marketplace in your kitchen. The television puts the theater in your living room. The telephone puts the public square in your hallway. The automobile puts the commuter train in your garage. The computer brings the library into your study. And now the cellphone and the networked tablet computer allow you to take all these information technologies with you into previously public space, the sidewalks and cafes where public opinion was born, and turn them into your own living room, study, or business office.

From the endpoint of the consumer, mobile privatization marks both an advance in convenience and a decline in governing power. There is literally no domain any more in which you can be in control of your space. Marketers or the NSA will find you anywhere. There is also no place where you need to be in the dark, and there is no situation in which you cannot raise your digital voice. But this does not mean that you are part of the public of public opinion. It means that you are always able to access a network public, but the identity of that public is different for each user.

In the network public, weak ties are more important than strong ties. Strong ties are like the ties you share with your family, ties that are durable and built up out of more than one shared interest. Weak ties are like the ties you share with other fans of Juventus. You may never root for any other team, and you will always have at least one thing in common with any other fan of Juventus, but a one-dimensional community is a very thin one. Traditional democratic theory assumed that citizens would have relatively strong ties in the political community. They would share not just membership in the state, but also a set of values, religious beliefs, public space, local resources, and so forth. All of these things become increasingly voluntary and personal in the age of mobile privatization. Instead, it becomes easier to mobilize ad hoc groups of individuals around movements or issues that are specific and often transitory.

The network public needs something to compensate for its tendency to fragmentation and evanescence. Journalism redefined might answer this need. The next new journalism will come, and it will be built on top of a set of material relationships, but it is hard to say what those will be. Perhaps it will emerge from the kinds of state sponsorship that have produced Al Jazeera and CCTV, and the populist journalisms of left governments in Latin America (Waisbord, 2011). Perhaps it will be nurtured by the new monopolists of the Internet age – Google, Apple, Time-Warner. If it is to provide us with more chips of messianic time, it will need to have the capacity to assemble the many voices of the public of "mass self-communication" (Castells, 2009) into something that the people who run things will hear as the voice of a supervising intelligence. And to do that it will have to have the active or passive participation of the great majority of ordinary people, which means the working class. Even given all those criteria, it will not be able to satisfy our tests of capacity unless it is able to work across national borders. Is that too much to hope for?

References

Abrahamson, David (1996). *Magazine-Made America: The Cultural Transformation of the Postwar Periodical*. Cresskill, NJ: Hampton Press.

Adams, John Quincy (1875). *Memoirs of John Quincy Adams*, ed. Charles Francis Adams, 12 vols. Philadelphia.

Alexander, Jeffery (2007). *The Civil Sphere*. New York: Oxford University Press.

Amar, Akhil Reed (1998). *The Bill of Rights: Creation and Reconstruction*. New Haven, CT: Yale University Press.

Arnold, Matthew (1887). "Up to Easter." *The Nineteenth Century*, CXXIII (May): 629–43.

ASNE (2013). "History: A Look at the Formation of ASNE." At <http://asne.org/content.asp?pl=24&sl=83&contentid=83>.

Athique, Adrian (2012). *Indian Media: Global Approaches*. Cambridge: Polity.

Auletta, Ken (2004). "Fortress Bush: How the White House Keeps the Press under Control." *New Yorker*, 19 January: 53–65.

Auletta, Ken (2009). *Googled! The End of the World as We Know It*. New York: Penguin.

Baldasty, Gerald (1992). *The Commercialization of News in the Nineteenth Century*. Madison, WI: University of Wisconsin Press.

Baldasty, Gerald (1999). *EW Scripps and the Business of Newspapers*. Urbana, IL: University of Illinois Press.

Barker, Hannah (1998). *Newspapers, Politics, and Public Opinion in Late Eighteenth-Century England*. Oxford: Oxford University Press.

Barnhurst, Kevin G. and Nerone, John (2001). *The Form of News: A History*. New York: Guilford Press.

Baron, Ava (1989). "Questions of Gender: Deskilling and Demasculinization in the US Printing Industry, 1830–1915." *Gender & History*, 1/2: 178–99.

Baron, Sabrina and Dooley, Brendan (2001). *The Politics of Information in Early Modern Europe*. London: Taylor and Francis.

Bayly, C. A. (2009). "The Indian Ecumene: An Indigenous Public Sphere." In Arvind Rajagopal, ed., *The Indian Public Sphere: Readings in Media History*. New Delhi: Oxford University Press, pp. 49–64.

Baym, Geoffrey (2009). *From Cronkite to Colbert: The Evolution of Broadcast News*. Boulder, CO: Paradigm Publishers.

Beckett, Charlie, and Ball, James (2012). *WikiLeaks: News in the Networked Era*. Cambridge: Polity.

Bederman, Gail (1992). "Civilization," the Decline of Middle-Class Manliness, and Ida B. Wells's Antilynching Campaign (1892–94)." *Radical History Review*, 52: 5–30.

Beniger, James R. (1986). *The Control Revolution: Technological and Economic Origins of the Information Society*. Cambridge, MA: Harvard University Press.

Benkler, Yochai (2006). *The Wealth of Networks: How Social Production Transforms Markets and Freedom*. New Haven, CT: Yale University Press.

Benson, Rodney (2013). *Shaping Immigration News: A French-American Comparison*. New York: Cambridge University Press.

Bergman, Tabe (2012). "The Dutch Media Monopoly." PhD Dissertation, University of Illinois at Urbana Champaign.

Black, Jeremy (1987). "Parliamentary Reporting in England in the Early Eighteenth Century: An Abortive Attempt to Influence the Magazines in 1744." *Parliament, Estates, and Representation*, 7/1: 61–9.

Bledstein, Burton (1976). *The Culture of Professionalism: The Middle Class and the Development of Higher Education in America*. New York: Norton.

Bleyer, Willard G. (1913). *Newspaper Writing and Editing*. Boston, MA: Houghton Mifflin.

Blondheim, Menahem (1994). *News over the Wires: The Telegraph and the Flow of Public Information in America, 1844–1896*. Cambridge, MA: Harvard University Press.

Botein, Stephen. (1975). "'Meer Mechanics' and an Open Press: The Business and Political Strategies of Colonial American Printers." *Perspectives in American History*, 9: 130–211.

Botein, Stephen (1980). "Printers and the American Revolution." In John Hench et al., eds, *The Press and the American Revolution*. Worcester, MA: American Antiquarian Society, pp. 23–45.

Botein, Stephen (1985). "Introduction." In Botein, ed., *"Mr. Zenger's Malice and Falshood": Six Issues of the New-York Weekly Journal, 1733–34*. Worcester, MA: American Antiquarian Society.

Bourdon, Jeffrey Normand (2011). "Compassionate Protector of America: The Symbolism of Old Hickory in a Jackson Woman's Mind." *American Nineteenth Century History*, 12/2: 177–201.

Bouton, Terry (2007). *Taming Democracy: "The People," the Founders, and the Troubled Ending of the American Revolution*. New York: Oxford University Press.

Braestrup, Peter, et al. (1977). *Big Story: How the American Press and Television Reported and Interpreted the Crisis of Tet 1968 in Vietnam and Washington*. Boulder, CO: Westview Press.

Brake, Laurel et al. (2012). *W. T. Stead: Newspaper Revolutionary*. London: British Library Publishing.

Braverman, Harry (1974). *Labor and Monopoly Capital: The Degradation of Work in the Twentieth Century*. New York: New York University Press.

Brewin, Mark (2008). *Celebrating Democracy: The Mass Mediated Ritual of Election Day*. New York: Peter Lang.

Briggs, Asa and Burke, Peter (2009). *A Social History of the Media: From Gutenberg to the Internet*. Cambridge: Polity.

Brown, Joshua (2002). *Beyond the Lines: Pictorial Reporting, Everyday Life, and the Crisis of Gilded-Age America*. Berkeley, CA: University of California Press.

Brown, Richard D. (1989). *Knowledge is Power: The Diffusion of Information in Early America, 1700–1865*. Oxford: Oxford University Press on Demand.

Calvo, Christopher W. (2012). "An American Political Economy: Industry, Trade, and Finance in the Antebellum Mind." PhD Dissertation, Florida International University.

Campbell, W. Joseph (2006). *The Year that Defined American Journalism: 1897 and the Clash of Paradigms*. New York: Routledge.

Carey, James W. (1983). "Technology and Ideology: The Case of the Telegraph." *Prospects*, 8/1: 303–25.

Carey, James W. (2009). "A Cultural Approach to Communication." *Communication as Culture*, 2nd edn. New York: Routledge, pp. 11–28.

Castells, Manuel (2009). *Communication Power*. New York: Oxford University Press.

Cecelski, David S. and Tyson, Timothy B., eds (1998). *Democracy Betrayed: The Wilmington Race Riot of 1898 and Its Legacy*. Chapel Hill, NC: University of North Carolina Press.

Cha, Jae Young (1994). "Media Control and Propaganda in Occupied Korea, 1945–1948: Toward an Origin of Cultural Imperialism." PhD Dissertation, University of Illinois at Urbana-Champaign.

Chandler, Alfred D. (1977). *The Visible Hand: The Managerial Revolution in American Business*. Cambridge, MA: Harvard University Press.

Chartier, Roger (1993). "Book Markets and Reading in France at the End of the Old Regime." In Carol Armbruster, ed., *Publishing and Readership in Revolutionary France and America*. Westport, CT: Greenwood Press, pp. 117–36.

Cheek, Timothy (1990). "Redefining Propaganda: Debates on the Role of Journalism in Post-Mao China." In King-Yuh Chang, ed., *Mainland China after the Thirteenth Party Congress*. Boulder, CO: Westview Press, pp. 419–46.

Chen, Peiqin (2011). "Social Movements and Chinese Literary Reportage." In John S. Bak and Bill Reynolds, eds, *Literary Journalism Across the*

Globe: Journalistic Traditions and Transnational Influences. Amherst, MA: University of Massachusetts Press, pp. 148–61.

Clark, Charles (1994). *The Publick Prints: The Newspaper in Anglo-American Culture, 1665–1740*. New York: Oxford University Press.

Clegg, Cyndia (2001). *Press Censorship in Jacobean England*. Cambridge: Cambridge University Press.

Cohen, Daniel A. (2006). *Pillars of Salt, Monuments of Grace: New England Crime Literature and the Origins of American Popular Culture, 1674–1860*. Amherst, MA: University of Massachusetts Press.

Commission on Freedom of the Press (1947). *A Free and Responsible Press*, ed. Robert D. Leigh. Chicago, IL: University of Chicago Press.

Cook, Timothy (1998). *Governing with the News*. Chicago, IL: University of Chicago Press.

Cornell, Saul (1999). *The Other Founders: Anti-federalism and the Dissenting Tradition in America, 1788–1828*. Williamsburg, VA: Omohundro Institute of Early American History and Culture.

Cowan, Brian (2004). "Mr. Spectator and the Coffee House Public Sphere." *Eighteenth-Century Studies*, 37/3: 345–66.

Cronon, William (1992). *Nature's Metropolis: Chicago and the Great West*. New York: Norton.

Crouse, Timothy (1973). *The Boys on the Bus*. New York: Random House.

Crouthamel, James L. (1969). *James Watson Webb: A Biography*. Middletown, CT: Wesleyan University Press.

Curran, James and Seaton, Jean (2009). *Power without Responsibility*. London: Routledge.

Daniel, Marcus (2009). *"Scandal and Civility": Journalism and the Birth of American Democracy*. New York: Oxford University Press.

Darnton, Robert (1979). *The Business of Enlightenment: A Publishing History of the Encyclopedie, 1775–1800*. Cambridge, MA: Harvard University Press.

Darnton, Robert (1982). *The Literary Underground of the Old Regime*. Cambridge, MA: Harvard University Press.

Darnton, Robert (1996). *The Forbidden Best-Sellers of Pre-Revolutionary France*. New York: Norton.

Darwin, Charles (1859/2003). *The Origin of Species*. New York: Signet.

Denning, Michael (1987). *Mechanic Accents: Dime Novels and Working-Class Culture in America*. New York: Verso.

Denning, Michael (1998). *The Cultural Front: The Laboring of American Culture in the Twentieth Century*. New York: Verso.

de Vivo, Filippo (2007). *Information and Communication in Venice: Rethinking Early Modern Politics*. Oxford: Oxford University Press.

Digby-Junger, Richard (1996). *The Journalist as Reformer: Henry Demarest Lloyd and Wealth against Commonwealth*. Westport, CT: Greenwood Press.

Dolan, Kevin (2011). "Whiteness and the News: The Interlocking Social Construction of 'Realities'." PhD dissertation, University of Illinois at Urbana-Champaign.

Dolber, Brian (2011). "From Socialism to 'Sentiment': Toward a Political Economy of Communities, Counterpublics, and Their Media Through Jewish Working Class History." *Communication Theory*, 21/1: 90–109.

Dooley, Brendan (1996). "Political Publishing and Its Critics in Seventeenth-Century Italy." *Memoirs of the American Academy in Rome*, 41: 175–93.

Douglas, Ann (1977). *The Feminization of American Culture*. New York: Macmillan.

Douglas, Susan (1999). *Listening In: Radio and the American Imagination*. New York: Times Books.

Eaton, Clement (1964). *The Freedom-of-Thought Struggle in the Old South*. New York: Harper & Row.

Eckhardt, Celia Morris (1984). *Fanny Wright: Rebel in America*. Cambridge, MA: Harvard University Press.

Eisenstein, Elizabeth (1979). *The Printing Press as an Agent of Change*. New York: Cambridge University Press.

Eisenstein, Elizabeth (1992). *Grub Street Abroad: Aspects of the French Cosmopolitan Press from the Age of Louis XIV to the French Revolution*. Oxford: Oxford University Press.

Epstein, Edward Jay (1975). *Between Fact and Fiction: The Problem of Journalism*. New York: Vintage Books.

Evans, Harold (2009). *My Paper Chase: True Stories of Vanished Times*. Boston, MA: Little, Brown.

Ewen, Stuart (2008). *PR!: A Social History of Spin*. New York: Basic Books.

Farrar, Ronald T. (1998). *A Creed for my Profession: Walter Williams, Journalist to the World*. Columbia, MO: University of Missouri Press.

Feller, Daniel (1997). "The Market Revolution Ate My Homework." *Reviews in American History*, 25/3: 408–15.

Foner, Eric (1976). *Tom Paine and Revolutionary America*. New York: Oxford University Press.

Formisano, Ronald P. (1983). *The Transformation of Political Culture: Massachusetts Parties, 1790s–1840s*. New York: Oxford University Press.

Foucault, Michel (1980). *Power/Knowledge: Selected Interviews and Other Writings, 1972–1977*. New York: Pantheon.

Fox, Elizabeth and Waisbord, Silvio (2002). *Latin Politics, Global Media*. Austin, TX: University of Texas Press.

Fox, Stephen R. (1984). *The Mirror Makers: A History of American Advertising and its Creators*. Urbana, IL: University of Illinois Press.

Furtwangler, Albert (1984). *The Authority of Publius: A Reading of the Federalist Papers*. Ithaca, NY: Cornell University Press.

Gans, Herbert J. (1979). *Deciding What's News: A Study of CBS News, NBC Evening News, Newsweek, and Time*. New York: Pantheon.

Gasaway, John G. (1999). "Tippecanoe and the Party Press Too: Mass Communication, Politics, Culture, and the Fabled Presidential Election of 1840." PhD dissertation, University of Illinois at Urbana-Champaign.

Gitlin, Todd (2002). Public Sphere or Public Sphericules? In James Curran and Tamar Liebes, eds, *Media, Ritual, and Identity*. New York: Routledge, pp. 168–74.

Glendon, Mary Ann (2002). *The World Made New: Eleanor Roosevelt and the Universal Declaration of Human Rights*. New York: Random House.

Goodman, Dena (1994). *The Republic of Letters: A Cultural History of the French Enlightenment*. Ithaca, NY: Cornell University Press.

Goodman, Paul (1988). *Towards a Christian Republic: Antimasonry and the Great Transition in New England, 1826–1836*. New York: Oxford University Press.

Gough, Hugh (1988). *The Newspaper Press in the French Revolution*. Chicago, IL: Dorsey.

Green, James N. (2000). "The Book Trade in the Middle Colonies, 1680–1720." In Hugh Amory and David D. Hall, *A History of the Book in America, Volume One: The Colonial Book in the Atlantic World*. New York: Cambridge University Press, pp. 199–223.

Gunderson, Robert Gray (1977). *The Log-Cabin Campaign*. Westport, CT: Greenwood Press.

Habermas, Jürgen (1989). *The Structural Transformation of the Public Sphere: An Inquiry into a Category of Bourgeois Society*. Cambridge: MIT Press.

Hallin, Daniel C. (1992). "The Passing of the High Modernism of American Journalism." *Journal of Communication*, 42/3: 14–25.

Hallin, Daniel C. and Mancini, Paolo (2004). *Comparing Media Systems: Three Models of Media and Politics*. Cambridge: Cambridge University Press.

Hammond, William M. (1998). *Reporting Vietnam: Media and Military at War*. Lawrence, KS: University Press of Kansas.

Hardt, Hanno and Brennen, Bonnie, eds (1995). *Newsworkers: Toward a History of the Rank and File*. Minneapolis, MN: University of Minnesota Press.

Harter, Eugene C. (1991). *Boilerplating America: The Hidden Newspaper*, ed. Dorothy Harter. Lanham, MD: University Press of America.

Harper, Robert S. (1951). *Lincoln and the Press*. New York: Harper & Row.

Hartsock, John C. (2011). "Literary Reportage: The 'Other' Literary Journalism." In John S. Bak and Bill Reynolds, eds, *Literary Journalism Across the Globe: Journalistic Traditions and Transnational Influences*. Amherst, MA: University of Massachusetts Press, pp. 23–46.

Harvey, David (2005). *A Brief History of Neoliberalism*. New York: Oxford University Press.

Headrick, Joan (1994). *Harriet Beecher Stowe: A Life*. New York: Oxford University Press.

Hening, W. W. (1810–23). *The Statutes at Large: Being a Collection of All the Laws of Virginia, from the First Session of the Legislature, in the Year 1619: Published Pursuant to an Act of the General Assembly of Virginia*, 13 vols. Richmond, Philadelphia, and New York.

Herbst, Susan (1993). *Numbered Voices: How Opinion Polling has Shaped American Politics*. Chicago, IL: University of Chicago Press.
Herbst, Susan (1998). *Reading Public Opinion: How Political Actors View the Democratic Process*. Chicago, IL: University of Chicago Press.
Herman, Edward S. and Chomsky, Noam (1988). *Manufacturing Consent: The Political Economy of the Mass Media*. New York: Pantheon.
Hertsgaard, Mark (1988). *On Bended Knee: The Press and the Reagan Administration*. New York: Farrar, Straus and Giroux.
Hill, Christopher (1978). *Milton and the English Revolution*. New York: Viking.
Hindman, Matthew (2008). *The Myth of Digital Democracy*. Princeton, NJ: Princeton University Press.
Hobsbawm, E. J. (1977). *The Age of Capital: 1848–1875*. New York: Scribner's.
Hochfelder, David (2012). *The Telegraph in America, 1832–1920*. Baltimore, MD: Johns Hopkins University Press.
Hofstadter, Richard (1969). *The Idea of a Party System: The Rise of Legitimate Opposition in the United States, 1780–1840*. Berkeley, CA: University of California Press.
Holton, Woody (2007). *Unruly Americans and the Origins of the Constitution*. New York: Hill & Wang.
Howe, Daniel Walker (2007). *What Hath God Wrought: The Transformation of America, 1815–1848*. New York: Oxford University Press.
Hughes, Frank L. (1950). *Prejudice and the Press: A Restatement of the Principle of Freedom of the Press with Specific Reference to the Hutchins-Luce Commission*. New York: Devin-Adair.
Infelise, Mario (2002). "Roman Avvisi: Information and Politics in the Seventeenth Century." *Court and Politics in Papal Rome, 1492–1700*. Cambridge: Cambridge University Press, pp. 212–28.
Infelise, Mario (2007). "From Merchants' Letters to Handwritten Political Avvisi: Notes on the Origins of Public Information." In F. Bethencourt and F. Egmond, eds, *Cultural Exchange in Early Modern Europe, III, Correspondence and Cultural Exchange in Europe 1400–1700*. Cambridge: Cambridge University Press, pp. 33–52.
Infelise, Mario (2010). "News Networks between Italy and Europe." In Brendan Dooley, ed., *The Dissemination of News and the Emergence of Contemporaneity in Early Modern Europe*. Farnham: Ashgate, pp. 51–65.
International Commission for the Study of Communication Problems (MacBride Commission) (1980). *Many Voices, One World*. Paris and New York: UNESCO.
Issenberg, Sasha (2012). *The Victory Lab: The Secret Science of Winning Campaigns*. New York: Crown.
Jackson, Kate (1997). "The Tit-Bits Phenomenon: George Newnes, New Journalism, and the Periodical Texts." *Victorian Periodicals Review*, 30/3 (Fall): 201–26.
James, Bessie Rowland (1972). *Anne Royall's USA*. New Brunswick, NJ: Rutgers University Press.

Jeffrey, Robin (2000). *India's Newspaper Revolution: Capitalism, Politics, and the English-Language Press, 1977–1999*. London: Hurst & Co.

Johanningsmeier, Charles (2002). *Fiction and the American Literary Marketplace: The Role of Newspaper Syndicates in America, 1860–1900*. New York: Cambridge University Press.

John, Richard R. (1995). *Spreading the News: The American Postal System from Franklin to Morse*. Cambridge, MA: Harvard University Press.

John, Richard R. (2010). *Network Nation: Inventing American Telecommunications*. Cambridge, MA: Harvard University Press.

Johns, Adrian (1998). *The Nature of the Book: Print and Knowledge in the Making*. Chicago, IL: University of Chicago Press.

Johnson, Karen Ramsay (2002). "Anne Royall's Apocalyptic Rhetoric: Politics and the Role of Women." *Women's Studies*, 31/5: 671–88.

Johnson, Richard (1982). *Making Histories: Studies in History-Writing and Politics*. London: Hutchinson Education.

Johnson, Richard R. (2009). "Intra-Imperial Communication, 1689–1775." In Jack P. Greene and J. R. Pole, eds, *A Companion to the American Revolution*. Oxford: Blackwell, pp. 14–15.

Jowett, Garth S., Jarvie, Ian C. and Fuller, Kathryn H., eds (1996). *Children and the Movies: Media Influence and the Payne Fund Controversy*. New York: Cambridge University Press.

Judge, Joan (1996). *Print and Politics:"Shibao" and the Culture of Reform in Late Qing China*. Stanford, CA: Stanford University Press.

Juergens, George (1966). *Joseph Pulitzer and the New York World*. Princeton, NJ: Princeton University Press.

Katz, Stanley N. (1972). "Introduction." In James Alexander, ed. Katz, *A Brief Narrative of the Case and Trial of John Peter Zenger*. Cambridge, MA: Harvard University Press, pp. 1–35.

Kemp, Geoff (2006). "L'Estrange and the Publishing Sphere." In Jason McElligott, ed., *Fear, Exclusion, and Revolution: Roger Morrice and Britain in the 1680s*. Aldershot: Ashgate, pp. 67–90.

Kim, Sae-Eun (2013). "Journalism History: Korea." In John Nerone, ed., *Media History and the Foundations of Media Studies*. Malden, MA: Wiley-Blackwell, pp. 279–96.

Kittler, Juraj (2009). "Historical Metamorphosis of the Athenian Agora: Changing Communication Technologies and the Enduring Quest for an Ideal Public Sphere." PhD Diss., Pennsylvania State University.

Kohli-Khandekar, Vanita (2006). *The Indian Media Business*, 2nd edn. New Delhi: Response Books.

Kovach, Bill and Rosenstiel, Tom (2007). *The Elements of Journalism: What Newspeople Should Know and the Public Should Expect, Completely Updated and Revised*. New York: Random House.

Kumar, Deepa (2008). *Outside the Box: Corporate Media, Globalization, and the UPS Strike*. Urbana, IL: University of Illinois Press.

Ladd, Jonathan M. (2012). *Why Americans Hate the Media and How it Matters*. Princeton, NJ: Princeton University Press.

Lake, Peter and Pincus, Steven (2007). "Rethinking the Public Sphere in Early Modern England." In Lake and Pincus, eds, *The Politics of the Public Sphere in Early Modern England*. Manchester: Manchester University Press.

Lawson, Linda (1993). *Truth in Publishing: Federal Regulation of the Press's Business Practices, 1880–1920*. Carbondale, IL: Southern Illinois University Press.

Leab, Daniel J. (1970). *A Union of Individuals: The Formation of the American Newspaper Guild, 1933–1936*. New York: Columbia University Press.

Leach, William (1993). *Land of Desire: Merchants Power and the Rise of a New American Culture*. New York: Pantheon.

Lears, T. J. Jackson (1994). *Fables of Abundance: A Cultural History of Advertising in America*. New York: Basic Books.

Lee, Chin-Chuan (2006). "The Conception of Chinese Journalists: Ideological Convergence and Contestation." In Hugo De Burgh, ed., *Making Journalists: Diverse Models, Global Issues*. London: Routledge, pp. 107–26.

Lehuu, Isabelle (2000). *Carnival on the Page: Popular Print Media in Antebellum America*. Chapel Hill, NC: University of North Carolina Press.

Leiserowitz, Anthony, et al. (2013). "Climategate, Public Opinion, and the Loss of Trust." *American Behavioral Scientist*, 57/6: 818–37.

Leonard, Thomas C. (1986). *The Power of the Press: The Birth of American Political Reporting*. New York: Oxford University Press.

Levy, Leonard (1985). *Emergence of a Free Press*. New York: Oxford University Press.

Lippmann, Walter (1920). *Liberty and the News*. New York: Harcourt, Brace.

Lippmann, Walter (1921). *Public Opinion*. New York: Macmillan.

Lippmann, Walter (1925). *The Phantom Public*. New York: Harcourt, Brace.

Loughran, Trish (2009). *The Republic in Print: Print Culture in the Age of US Nation Building, 1770–1870*. New York: Columbia University Press.

Lunt, Peter and Stenner, Paul (2005). "The Jerry Springer Show as an Emotional Public Sphere." *Media, Culture & Society*, 27/1: 59–81.

Lynd, Robert and Lynd, Helen (1929). *Middletown: A Study in Contemporary American Culture*. New York: Harcourt, Brace.

McChesney, Robert W. (1991). "Press-Radio Relations and the Emergence of Network, Commercial Broadcasting in the United States, 1930–1935." *Historical Journal of Film, Radio and Television*, 11/1: 41–57.

McChesney, Robert W. (1999). *Rich Media, Poor Democracy: Communication Politics in Dubious Times*. Urbana, IL: University of Illinois Press.

McChesney, Robert Waterman and Nichols, John (2011). *The Death and Life of American Journalism: The Media Revolution That Will Begin the World Again*. New York: Nation Books.

McChesney, Robert W. and Scott, Ben, eds (2004). *Our Unfree Press: 100 Years of Radical Media Criticism*. New York: New Press.

McDougall, Curtis D. (1938). *Interpretative Reporting*. New York: Macmillan.

McElligott, Jason (2007). *Royalism, Print, and Censorship in Revolutionary England*. Woodbridge: Boydell Press.

McGerr, Michael (1986). *The Decline of Popular Politics: The American North, 1865–1928*. New York: Oxford University Press.

McIntyre, Sheila (1998). "'I Heare It So Variously Reported': News-Letters, Newspapers, and the Ministerial Network in New England, 1670–1730." *The New England Quarterly*, 71/4: 593–614.

McKendry, Virginia (1994). "The Illustrated London News and the Invention of Tradition." *Victorian Periodicals Review*, 27/1: 1–24.

Mackie, Erin (1999). *Market a la Mode: Fashion, Commodity, and Gender in the Tatler and the Spectator*. Baltimore, MD: Johns Hopkins University Press.

MacKinnon, Stephen R. (1997). "Toward a History of the Chinese Press in the Republican Period." *Modern China*, 23/1: 3–32.

MacNeil, Robert (1985). *The Mass Media and Public Trust*. New York: Gannett Center for Media Studies.

Maier, Pauline (1997). *American Scripture: Making the Declaration of Independence*. New York: Vintage.

Manning, William (1993). *The Key of Liberty: The Life and Democratic Writings of William Manning, "A Laborer," 1747–1814*. Cambridge, MA: Harvard University Press.

Martin, Christopher R. (2008). "Writing off Workers: The Decline of the US and Canadian Labor Beat." In Catherine McKercher and Vincent Mosco, eds, *Knowledge Workers in the Information Society*. Lanham, MD: Lexington Books, pp. 19–36.

Martin, Michèle (2006). *Images at War: Illustrated Periodicals and Constructed Nations*. Toronto: University of Toronto Press.

Matheson, Donald (2000). "The Birth of News Discourse: Changes in News Language in British Newspapers, 1880–1930." *Media, Culture & Society*, 22/5: 557.

Mattelart, Armand (1996). *The Invention of Communication*. University of Minnesota Press.

Mattelart, Armand (2006). *The Invention of Communication*. Minneapolis, MN: University of Minnesota Press.

Mayer, Henry (1998). *All on Fire: William Lloyd Garrison and the Abolition of Slavery*. New York: Norton.

Melville, Lewis (1913). *The Life and Letters of William Cobbett in England and America*, 2 vols. London: John Lane.

Mendle, M. (1995). "De Facto Freedom, de Facto Authority: Press and Parliament, 1640–1643." *The Historical Journal*, 38/2: 307–32.

Merritt, Davis (1998). *Public Journalism and Public Life: Why Telling the News is Not Enough*. New York: Routledge.

Mill, John Stuart (1859). *On Liberty*. London: John W. Parker and Son.

Miller, John Chester (1951). *Crisis in Freedom: The Alien and Sedition Acts*. Boston, MA: Little, Brown.

Mindich, David T. Z. (1998). *"Just the Facts": How Objectivity Came to Define American Journalism*. New York: New York University Press.

Mishra, Pamkaj (2012). *From the Ruins of Empire: The Intellectuals who Remade Asia*. New York: Macmillan.

Mittler, Barbara (2004). *A Newspaper for China?: Power, Identity, and Change in Shanghai's News Media, 1872–1912*. Cambridge, MA: Harvard University Press.

Montgomery, David (1989). *The Fall of the House of Labor: The Workplace, the State, and American Labor Activism, 1865–1925*. New York: Cambridge University Press.

Moran, James (1973). *Printing Presses: History and Development from the Fifteenth Century to Modern Times*. Berkeley, CA: University of California Press.

Morrison, Howard Alexander (1981). "Gentlemen of Proper Understanding: A Closer Look at Utica's Anti-Abolitionist Mob." *New York History*, 62/1: 61–82.

Mott, Frank Luther (1950). *American Journalism: A History of Newspapers in the United States through 260 Years: 1690 to 1950*. New York: Macmillan.

Munsell, Joel (1850). *Typographical Miscellany*. Albany, NY: Joel Munsell.

Murphy, Paul L. (1979). *World War I and the Origin of Civil Liberties in the United States*. New York: Norton.

Murray, Robert K. (1955). *Red Scare: A Study of National Hysteria, 1919–1920*. Minneapolis, MN: University of Minnesota Press.

Nalbach, Alex (2003). " 'The Software of Empire': Telegraphic News Agencies and Imperial Publicity, 1865–1914." In Julie F. Codell, ed., *Imperial Cohistories: National Identities and the British and Colonial Press*. Madison, Teaneck: Fairleigh Dickinson University Press.

Nasaw, David (1993). *Going Out: The Rise and Fall of Public Amusements*. New York: Basic Books.

Nasaw, David (2000). *The Chief: The Life of William Randolph Hearst*. New York: Houghton Mifflin.

Nash, Gary B. (1979). *The Urban Crucible: Social Change, Political Consciousness, and the Origins of the American Revolution*. Cambridge, MA: Harvard University Press.

Nerone, John (1987). "The Mythology of the Penny Press." *Critical Studies in Mass Communication*, 4 (December): 376–404.

Nerone, John (1989). *The Culture of the Press in the Early Republic: Cincinnati, 1793–1848*. New York: Garland.

Nerone, John (1993). "A Local History of the Early U.S. Press: Cincinnati, 1793–1848." In William S. Solomon and Robert W. McChesney, eds, *Ruthless Criticism: New Perspectives in U.S. Communication History*. Minneapolis, MN: University of Minnesota Press, pp. 38–40.

Nerone, John (1994). *Violence against the Press: Policing the Public Sphere in US History*. New York: Oxford University Press.

Nerone, John (2008). "Newswork, Technology, and Cultural Form, 1837–1920." In Barbie Zelizer, ed., *Explorations in Communication and History*. New York: Routledge, pp. 136–56.

Nerone, John (2013). "The Historical Roots of the Normative Model of Journalism." *Journalism*, 14/4 (May): 446–58.

Nerone, John and Barnhurst, Kevin G. (2003). "US Newspaper Types, the Newsroom, and the Division of Labor, 1750–2000." *Journalism Studies*, 4/4: 435–49.

Nerone, John and Barnhurst, Kevin G. (2012). "Stead in America." In Laurel Brake et al., *William T. Stead: Newspaper Revolutionary*. London: British Library Publishing, pp. 98–114.

Nimkoff, Mark (2008). "Media Memories: The Newseum Story of News." PhD dissertation, University of Illinois at Urbana-Champaign.

Nord, D. P. (1990). "Teleology and News: The Religious Roots of American Journalism, 1630–1730." *The Journal of American History*, 77/1: 9–38.

Nord, David Paul (2004). *Faith in Reading: Religious Publishing and the Birth of Mass Media in America*. New York: Oxford University Press.

Nye, Russel Blaine (1964). *Fettered Freedom; Civil Liberties and the Slavery Controversy, 1830–1860*. Michigan: Michigan State University Press.

Orsini, Francesca (2002). *The Hindi Public Sphere, 1920–1940: Language and Literature in the Age of Nationalism*. New York: Oxford University Press.

Packer, Jeremy and Robertson, Craig (2006). *Thinking with James Carey: Essays on Communications, Transportation, History*. New York: Peter Lang.

Pasley, Jeffrey L. (2001). *The Tyranny of Printers: Newspaper Politics in the Early Republic*. Charlottesville, VA: University Press of Virginia.

Peters, John Durham (1999). *Speaking into the Air: A History of the Idea of Communication*. Chicago, IL: University of Chicago Press.

Peters, John Durham (2004). "The Marketplace of Ideas: History of a Concept." In Andrew Calabrese and Colin Sparks, eds, *Toward a Political Economy of Culture: Capitalism and Communication in the Twenty-First Century*. Boulder, CO: Rowman & Littlefield, pp. 65–82.

Pettegree, Andrew (2010). *The Book in the Renaissance*. New Haven, CT: Yale University Press.

Pettegree, Andrew (2014). *The Invention of News: How the World Came to Know about Itself*. New Haven, CT: Yale University Press.

Petronius (1959). *Satyricon*. Trans. William Arrowsmith. Ann Arbor, MI: University of Michigan Press.

Phillips, Kevin (2012). *1775: A Good Year for Revolution*. New York: Viking Press.

Phillips, Kim T. (1989). *William Duane: Radical Journalist in the Age of Jefferson*. New York: Garland.

Pickard, Victor (2010). " 'Whether the Giants Should Be Slain or Persuaded to Be Good': Revisiting the Hutchins Commission and the Role of Media in a Democratic Society." *Critical Studies in Media Communication*, 27/4: 391–411.

Pickard, Victor (2014). *America's Battle for Media Democracy: The Triumph of Corporate Libertarianism and the Future of Media Reform*. New York: Cambridge University Press.

Pincus, Steve (2009). *1688: The First Modern Revolution*. New Haven, CT: Yale University Press.
Pollock, Anthony (2009). *Gender and the Fictions of the Public Sphere*. New York: Routledge.
Popkin, Jeremy (1990). *Revolutionary News: The Press in France, 1789–1799*. Durham, NC: Duke University Press.
Powell, Colin (1995). *My American Journey*. New York: Random House.
Prather, H. Leon (1984). *We Have Taken a City: Wilmington Racial Massacre and Coup of 1898*. Rutherford, NJ: Fairleigh Dickinson University Press.
Pratte, Paul A. (1995). *Gods Within the Machine: A History of the American Society of Newspaper Editors, 1923–1993*. Westport, CT: Greenwood Publishing Group.
Pred, Allan Richard (1973). *Urban Growth and the Circulation of Information: The United States System of Cities, 1790–1840*. Cambridge, MA: Harvard University Press.
Pretzer, William S. (1985). "'The British, Duff Green, the Rats and the Devil': Custom, Capitalism, and Conflict in the Washington Printing Trade, 1834–36." *Labor History*, 27/1: 5–30.
Pulitzer, Joseph (1904). "The College of Journalism." *North American Review*, CLXXVIII (May): 641–80.
Putnam, Robert (1995). "Bowling Alone: America's Declining Social Capital." *Journal of Democracy*, 6 (January): 65–78.
Rajagopal, Arvind (2001). *Politics after Television: Hindu Nationalism and the Reshaping of the Public in India*. New York: Cambridge University Press.
Rantanen, Terhi (1997). "The Globalization of Electronic News in the 19th Century." *Media, Culture & Society*, 19/4: 605–20.
Raymond, Joad (1996). *The Invention of the Newspaper: English Newsbooks, 1641–1649*. Oxford: Clarendon Press.
Redfern, Walter (2004). *Writing on the Move: Albert Londres and Investigative Journalism*. New York: Peter Lang.
Reed, Annette Gordon (2008). *The Hemingses of Monticello: An American Family*. New York: Norton.
Reynolds, David S. (1988). *Beneath the American Renaissance: The Subversive Imagination in the Age of Emerson and Melville*. New York: Random House.
Richards, Leonard L. (1970). *Gentlemen of Property and Standing: Anti-abolition Mobs in Jacksonian America*, vol. 347. New York: Oxford University Press.
Richards, Leonard L. (2000). *The Slave Power: The Free North and Southern Domination, 1780–1860*. Baton Rouge, LA: Louisiana State University Press.
Robbins, Sarah (1997). "Gendering the History of the Antislavery Narrative: Juxtaposing Uncle Tom's Cabin and Benito Cereno, Beloved and Middle Passage." *American Quarterly*, 49/3: 531–73.

Roberts, Gene and Klibanoff, Hank (2006). *The Race Beat: The Press, the Civil Rights Struggle, and the Awakening of a Nation.* New York: Knopf.

Rodgers, Daniel T. (1977). "Tradition, Modernity, and the American Industrial Worker: Reflections and Critique." *The Journal of Interdisciplinary History*, 7/4: 655–81.

Rogers, Charles E. (1942). "The Role of the Weekly Newspaper." *Annals of the American Academy of Political and Social Science*, 219: 151–7.

Rorabaugh, William Joseph (1986). *The Craft Apprentice: From Franklin to the Machine Age in America.* New York: Oxford University Press.

Rosen, Jay (1999). *What Are Journalists For?* New Haven, CT: Yale University Press.

Rosenberg, Norman L. (1986). *Protecting the Best Men: An Interpretive History of the Law of Libel.* Chapel Hill, NC: University of North Carolina Press.

Rothenbuhler, Eric and McCourt, Tom (2002). "Radio Redefines Itself, 1947–1962." In Michelle Hilmes and Jason Loviglio, eds, *The Radio Reader: Essays in the Cultural History of Radio.* New York: Routledge, pp. 367–87.

Rudenstine, David (1998). *The Day the Presses Stopped: A History of the Pentagon Papers Case.* Berkeley, CA: University of California Press.

Ryan, Mary P. (1997). *Civic Wars: Democracy and Public Life in the American City during the Nineteenth Century.* Berkeley, CA: University of California Press.

Sabato, Larry (1991). *Feeding Frenzy: How Attack Journalism Has Transformed American Politics.* New York: Free Press.

Sarna, Jonathan D. (1981). *Jacksonian Jew: The Two Worlds of Mordecai Noah.* New York: Holmes & Meier.

Saxton, Alexander (1984). Problems of Class and Race in the Origins of the Mass Circulation Press. *American Quarterly*, 36/2: 211–34.

Schiller, Dan (1981). *Objectivity and the News: The Public and the Rise of Commercial Journalism.* Philadelphia, PA: University of Pennsylvania Press.

Schiller, Herbert I. (1976). *Communication and Cultural Domination.* White Plains, NY: International Arts and Sciences Press.

Schivelbusch, Wolfgang (1986). *The Railway Journey: The Industrialization of Space and Time.* Berkeley, CA: University of California Press.

Schudson, Michael (1978). *Discovering the News: A Social History of American Newspapers.* New York: Basic Books.

Schudson, Michael (1992). *Watergate in American Memory: How We Remember, Forget, and Reconstruct the Past.* New York: Basic Books.

Schwarzlose, Richard A. (1989). *The Nation's Newsbrokers: Vol. 1: The Formative Years, from Pretelegraph to 1865.* Chicago, IL: Northwestern University Press.

Schwarzlose, Richard Allen (1990). *The Nation's Newsbrokers: Vol. 2: The Rush to Institution, from 1865 to 1920.* Chicago, IL: Northwestern University Press.

Sellers, Charles G. (1994). *The Market Revolution: Jacksonian America, 1815–1846*. Oxford: Oxford University Press.

Siebert, F. S. (1952). *Freedom of the Press in England, 1476–1776: The Rise and Decline of Government Controls*. Urbana, IL: University of Illinois Press.

Sinclair, Upton (1920). *The Brass Check: A Study of American Journalism*. New York: The author.

Sloan William, David and Williams, Julie Hedgepeth (1994). *The Early American Press, 1690–1783*. Westport, CT: Greenwood Press, pp. 8–10.

Slotkin, Richard (1992). *Gunfighter Nation: The Myth of the Frontier in the Age of Industrialization*. New York: Harper.

Smelser, Marshall (1958). "The Federalist Period as an Age of Passion." *American Quarterly*, 10/4: 391–419.

Smelser, Marshall (1972). *The Winning of Independence*. Chicago, IL: Quadrangle.

Smith, Culver H. (1977). *The Press, Politics, and Patronage: The American Government's Use of Newspapers, 1789–1875*. Athens: University of Georgia Press.

Smith, David Clayton (1971). *History of Papermaking in the United States, 1691–1969*. New York: Lockwood Publishing.

Smith, James Morton (1956). *Freedom's Fetters: The Alien and Sedition Laws and Civil Liberties*. Ithaca, NY: Cornell University Press.

Smith, Jeffery Alan (1988). *Printers and Press Freedom: The Ideology of Early American Journalism*. New York: Oxford University Press.

Smith, W. (1916). "The Colonial Post-Office." *The American Historical Review*, 21/2: 258–75.

Smythe, Ted Curtis (1980). "The Reporter, 1880–1900: Working Conditions and their Influence on the News." *Journalism History*, 7/1: 1–10.

Soderlund, Gretchen (2011). "The Rhetoric of Revelation: Sex Trafficking and the Journalistic Exposé." *Humanity: An International Journal of Human Rights, Humanitarianism, and Development*, 2/2: 193–211.

Soderlund, Gretchen (2013). *Sex Trafficking, Scandal, and the Transformation of Journalism, 1885–1917*. Chicago, IL: University of Chicago Press.

Solomon, Martha and Watson, Martha, eds (1991). *A Voice of Their Own: The Woman Suffrage Press, 1840–1910*. Tuscaloosa, AL: University of Alabama Press.

Solomon, William S. (1995). "The Site of Newsroom Labor: The Division of Editorial Practices." In Hanno Hardt and Bonnie Brennen, eds, *Newsworkers: Toward a History of the Rank and File*. Minneapolis, MN: University of Minnesota Press, pp. 110–34.

Standiford, Les (2012). *Desperate Sons: Samuel Adams, Patrick Henry, John Hancock, and the Secret Bands of Radicals Who Led the Colonies to War*. New York: Harper.

Starr, Paul (2004). *The Creation of the Media: Political Origins of Modern Communications*. New York: Basic Books.

Starr, Paul (2009). "Goodbye to the Age of Newspapers (Hello to a New Age of Corruption)." *New Republic* (March 4): 28–35.

Stearns, Peter N. (1993). *The Industrial Revolution in World History*. Boulder, CO: Westview Press.

Steel, Ronald (1980). *Walter Lippmann and the American Century*. Boston, MA: Little, Brown.

Stephens, Mitchell (2007). *A History of News*. Oxford: Oxford University Press.

Stocking, George W. (1968). *Race, Culture, and Evolution: Essays in the History of Anthropology*. Chicago, IL: University of Chicago Press.

Stott, William (1973). *Documentary Expression and Thirties America*. New York: Oxford University Press.

Stowe, Harriet Beecher (1969). *Uncle Tom's Cabin, or, Life among the Lowly*. Columbus: Charles Merrill.

Stroud, Natalie Jomini (2011). *Niche News: The Politics of News Choice*. New York: Oxford University Press.

Strunsky, Simeon (1924). "About Books, More or Less: In the Matter of Style, Perspective, and Related Subjects." *New York Times*, February 17, pp. 4–5.

Tarbell, Ida Minerva (1939). *All in the Day's Work: An Autobiography*. Urbana, IL: University of Illinois Press.

Taylor, George Rogers (1951). *The Transportation Revolution, 1815–1860*. New York: Rinehart.

Thomas, John L. (1963). *The Liberator, William Lloyd Garrison: A Biography*. Boston, MA: Little, Brown.

Thompson, Anthony B. (1998). "Licensing the Press: The Career of G. R. Weckherlin during the Personal Rule of Charles I." *Historical Journal*, 41/3: 653–78.

Thompson, Edward P. (1967). "Time, Work-Discipline, and Industrial Capitalism." *Past & Present*, 38: 56–97.

Thussu, Daya Kishan (2006). "Adapting to Globalization: The Changing Contours of Journalism in India." In Hugo De Burgh, ed., *Making Journalists: Diverse Models, Global Issues*. London: Routledge, pp. 127–46.

Tocqueville, Alexis de (2003). *Democracy in America and Two essays on America*. London: Penguin.

Tuchman, Gaye (1972). "Objectivity as Strategic Ritual: An Examination of Newsmen's Notions of Objectivity." *American Journal of Sociology*, 77: 660–79.

Tusan, Michelle Elizabeth (2005). *Women Making News: Gender and Journalism in Modern Britain*. Urbana, IL: University of Illinois Press.

Underwood, Doug (1995). *When MBAs Rule the Newsroom*. New York: Columbia University Press.

US Congress (1836). Senate, Tuesday, January 19, 1836, 24th Congress, First Session. In *Register of Debates in Congress*, vol XII. Washington, DC: Gales and Seaton, pp. 203–8.

Usher, Nikki (2014). *Making News at the New York Times*. Ann Arbor, MI: University of Michigan Press.

Van Deusen, Glyndon (1947). *Thurlow Weed: Wizard of the Lobby*. Boston, MA: Little, Brown.

Van Buren, Martin (1836). Letter to William C. Rives, January 17, 1836. In Rives Collection, Library of Congress.

Verba, Sidney, Schlozman, Kay Lehman and Brady, Henry E. (1995). *Voice and Equality: Civic Voluntarism in American Politics*. Cambridge, MA: Harvard University Press.

Waisbord, Silvio (2011). "Between Support and Confrontation: Civic Society, Media Reform, and Populism in Latin America." *Communication, Culture & Critique*, 4/1: 97–117.

Walker, Stanley (1934). *City Editor*. New York: Blue-Ribbon Books.

Wang, Robin R. (2004). *Chinese Philosophy in the Age of Globalization*. Albany, NY: State University of New York Press.

Warner, Michael (1990). *The Letters of the Republic: Publication and the Public Sphere in Eighteenth-Century America*. Cambridge, MA: Harvard University Press.

Warren, Samuel D. and Brandeis, Louis D. (1890). "The Right to Privacy." *Harvard Law Review*, 4/5: 193–220.

We the People and Old Colony Press (1830–36). *Business Records*. Worcester, MA: American Antiquarian Society.

Weed, Thurlow (1883–4). *Life of Thurlow Weed, Including His Autobiography and a Memoir*. Boston, MA: Houghton Mifflin.

Welke, M. and Wilke, Jurgen (2008). *400 Jahre Zeitung: Die Entwicklung der Tagespresse im Internationalen Kontext*. Bremen: Edition Lumiere.

Wells-Barnett, Ida B. (1972). *Crusade for Justice: The Autobiography of Ida B. Wells*. Chicago, IL: University of Chicago Press.

White, Hayden (1973). *Metahistory: The Historical Imagination in Nineteenth-Century Europe*. Baltimore, MD: Johns Hopkins University Press.

White, Horace (1904). "The School of Journalism." *North American Review*, CLXXVII (January): 25–32.

Wiener, Joel H. (1983). *Radicalism and Freethought in Nineteenth-Century Britain: The Life of Richard Carlile*. Westport, CT: Greenwood Press.

Wiener, Joel H. (2012). *The Americanization of the British Press, 1830s–1914: Speed in the Age of Transatlantic Journalism*. New York: Palgrave Macmillan.

Wilentz, Sean (1984). *Chants Democratic: New York City and the Rise of the American Working Class, 1788–1850*. New York: Oxford University Press.

Wilke, Jurgen (2003). "The History and Culture of the Newsroom in Germany." *Journalism Studies*, 4/4: 465–77.

Wilke, Jurgen (2008). *Grundzuge der Medien- und Kommunikationsgeschichte*. Cologne: Bohlau.

Wilke, Jurgen (2013). "Journalism History: Europe." In John Nerone, ed., *Media History and the Foundations of Media Studies*. Malden, MA: Wiley Blackwell, pp. 262–78.

Williams, Bruce A. and Delli Carpini, Michael X. (2011). *After Broadcast News: Media Regimes, Democracy, and the New Information Environment*. New York: Cambridge University Press.

Williams, Kevin (2010). *Read All About It: A History of the British Newspaper*. London: Routledge.
Williams, Raymond (1965). *The Long Revolution*. London: Penguin.
Williams, Raymond (1974). *Television: Technology and Cultural Form*. London: Fontana.
Wilson, Christopher (1985). *The Labor of Words: Literary Professionalism in the Progressive Era*. Athens, GA: University of Georgia Press.
Wilson, Harold S. (1970). *McClure's Magazine and the Muckrakers*. Princeton, NJ: Princeton University Press.
Wood, Gordon S. (1991). *The Radicalism of the American Revolution*. New York: Vintage.
Young, Alfred Fabian (1976). *The American Revolution*. DeKalb, IL: Northern Illinois University Press.
Zboray, Ronald J. (1986). "The Transportation Revolution and Antebellum Book Distribution Reconsidered." *American Quarterly*, 38/1: 53–71.
Zboray, Ronald J. and Zboray, Mary Saracino (2010). *Voices without Votes: Women and Politics in Antebellum New England*. Lebanon, New Hampshire: University Press of New England.
Zelizer, Barbie (1992). *Covering the Body: The Kennedy Assassination, the Media, and the Shaping of Collective Memory*. Chicago, IL: University of Chicago Press.
Zhao, Yuezhi and Xing Guoxin (2012). "Provincial Papers, National Power: The Scaling Up of Nanfang Daily Media Group." In Wanning Sun and Jenny Chio, *Mapping Media in China: Region, Province, Locality*. London and New York: Routledge.
Zunz, Olivier (1990). *Making America Corporate: 1870–1920*. Chicago, IL: University of Chicago Press.

Index